D1218029

KEEP
BUSINESS
FLYING

KEEP BUSINESS FLYING

A History of
The National Business Aircraft
Association, Inc.

1946–1986

By
JOHN H. WINANT

NATIONAL
BUSINESS AIRCRAFT
ASSOCIATION, INC.

KEEP BUSINESS FLYING *Copyright © 1989*
by The National Business Aircraft Association, Inc.

All rights reserved. This book may not be reproduced in whole or in part by any means, whether mechanical or electronic, without the written permission of the publisher, The National Business Aircraft Association, Inc., 1200 Eighteenth Street NW, Washington, DC 20036, except for brief passages used in a review.

FIRST EDITION

For all whose lives
will be enriched by flight,
now and in the future, but mostly
for Katey, Ashby and Tad.

&

CONTENTS

Chapters

Appendices

PREFACE

"Man without writing cannot long retain his history in his head. His intelligence permits him to grasp some kind of succession of generations; but without writing, the tale of the past rapidly degenerates into fumbling myth and fable."[1]

NOW THE TIME IS RIGHT FOR PUTTING INTO WRITING THE principal events of the first four decades in the life of the National Business Aircraft Association. Already too many of the players are gone forever from the stage and memories are growing dim.

The book is based mostly on written association records, but it has been richly supplemented by interviews, letters and notes from many, many persons whose devotion to the organization is strong. On more than a few occasions their memories and the author's did not comport with written source materials. Where the written matter appeared authoritative it was accepted as factual and used.

I have tried to produce a useful reference work rather than an anecdotal memoir. To make it so, the text is chronological rather than topical. The book is intended for use by those who have a serious interest in business aviation; there has been no attempt made to popularize the subject.

Where sources are not stated in the text or in the chapter notes, the material comes from association publications, mailings, and minutes books. Names of persons are stated in full in the first reference in each chapter; subsequent use in the chapter is by surname only.

I have two disappointments concerning the work. It has been impossible even to consider listing the names of all the persons who deserve mention for their contributions to NBAA history and lore. It also was necessary on many occasions to exercise choice about the relative importance of events. Many interesting matters were thus excluded, but only in order to keep the total work within reasonable limit. In both of these regrettable cases I have learned that all historians must exercise subjective judgements, and that history is thus unintentionally biased by the story teller.

Valuable contributions came from many persons, but the following merit special mention. All have my grateful thanks for helping to inject a humanizing element into what otherwise would be a simple recitation of events:

John B. Bean, Earle W. Bauer, Robert W. Burke, Joseph B. Burns, Dorothy W. Cheek, John W. Davis, Ann W. Devers, Malcolm R. Doak, Raleigh E. Drennon, E. E. Dunsworth, Donald Esser, Howard O. Evans, Peter J. Fetterer,

Edwin J. Fox, Les B. Gerlach, William F. Gilbert, Leddy L. Greever, John W. Griese, J. W. Groll, Richard W. Groux, Ronald J. Guerra, Richard I. Hornbeck, T. William Hotze, Dean Humphrey, Stanley L. Kuck, Richard Lampl, Jerome Lederer, J. Sheldon Lewis, Harry C. McCreary, Frederick B. McIntosh, Scott E. Miller, Norman L. Mitchell, Cole H. Morrow, Walter C. Pague, Preston S. Parish, William L. Patrick, David L. Pease, Ralph E. Piper, John A. Pope, Lee L. Robbins, David M. Sheehan, Thomas J. Simpson, Ross R. Stephenson, William H. Stine, II, William G. Robinson, D. M. Teel, David M. Woodrow, Eugene J. Zepp and C. F. Zimmerman. Thanks also go to the History of Aviation Collection, University of Texas, and to three of its principals, George E. Haddaway, G. Edward Rice and Bob Kopitzke; special gratitude goes to *Flying* magazine and Jay Durfee for granting me access to archival collections of predecessor magazines published in the 1920's and early 1930's.

John H. Winant
Alexandria, Virginia
August, 1988

---

[1]*Loren Eisley, Anthropologist*

GLOSSARY

MOST INDUSTRIES HAVE THEIR OWN PECULIAR LANGUAGE; their literature and conversation are filled with acronyms and abbreviations. Aviation is no exception, as is illustrated by this list of abbreviations used in this book:

AAAE	—American Association of Airport Executives
ACC	—Air Coordinating Committee
ADF	—Automatic Direction Finder (Navigation)
ADMA	—Aviation Manufacturers and Distributors Association
AIA	—Aircraft (later Aerospace) Industries Association
ALPA	—Air Line Pilots Association
ANDB	—Air Navigation Development Board
AOCI	—Airport Operators Council International
AOPA	—Aircraft Owners and Pilots Association
ARO	—Airport Reservations Office (FAA)
ARTCC	—Air Route Traffic Control Center
ASO	—Aviation Service Organization (also known as Fixed Base Operator)
ATA	—Air Transport Association of America
ATPAC	—Air Traffic Procedures Advisory Committee
BAUA	—Business Aircraft Users Association (United Kingdom)
BDI	—Bundesverband der Deutschen Industrie (Federal Republic of Germany)
CAA	—Civil Aviation Administration
CAAA	—Commuter Air Line Association of America
CAB	—Civil Aeronautics Board
CAOA	—Corporation Aircraft Owners Association
CBAA	—Canadian Business Aircraft Association
CECAI	—Council of European Corporate Aircraft Interests
CVF	—Controlled Visual Flight (Rules)
DECCA	—A British-manufactured navigation system
DME	—Distance Measuring Equipment (Navigation)
DOT	—Department of Transportation
EBAA	—European Business Aviation Association
EEC	—European Economic Community
EPA	—Environmental Protection Agency
FAA	—Federal Aviation Agency (1958–1966); Federal Aviation Administration (1966 and later)
FAR	—Federal Aviation Regulation
FASST	—Fly Around Saturated Sectors and Terminals (NBAA Informational Program)

FBO	— Fixed Based Operator (also known as Aviation Service Organization)
FCC	— Federal Communications Commission
FEC	— Federal Election Commission
FEO/FEA	— Federal Energy Office; later, Federal Energy Administration
FSF	— Flight Safety Foundation
GENAVAC	— General Aviation Associations Council
GAC	— General Aviation Council
GAFPG	— General Aviation Facilities Planning Group
GAMA	— General Aviation Manufacturers Association
GAR	— General Aviation Reservation System
HAI	— Helicopter Association International
HBAA	— Holland Business Aircraft Association
IBAA(E)	— International Business Aircraft Association (Europe)
ICAO	— International Civil Aviation Organization
IFR	— Instrument Flight Rules
ILS	— Instrument Landing System
IRS	— Internal Revenue Service
JAR	— Joint Airworthiness Regulation
NAR	— National Airspace Review
NASA	— National Aeronautics and Space Administration
NASAO	— National Association of State Aviation Officials
NATA	— National Aviation Trades Association; later, National Air Transportation Association
NATC	— National Air Taxi Conference
NBAA	— National Business Aircraft Association, Inc.
NPA	— National Pilots Association
NPRM	— Notice of Proposed Rule Making
NTSB	— National Transportation Safety Board
OMB	— Office of Management and Budget
PATCO	— Professional Air Traffic Controllers Organization
RAP	— Reliever Airport Program
RTCA	— Radio Technical Commission for Aeronautics
SENEL	— Single Event Noise Exposure Level
TACAN	— Tactical Air Navigation System
TCA	— Terminal Control Area
TRSA	— Terminal Radar Service Area
UAC	— Utility Aircraft Council; later, GAMA
VOR	— Very High Frequency Omni Range System (Navigation)
VORTAC	— Combined VOR and TACAN systems
WCAAC	— Westchester County Airport Advisory Committee

PRELUDE: 1918–1945

IF AN AIRPORT-AIRWAY CAPACITY CRUNCH HAD NOT turned into a crisis in the spring of 1946, there might be no National Business Aircraft Association (NBAA).

Crisis raised the possibility that business-use aircraft would be excluded from many key airports. To prevent such drastic action, a small group of men soon created a community of interest which later became the NBAA. This marshalling of forces, modestly begun in late 1946 as the Corporation Aircraft Owners Association (CAOA), was of major historic importance to the world of aviation. It was affirmation that business aviation had come of age.

But evidence of the event that was business aviation's birth seems not to exist. The years between Kitty Hawk and World War I yield stories which link aircraft to business purposes but virtually all seem to be of doubtful or partial authenticity. Documentation is scarce and points primarily to company-sponsored "barnstorming" tours which served the twin purposes of introducing products and aviation to an eager, enthusiastic American public. At the core was a group of pioneering aviators who for the most part lived from hand to mouth, yet in joyous, free spirited circumstances.

The first World War proved the airplane a fearsome tactical weapon and a sophisticated means of surveillance. Great emphasis was laid during the war on development of sturdy, easily maintained and highly maneuverable aircraft capable of achieving high speed and extended range. Equal prominence was placed on the training of pilots, many of whom sought careers in the civil aviation community that grew in the post-war period as improvements were made on aircraft introduced during the war.

Business aviation began as a recognizable activity during this period but it took many, many years for its principal purpose to become the transportation of people. This mature mission developed slowly through a long evolutionary process and, while foreseen in the early 1920's, did not take pre-eminence until after World War II.

Meanwhile, the years from World War I until far into the 1920's produced a business aviation community that was involved principally in product promotion and direct marketing. The routine carriage of passengers on business missions gained only tenuous acceptance until Lindbergh proved in his historic transatlantic flight to Paris in May, 1927 that air transportation was reliable, and more important, safe.

Time would show that Lindbergh's epic flight was much more than an awesome display of piloting skill and technical achievement. It was the great transitional event between demonstration of man's capability to fly and the slow emergence of an organized air transportation system. Almost overnight people became aviation enthusiasts, but a faddish reaction soon followed. A host of imitators rushed in, often poorly prepared, sometimes tragically so, trying to go Lindbergh one better. Others, however, realized that the true message of Lindbergh's victory was being lost. *Popular Aviation* editorially lamented the craze, saying "this is no attempt to belittle the courage or results" of such attempts. But, the magazine urged, "it is the coldly practical, the commercial-minded dollars and cents attitude that we need now. . . After all, aviation is (now) *Transportation, Fast — Clean — Safe.*"[1]

Earlier, in the formative days just after World War I, business aviation was epitomized in the Heddon Company's JN 4-D "Jenny" biplane, (1919) painted so as to make the fuselage look like a scaly fish. Gills and eyes adorned the engine cowling, and the fish's mouth was painted wide open to make it appear that the propeller was about to be swallowed. Heddon, a Dowagiac, Michigan manufacturer of fishing lures, may have been the first company to use a fixed-wing aircraft on a regular basis for business promotion. There is a belief that Heddon's pilot was Frank Hawks, a renowned aviator who established many world records during a period when the outlines of business aviation as a profession were dimly sketched.[2] Heddon later acquired a lighter version of the Jenny, commonly known as the Canuck, and used both aircraft extensively for theatrically-staged delivery of products and for broadening name recognition of the company and its line of fishing lures. It is improbable Hawks worked as a pilot for Heddon. His 1918–1926 activities as barnstormer and entrepreneur in Texas and Mexico are well documented. In 1927, he joined the Texas Company (Texaco) as Superintendent of its Aviation Division.[3]

At about the same time Heddon's fish was plying its way through the air, the Simmons Hardware Company of St. Louis acquired a Curtiss Oriole biplane for $7,500 and had the words "KEEN KUTTER" painted in extraordinarily large form on the fuselage and tail. The pilot was Lt. A(rmor) M. Alcorn, late of the British Royal Flying Corps.[4] A dashing figure, Alcorn took on the mission of promoting the Simmons line of hardware and tools in imaginative ways. A letter dated February 7, 1920, signed by Frank Meigs of the Meigs Hardware Store in Centreville, Alabama, tells this triumphant but complex story:

> *To the best of my knowledge my town is the first in the United States to be visited by a travelling salesman travelling in an aeroplane, and I am the first man to place an order with a travelling salesman travelling in an aeroplane . . . I bought an order of KEEN KUTTER hardware . . . and I am free to pronounce this (unique way of advertising) the biggest thing ever pulled off by the SIMMONS HARDWARE COMPANY.*

In a later sales foray, Lt. Alcorn made a drop of sales literature over Montgomery (apparently Alabama). It announced that a limited number of persons who purchased KEEN KUTTER safety razors would qualify for a drawing, with the winners given free rides in the Oriole. "On a certain day, at a specified time," read a subsequent air drop communication, "the drawing was held and the first numbers drawn from the box indicated those successful in securing the flight." Both the coupon used in the drawing and the "ticket" issued to the lucky few winners described the prize as a "Free KEEN KUTTER FLIGHT in the $7,500 Curtiss Aeroplane."

One individual who was known to have used aircraft for professional reasons as early as 1919 was Frank Brewster, M.D., of Beaver City, Nebraska. With Wade Stevens as his pilot, Dr. Brewster was flown more than a million miles in his two-place Jenny during a 15-year period. Visiting patients throughout Nebraska and Kansas, he is also said to have financed or built five hospitals and five airports in the region. "I got my first airplane ride in Dr. Brewster's plane in 1919. My dad paid $5 for it," said Dill M. "Don" Teel many years later.[5] "I thought it was the greatest thing in the world." In 1927 Teel learned to fly. In time he became an internationally known figure as general manager of U.S. Steel's aircraft division and as a Director and officer of NBAA.

The year 1920 brought an oil boom to Kansas. By mid-1921 the L.M.C. Drilling and Producing Co. of Wichita was the recorded owner of a Laird-Swallow. It is thought the airplane was used for promotional flights and for transportation to drilling sites. Great significance must be given to the fact that this business aircraft was the first airplane to be registered in the United States in accordance with international conventions; its credentials were "N-ABCB c/m 113."[6] Other company aircraft were purchased circa 1921–1922 by the Chicago Tribune Company (a Curtiss C-6 Seagull) and Brooks, Banks and Smith Corp., Framingham, Massachusetts (an Avro 504-K). Businessmen owners of aircraft prior to February, 1922 included John W. Schroeder, Chicago; Walter Becker, Newark, N.J.; John M. Larsen, New York; and John A. Hambleton, Baltimore, a 504-K owner, financier and one of the principal backers of Pan American World Airways.[7]

The 1920's were a period of ripening for business aviation, with a slow but inevitable movement away from what was contemporaneously described as the "spectacular phase" of flying and toward development of a utilitarian role. Before the end of the decade, the first of the "purpose built" aircraft were manufactured, creating a small yet defined business transportation marketplace.

Joining the ranks of business aircraft users during the early part of the decade were such well known companies as Wildroot Hair Tonic and the Prestolite Company.[8]

The Travel Air Manufacturing Company produced its first airplane in 1924 — a 3-place, open cockpit biplane. It was powered by the renowned Curtiss OX-5 engine. Aircraft No. 1 went to O. E. Scott, a St. Louis automobile dealer whose first flight was to Detroit to call on Henry Ford himself.

Competition to the Travel Air soon appeared, and in 1926 the Alexander Film Company of Denver started turning out a 3-place aircraft also powered by the OX-5 which was aimed directly at the business market. The first model, called the "Eaglerock," offered in a 1928 advertisement for "$2475 Denver," was soon converted into a biplane and two other models, the "Bullet" and the "Flyabout"

Photograph courtesy of History of Aviation Collection, University of Texas

B. G. Dahlberg, sugar cane and by-products tycoon, logged more than 300,000 miles in the Fairchild Wasp he purchased in 1927. Celotex was the name of his principal company.

followed. By the end of the decade the Alexander Company had manufactured some 1,100 aircraft but by 1931 the great depression plunged it into bankruptcy.

Stinson was another familiar name in the 1920's and its Model A, a cabin type, was used by Gannett News and Reynolds Tobacco. Lavish praise for business aircraft was expressed by B.G. Dahlberg, sugar cane and byproducts tycoon who bought a Stinson-Detroiter in 1927. Named "The Celotex" after one of his several companies, the airplane was in constant movement through the Southern states and by 1929 its owner had logged more than 300,000 miles. "The cabin is arranged," he wrote, "so that I can work with my secretary, going over the mail and papers on hand and having them all cleaned up by the time we finish our 'hop'." While it was simply impossible for him to estimate either the time saved, or efficiency increased, through air travel, Dahlberg said: "In fact, after having used an airplane for business traveling, it would be as difficult to do without it as to go back to the horse and buggy after the automobile."[9]

Major U.S. oil companies began to realize by the late 1920's that there was a three-fold purpose to be achieved in operating their own aircraft: provision of transportation, demonstration of the speed and safety of aircraft, and promotion of the sale of their products. Standard Oil Company (Indiana) laid emphasis on the first of these when it took delivery of an enormous, cabin-class Ford Trimotor monoplane May 21, 1927. Transportation of executives was the reason, making possible "safe, fast and comfortable trips . . . to oil producing regions, division headquarters and outlying refineries." Lest the uninitiated not comprehend the comfort factor, it was

Photograph courtesy of History of Aviation Collection, University of Texas

An early user of the famed Ford Trimotor was Standard Oil of Indiana. Company publicists pointed out that passengers were not required to "wear helmets, leather coats or any special clothing."

pointed out that "it is not necessary for either pilots or passengers to wear helmets, leather coats or any special clothing ... There is less vibration and jar than is apparent in a modern parlor car ..." With a wing span of 71 feet and length of 49 feet, the Trimotor was the largest business aircraft yet to be seen, but its empty weight was only 5,200 pounds. Evidently a solid hit with the company, it caused Colonel Robert W. Stewart, Chairman, to conclude that speed and point-to-point routing versus train travel "more than compensate for the expense and make the airplane an economical method of travel ... as safe and comfortable as transcontinental train."[10]

Phillips Petroleum Company, headed by air minded Frank Phillips, bought its first company plane in 1927. It was a Travel Air with open cockpit, based at the company's headquarters in Bartlesville, Oklahoma. In addition to using aircraft for personnel transportation, Phillips became a leader in dramatic forms of product promotion. It was the sponsor of celebrated aviator Wiley Post and his world famed airplane, Winnie Mae. In it Post set record after record, not only in point-to-point flights and the setting of new altitude records, but in around-the-world solo flight as well.

Exploitation of speed, safety and product promotion goals led other oil companies to hire well known pilots. Notable among such associations were Texaco and Frank Hawks; Gulf and Al Williams; Standard Oil of New Jersey and Edwin Aldrin (father of lunar astronaut "Buzz" Aldrin); Gilmore Oil and Roscoe Turner; and Shell and Jimmy Doolittle.

In December, 1927 the Texas Company (Texaco) entered this innovative phase of business aviation by investing the then-huge sum of $48,223 in a Ford Trimotor monoplane (NC 3443).[11]

Photograph courtesy of History of Aviation Collection, University of Texas

After entering the business aviation field in 1927, Phillips Petroleum moved up from open cockpit airplanes to the comfort of the cabin class Travel Air.

Chosen to head Texaco's planned "National Aviation Program," a major flying/marketing effort, was Frank Hawks, a remarkable figure who had risen in World War I to the position of assistant officer in charge of flying at the U.S. Army Instructors' School of Advanced Flying, Brooks Field, San Antonio, Texas. From that springboard Hawks went on to renown as a barnstormer in the United States and in Mexico, where he conducted an "aerial circus" for the government during the Centennial Exposition in Mexico City.

Hawks' exploits led him to the business of flying payrolls throughout the bandit-infested oil fields of Mexico, a business which he moved in 1926 to a base in Houston. Along the way he picked up numerous awards for efficiency and speed in aircraft races.

As the first Superintendent of Texaco's Aviation Division Hawks set out to make the Ford Trimotor do four things well: "It is spreading Texaco good will, creating greater interest in aviation, and giving Texaco airplane products severe and practical tests and demonstrating their high quality," said the May, 1928 issue of the *Texaco Star.*

Immediately after taking delivery of the Trimotor in February, 1928, Hawks set out from Dearborn, Michigan, on a whirlwind tour of the American South and Southwest which clearly demonstrated the new Superintendent's will to fulfill his missions. Included were stops, some necessary but unscheduled, at Lexington and Louisville, Kentucky; Atlanta, Georgia; Gainesville, Tampa, Miami, and Jacksonville, Florida; New Orleans, Louisiana; Houston, Port Arthur, Galveston, (aborted because of foul weather), San Antonio, Austin, Waco, Fort Worth, Dallas, Wichita Falls, and Amarillo, Texas; Oklahoma City and Tulsa, Oklahoma; and Little Rock, Arkansas. Hawks reached the final destination of the tour on April Fools Day, 1928, having within 41 days established mountains of good will and recognition.

Illustrative of the conditions he faced were those of the second day of the tour:

On Wednesday, February 22, at 6:45 a.m., we took off from Louisville against a strong southeast wind. The Weather Bureau reported that the low pressure was traveling east from Texas, carrying with it heavy rains, but advised me it would be quite possible, with an early start, to make Atlanta before the bad weather set in.

After an hour's flying it appeared to me that the weather man miscalculated ... It was, without a doubt, the worst storm I have ever encountered, and as I was flying a new ship, and a costly one, I picked my way very cautiously.

The fury of the storm came upon us in Tennessee over the mountains. It was closing down, raining heavily with a terrific wind coupled with several line squalls which threshed the large plane around like a leaf. Twice I was thrown out of my seat.

Despite this and other severe weather obstacles met along the way, the airplane carried several United States Senators, Governors, prominent community leaders, customers of the company, employees and a host of ordinary, highly inquisitive citizens. By the time he had reached Fort Worth, Hawks complained "the question of carrying passengers is getting more and more serious. Everybody wants to go in the Texaco airplane and I am having a serious problem limiting these flights." Crowds grew as the odyssey continued and by the time Little Rock was reached some 10,000 citizens waited at the airport to greet Hawks. The Governor was enthused and Hawks' trip diary reported that "plans are being made to make a little side flight down to Pine Bluff with the Governor, and the National Guards (sic) are so enthusiastic that they are also going to send an escort of five or six airplanes."

With understandable pride, Hawks closed his diary on the 1928 good will-promotional tour by noting that the 41-day journey covered "over ten thousand miles on schedule and without the slightest mishap. We have carried ... 1,368 passengers ... Everybody is enthusiastic and especially those who are trying to forward aviation."

A tragic footnote is appended to the triumphal story of the Ford Trimotor's maiden tour. Texaco aircraft records, maintained meticulously for every craft owned by the company, tersely state the final disposition of Ford NC 3443: "Wrecked in Texas, December 22, 1928." The Trimotor's life was brief but her great contribution to promoting aviation, and in particular to linking aircraft to business, was inestimable.

Prior to making the odyssey in the new Trimotor Hawks conducted the first good will trade extension air tour from the United States (Houston) to Mexico

City. The return leg produced an additional benefit in the form of a new elapsed time speed record of 8 hours, 20 minutes, and a flying time record of 6 hours, 50 minutes. Several transcontinental speed records followed as Hawks concentrated on demonstrating the high speed of air travel as well as its dependability and safety. One record setting flight was said by him to be a means of "establishing a fast 'pony express' service between the east and west coasts."

Commenting on a critical article, "What's Wrong with Aviation?," which appeared in the widely read magazine *Liberty*, Hawks in 1931 said "what American air transport needs is faster and more frequent service . . . Air transportation is going to progress not by carrying more people at one time than the old forms . . . but by carrying people faster and further (sic) in a given time . . ."

Perhaps anticipating the huge, largely untapped potential for business aircraft use, Hawks wrote that,

> *When businessmen, and especially men from the big metropolitan centers . . . can be shown that there is actually a saving of time on the air routes, then I believe that the aviation industry will be on a firm footing with some definite prospects for sound financial development.*

Several of Hawks' record flights were made in Texaco 13 (thirteenth aircraft to be owned by the company), a Travel Air monoplane which was described by the manufacturer as a "mystery ship" powered by a Wright Whirlwind "motor." Extending his mission of good will and education, Hawks took this airplane to Europe (making the transatlantic legs by ship). Between April and June of 1931, he made a number of trips back and forth between principal cities, including London, Paris, Rome, Brussels, Stockholm, and Lausanne. Reflecting the kind of strong and durable bond which aviation created among men, Hawks unaffectedly wrote: "The aviators over here are friendly, the governments are friendly, and I can't help but feel everybody is friendly if a fellow comes over here with the idea of being likewise himself."

The relatively easy accessibility by air of one European capital to the next evidently made a deep impression, one which would logically carry over into comparisons involving key United States cities. "I am still in Paris," wrote Hawks on May 30, "but I have been places this past week." His diary then tells of breakfast in London, lunch in Berlin, and Paris for dinner and the 'Follies' . . . "Please don't think it egotism which prompts me to mention these little trips. I do so only to show that with greater speed a man can see and do much more in a day." Then, in an observation used in countless forms over the years by promoters of business aircraft, he concluded that because of mobility provided by the airplane, "man's . . . business opportunities are greatly increased."

Having made a major contribution to the development of business aviation, particularly in the form of more closely defining its capabilities and promise, Hawks left Texaco in May, 1934. While taking off on a demonstration flight

Photograph courtesy of History of Aviation Collection, University of Texas

Frank Hawks was one of the celebrated airmen who joined forces with petroleum companies in the 1920's to promote products and demonstrate the efficiency of business air transportation. Flying Texaco 13, Hawks spread the message throughout Europe during a three-month tour in 1931.

in East Aurora, New York, in August, 1938, Hawks, then only 41, crashed into telephone wires. His passenger was killed outright. Hawks died in a Buffalo hospital a few hours later.

Left behind were memories of an ambition which had moved business aviation far ahead, and a tradition which Texaco enlivened by its continuous, extensive use of business aircraft over the years. Among those early on who, like Hawks, used aircraft directly to promote products and solicit orders were Texaco's J. P. Henning, who started his "flying salesman" activities in southern regions in 1929, J. D. "Duke" Jernigan, who began in general domestic sales in 1930, and Aubrey Keif. Destined to be elected president and chief executive officer of NBAA

1964–1965, Keif as early as 1932 was piloting a Stearman 4D (Texaco 14) on sales solicitation flights in the central and northern sales division.

At almost the moment of Texaco's entry into business aviation, Lindbergh's great year, 1927, came to a close. Rightly, its final event was a major aviation industry meeting in Washington which breathed life into the new Air Commerce Act. Clearly stated by Secretary of Commerce Herbert Hoover was the department's policy to cooperate with the industry and promote its welfare. Decisions made included the resolve to create a code of airplane design and construction; further, the meeting recommended that "war surplus planes should be used only so long as they remain airworthy." Flying schools were to be classified and airports examined and rated. Lindbergh, whose achievement had helped speed the convening of the group, told the conference: "It is now time for a step forward by inaugurating regulations which will assure the traveling public of as great safety in every form of air activity as they have at present in our organized air lines."[12]

And at the same conference data were circulated showing "by far the greatest volume of flying is done by fixed base and itinerant operators, both individuals and firms . . . A large number of unexpected purchasers . . . are the corporations and individual business men who have bought the most modern planes for business travel.[13] Quietly and in "unexpected" ways business aviation was taking a central position on the stage.

In 1928 Shell Aviation began its long and distinguished history. By the following year, Shell Oil of San Francisco set up an aviation department and hired the accomplished Army flier, Major John A. Macready. He encouraged the St. Louis Shell Company to hire Army pilot James A. Doolittle. This they did, with Doolittle becoming Aviation Manager[14] and another Army officer, James G. Haislip, his assistant. *Shell Wings* noted that the "speed flights performed by this small racing stable certainly did much to prominently display the Shell name before the eyes of the consumer, but their record-breaking feats were even more formidable."

Doolittle's introduction into business flying was not without problems. Deciding that a high speed transport plane was a necessity, he talked Shell into purchasing a $25,000 Lockheed Vega. Picking up the new aircraft in Burbank, Doolittle and his wife flew it east to Mitchell Field, Long Island where they loaded it with possessions and family for the flight to their new home in St. Louis. "It was a cold, blustery winter day and during the take-off run the landing gear began to collapse; the plane settled on its belly" reported *Shell Wings*, "and skidded to a halt on the frozen turf." Ten thousand dollars later the Vega was as good as new and brought speed records to Shell, including the Transport Race at the 1930 National Air Races. For several years thereafter, Doolittle and Haislip alternatively flew the Vega out of St. Louis on company transportation missions or criss-crossed the nation in specially built racing planes, always seeking to set new records.

On one notable day, September 4, 1931, Doolittle was aloft virtually every minute from 5:35 a.m. Pacific time until 10:20 p.m. Central time. During that lengthy period he won the Burbank to Cleveland race of that year, and then went on

Photograph courtesy of History of Aviation Collection, University of Texas

Shell's United States air transport operations began in 1928, one year after those of its European parent organization. A three engine Fokker was a mainstay of Shell's early American fleet.

immediately to New York, setting a new transcontinental record of 11 hours, 16 minutes, and 10 seconds. Returning to the Cleveland Air Races site, he claimed his trophy and hopped aboard another Shell airplane to travel to St. Louis. Arriving at 10:20 p.m. in the evening he went at once to a victory celebration which had been hastily organized by Shell executives.

Not only an exceptional pilot, Doolittle was a Phi Beta Kappa member and held Master's and Doctor's degrees in aeronautical engineering from the Massachusetts Institute of Technology. Academic rigor no doubt led to meticulous planning of his flights and mathematical precision in carrying them out.

Exemplary was an unusual flight he conducted in a Lockheed Orion which he used mostly for executive transport. The time was 1932 and the flight carried the imposing title of the George Washington Bicentennial Airplane Flight. The idea was to retrace by air all of the routes traveled by Washington during his entire lifetime. Ancillary to this goal was the aim to promote use of air mail, so a plan evolved whereby a mail pouch would be dropped over thirty communities along the route. To add yet another dimension, Ann Madison Washington, a descendant of George, was a passenger. Doolittle carried out all the arrangements flawlessly and after flying 2,600 miles on a circuitous route from Maine to Newark, New Jersey, terminated the flight 15 hours and 40 minutes after engine start.

One of Doolittle's major contributions to aviation lay in his successful persuasion of Shell that it should produce 100 octane fuel. Along the way this decision was criticized as "Doolittle's Folly," but in 1938 the higher octane fuel was adopted as standard by the Army Air Corps. The significantly superior margin of performance it gave to American airplanes in World War II is given credit as a major reason for Allied victory.

After gallant service in that war, Doolittle returned to Shell as a vice president and became one of many American business leaders to travel in a surplus B-25 bomber, converted to civilian transportation configuration.

He and Shell continued to play prominent roles in business aviation. In 1959 NBAA conferred on him its Award for Meritorious Service to Aviation, the highest distinction given by the Association.

In 1928, at about the same time as Shell's launch, Atlantic Richfield acquired its first business aircraft, with Dudley Steel acting as its manager and chief pilot. Soon after, an article describing growth in business aviation said "then came Richfield Oil. They brought a plane costing $82,000, the last word in airplane construction and refinement. Use of the Richfield plane is limited to the president of the company and some of their major officials."[15] Steel was to have a long career in aviation and subsequently became manager of the Lockheed Air Terminal airfield in Burbank, California.

Yet another oil company aircraft operation began when on October 23, 1928, Continental Oil Company (later Conoco) took possession of a Ryan B-1 monoplane previously owned by its chairman. Soon the Ryan was sold in an upgrade move to a Travel Air cabin class airplane. Conoco's red triangle trademark appeared on the fuselage along with an advertising message, "Germ Processed Airplane Oils." Over the years the Conoco fleet grew to impressive size and complexity and in 1951 it began one of the pioneer daily business aircraft shuttle operations between various key company facilities, first utilizing DC-3 aircraft.

The same year one of the late 1920's Travel Air biplanes went to the Missouri-Pacific Railroad, making it the first landlocked transportation company to become a business aircraft user.

And 1928, according to Cole H. Morrow, one of CAOA's early Chairmen, witnessed completion of the "first multi-engine aircraft designed and built specifically for business use."[16] It was the Chapman/Burnelli CB-16, built for banker Paul W. Chapman. Ordered in May, it flew in December, piloted by Lieutenant Wade Leigh, one of the airmen on the first round-the-world flight. Capable of carrying 16 passengers, the CB-16 was described by Morrow as having 145 miles per hour cruise speed, a climb rate of 800 feet per minute and non-stop range from coast to coast. It also was "the first multi-engine aircraft to incorporate a retractable landing gear." The airplane was lost at sea in 1929 during a disastrous attempt to

Photograph courtesy of History of Aviation Collection, University of Texas

Richfield Oil bought its first airplane in 1929. The next year it purchased this Fokker and put 30,000 miles on it in the first three months.

pick up mail on the fly from the luxury liner S.S. Leviathan. Fortunately there were no injuries to pilot or passengers.

Among well known persons owning business aircraft in 1928 was Walter J. Kohler, chief executive officer of the Kohler Co., Kohler, Wisconsin almost continuously from 1905 to 1940. His only break in service was from 1928 to 1930 when he was Governor of the state. To help in his lively campaign he purchased a Ryan monoplane, sister ship to Lindbergh's, in June, 1928 and named it the "Village of Kohler." The candidate covered 7,280 miles in 104 flights and continued to use the aircraft during his gubernatorial term and later in Kohler Co. business. His pioneering efforts created a lasting air-mindedness in the Kohler company for in 1987 it still operated business aircraft.[17]

As the 1920's drew to a close and American business flourished in one of its greatest periods of exuberant growth, several major product innovations helped to speed the development of business aviation.

The implications of Lindbergh's epic achievement were by then more fully realized and its revolutionary effects on transportation were beginning to take form. An awareness grew which recognized that business aviation's role would be essential to the peaceful revolution. A contemporary article put the case in almost

Continental Oil was another of the petroleum companies that helped pioneer business aviation. This early Boeing model, with open cockpit and enclosed passenger cabin, was in the company's growing fleet in the late 1920's.

do-or-die terms: "The man who has the pocketbook to buy an airplane and hire a pilot is primarily a business man and he is not yet air minded. He still considers it a hazardous means of travelling." Yet, the author observed, ". . . business is turning rapidly to the airplane as its newest arm . . . The next large field open to the airplane is that in which the corporation executive moves. And unfortunately for the executive, I think it makes little difference whether he wishes to ride in airplanes. He will be forced to accept aviation or he will step down in favor of the man who will fly."[18]

At about this time the Travel Air Company merged with Curtiss-Wright to become the Curtiss-Wright Travel Air Division and soon a new Travel Air appeared, vastly changed from the open cockpit versions introduced in 1924. The new airplane was cabin class, offering a true "flight deck" for the pilot and limited yet comfortable interior seating for up to six passengers.

In a far-sighted sales literature statement of the late 1920's, the company accurately judged that a new phase had begun: "The spectacular phase of flying has passed. The daredevils of the air have ceased to fly for entertainment and now fly for business . . ." The company accordingly set a course which would dominate major future marketing orientation.

Advertising copy capitalized on the theme:

450 miles since morning — two engagements filled and home in time for dinner.

Walter J. Kohler was chief executive of his company for almost 35 years. He purchased a Ryan monoplane to assist in his successful campaign to become Governor of Wisconsin in 1928.

Breakfast at home — leisurely attention to office mail — Indianapolis in time for luncheon — important engagements filled and back to Chicago by early evening. Not an idle dream, but an every day occurrence for the modern business executive who travels by air.

How to Save a Day — how to gain a day on competition, is fully answered by using the Travel Air cabin monoplane. It takes off quickly and smoothly; climbs fast; cruises at 100 miles per hour and lands slowly, without shock...[19]

A flurry of other innovative products appeared at about the same time. Fairchild introduced its Model 71. Cessna, in 1929, started production of the single engine DC-6 model, a long, low, racy high wing ancestor of the Airmaster. Among the first of the business use airplanes designed by Cessna, it achieved the astonishing speed of 115 miles per hour, powered by a 170 hp Curtiss Challenger engine.

Other late 1920's business owners, according to material in the History of Aviation Collection, University of Texas, were Reid, Murdock and Co. grocers (Ford Trimotor), Cook Paint and Varnish, St. Louis (Fairchild 71), The Kellogg Company (Fokker), Standard of Ohio (Ryan), Des Moines Register-Tribune (Fairchild FC-2), and Allen Oil Co., Hobart, Oklahoma (American Eagle A-1).

General D. Harold Byrd, a Texan and cousin of the noted Admiral Richard E. Byrd, was reported to have owned many business use airplanes, the last of which was a Lodestar. Byrd, a pioneering oil driller, is said to have sunk 59 dry holes before making major strikes. Unusually air minded, he was one of the leaders of the campaign to make the Civil Air Patrol the official auxiliary of the U.S. Air Force.

Growing acceptance of business aviation by major corporations did not go unnoticed. "When you find such organizations as General Motors taking it up and going into it with their resources, the question of its assured success is answered," said the same writer who declared businessmen must fly "or else".[20] Long involved in manufacture of aircraft and components, GM came into business aviation operations through purchase in 1929 of a four engine Fokker (GM held a substantial interest in Fokker Corporation of America) by Larry P. Fisher, one of the original Fisher brothers. This Fisher, general manager of the Cadillac motor car division, based his airplane at Detroit City Airport; later most of its flight and ground crew personnel became employees of the General Motors Air Transport Section,[21] a leading element in business aviation in the years ahead.

In 1929, the United States Line became airborne by means of a Chapman/ Burnelli airplane, and in the same year Sikorsky introduced its Model S-38 amphibian, initiating a vogue which was to become widespread in business aviation during the 1930's.

Sikorsky and Grumman, the latter producing the popular Goose, Widgeon, and Mallard, dominated the amphibian business aircraft market. Among reasons for the popularity of the amphibian were its very large size and comfort and the fact that it offered a practicable way to get around the dearth of airports. Among companies owning Grumman products were General Motors, Ford, General Foods, General Tire, and 20th Century Fox.

Charles Lindbergh himself was at the controls of the early Sikorsky S-38 flights which in February, 1929, first transported mail by air between Miami and the Panama Canal Zone. The airplane was slightly larger than any previously tailored to personal and business use, having a 71 foot, 8 inch wing span and carrying capacity of eight passengers.

Among the early business users were Grigsby-Grunow, manufacturers of the ubiquitous Majestic radio. The multimillionaire John Hay Whitney, newspaper publisher and owner of the great racing horse stables, purchased one for personal transportation. Sikorsky described his airplane as "probably the finest private flying yacht yet produced in this country." It has a "comfortable spring couch" with soft

Photograph courtesy of History of Aviation Collection, University of Texas

Pioneering Texan oil driller D. Howard Byrd, right, reputedly sank 59 dry holes before striking it rich. An avid business aircraft user, he also was instrumental in forming the Civil Air Patrol.

leather cushions, "heavy plush carpet, four special high-backed chairs, a highly polished cabinet with drawer and folding top, ash receivers, carafe, vanity case and special flight instruments for the convenience of passengers."[22]

This glowing description helped inadvertently to create an erroneous impression which has persisted over the years as a thorny and vexing problem for business aviation. Failure of many critics to perceive a clear line between personal and business purposes has perpetuated the myth. The high visibility of aircraft has reinforced it. These factors have manufactured an image of business aircraft use as a self-indulgent and elitist activity, centered more on personal satisfactions than business promotion. As years passed, terms such as "yacht" or "royal barge" have been used by critics to demean business aircraft use, even though the factual record has consistently shown that these are gross inaccuracies.

Exemplary of business use aircraft of the late 1920's were cabin class machines used by The Automatic Washer Company, Newton, Iowa, and "The Vision of Prestolite." In both cases, the airplane served as a spartan, highly functional "office in the sky."

"Smiling Thru," a Travel Air configured as a true "private air office," was used by H. L. Ogg, President of the Automatic Washer Company to promote face-to-face business contacts and to popularize the company's name. Wilfred Gerbracht, right, was Ogg's full time pilot. The lady is not identified.

Memories of the Automatic Washer aircraft, a Travel Air whose fuselage bore the name "Smiling Thru" in large gold letters, were collected some 50 years later by David M. Woodrow, Director of Aviation, 3M. Woodrow's father was an executive with Automatic Washer and the younger Woodrow, who was Chairman of the Board of NBAA from 1981 to 1983, had his first airplane ride on "Smiling Thru."

Neatly painted lettering on the door of the airplane identified it as the "Private Air Office of H. L. Ogg, President" of the washer machine company. A remarkable man, Ogg overcame the loss of his right arm to build the company into one of the major elements of its field, using a florid sense of showmanship as one of his many personal tools.

When the airplane was flown in 1929 from the factory in Wichita to its christening in Newton, it was accompanied by an escort of nine other planes flying in formation. Mrs. Ogg broke a bottle of champagne on "Smiling Thru's" propeller hub, and an elegant luncheon attended by many publishers followed. The event became first page news.

The decor and fitting out of the airplane were remarkable. In addition to the foot-high lettering on the sides of the fuselage and the inscription on the door, the wings were painted a deep orange and the company's slogan, reminding all who saw it that Monday was washday, was painted on the leading edges: "Start the Week with a Smile." Inside the cabin were seats for five, a washroom and toilet, and an intercom which permitted conversation with the full-time, uniformed pilot, Wilfred Gerbracht. There was also a typing table with portable Corona, electric outlet for a dictation machine and provision for up to four washing machines (the maximum attainable by removing some of the seats).

Besides using the airplane for transportation connected with management of the company, Ogg carried on the early tradition of exploiting good public recognition and relations through the mere presence of a business aircraft. "Smiling Thru" was used with good dramatic effect for product demonstrations, and for providing free rides to employees and fortunate potential customers as well. Above all, the Automatic Washer Company airplane was a no-nonsense business machine; an article about it in 1980[23] concluded that:

Far more important than the list of equipment aboard, some of which now appears almost quaint, was Ogg's philosophy about the use of an airplane for business. His 'private air office' embodied precepts that even today are being learned and applied by new business aviation operations.

The "Vision of Prestolite" a single-engine, cabin class aircraft identified as a sister ship to Lindbergh's "Spirit of St. Louis" also served a dual role as a no-frills transportation machine and a publicity generating phenomenon. Its cabin was a spartan office in the sky, fitted out with a polished wood knee-hole desk containing four drawers, a large working surface, water thermos and drinking glass, and a large dictating machine. Prestolite's general manager is quoted as saying he could crowd almost six months of travel time by other means into sixty days by using this early "time machine."[24]

As America moved from the fast track of the 1920's into the deep trough of the great depression which brought the world's economy to its knees, the pace of business aviation growth slowed.

And yet, during the depression years, a significant number of new products were introduced. More and more companies, accepting the airplane as a tool for promoting and expediting business, joined the ranks of owners. Even at the lowest depths there was realization of the business aircraft's worth. "At first we thought it was a gamble . . . but after six months' trial we wholeheartedly realized that . . . the airplane . . . was the (sales) stimulant needed in these days of depression, and the panacea for the majority of our ills and business worries," said a company president who had two monoplanes in use.[25] The 1932 article quoting this enthusiast added that "the American public is becoming airminded more and more each day and it remains for the business men of America to discard their antiquated ideas of getting business and adopt 1930 methods."

Photograph courtesy of History of Aviation Collection, University of Texas

Prestolite, the battery manufacturer, used its Ryan, a sister ship to Lindbergh's, as a flying office, equipping it with a large desk and a dictating machine.

During the same period E.L. Cord of motor car fame described how invaluable an aircraft was to making his use of time more productive. "In our judgment," he said, "it is time for the industry to quit talking about the 'future of aviation.' To us aviation today offers an improved type of transportation, practical and safe and one which the public vitally needs."[26]

John Morrell & Company, the meat packers, acquired a cabin class Travel Air in 1930. And during the same year Socony-Vacuum (later Mobil Corporation) took the plunge into aircraft ownership. After having used chartered planes for several years Vacuum Oil purchased three planes in 1930, a Curtiss-Robin, a Fairchild 34 and Stinson-Junior, planning to use them strictly as sales builders. A year later a merger created Socony-Vacuum. Socony bought an Autogiro, a strange looking ship with a propeller in front but with a rotor substituting for wings, creating lift as the ship gained forward speed. For many years the Mobil operation was headed by Colonel Harley W. Lake, a colorful, strong-willed and rather impulsive aviation pioneer who was an original but non-participating Director of CAOA. Later, under Charles E. Morris, the Mobil fleet was recognized as the largest business aircraft operation in the world, with headquarters at the Westchester County Airport in New York, and other elements based at 10 locations spread from California to Canada, Saudi Arabia to Tripoli, Nigeria to Singapore.[27]

A spate of amphibian purchases took place during the early 1930's. The Esso (later EXXON) Company brought a 6-place Douglas Dolphin on line and the Walgreen Drug Store chain bought a Sikorsky S-38 amphibian. Continental Oil (later Conoco), Gulf Oil, McFadden Publications, and the Noble Drilling Corporation added their names to the growing list of petroleum industry amphibian users.

In 1932, Walter and Olive Ann Beech went independent by creating the Beech Aircraft Corporation out of the Curtiss-Wright Travel Air Division. Walter was to remain president of the new enterprise until his death in 1950, and Olive Ann carried on her husband's leadership for a further period of some 35 years. The first of the "Beechcraft" line, a model 17, was sold to the Ethyl Corporation in 1933 for $17,000. Popularity of the 17 was evidenced by the fact that it remained in production until 1948. And Clyde Cessna, aided mightily by his nephew, Dwane Wallace, also persevered during the lean years of the depression, steadily increasing market share by making continuous product improvements and innovations.

Lockheed became an active business aircraft manufacturer during the period, with its Model 10 going to such companies as Fleishmann's Yeast and A.O. Smith. The latter, based in Milwaukee, received the second Model 10 airplane and hired Ed Pavla, a seasoned Northwest Air Lines pilot, to operate it. In 1935, Lockheed, in response to a competition sponsored by the U.S. Department of Commerce, designed the Model 12 Electra Junior, a purpose-built, scaled down version of its popular airline transport aircraft. The smaller machine carried six passengers, a crew of two, and cruised at 200 miles an hour. It had the distinctive triple tail which was a Lockheed "trademark" up through the Constellation series. It also is believed to have been the first airplane to use transport tricyle gear and thermal wing deicing. Of particular historic significance was the fact that the Model 12 was designed for business rather than general use; added lustre came from its leading position in the government's design competition.

Nineteen thirty-five witnessed birth of company aircraft operations at Cities Service Oil Company. A DC-2 was purchased that year and a photograph of its interior, showing a comfortable cabin arrangement with art deco tables, plush-covered couch and four upholstered chairs was featured in a *Fortune* magazine article. In the mid-30's the DC-2 was much in demand, taking the place of the Ford Trimotor in the inventory of many airlines. Thomas J. Simpson, Captain for Cities Service in 1987, said he believed the DC-2 which founded the company's fleet was lost in World War II when it was being flown by the U.S. Army. The replacement aircraft was one of the final production models of the DC-3, a backbone airplane of the post-war business and airline fleets.

While new business-use aircraft developed by Cessna, Beech, Lockheed, and others were tailored to meet transportation needs, the original thread of sales promotion use of business aircraft still remained in the fabric of the 1930's. There is a tale of a resourceful but unidentified fruit basket salesman who in 1936 bought one of the earliest of the Piper Cub trainer aircraft. It enabled him to land almost at the door of his customers' barns. His unique sales approach is alleged to have doubled his business within the year.

Technological advances of the depression years coupled innovative aircraft design to a new generation of engines. Together these developments gave the community impetus and renewed vigor.

The Wright Whirlwind and Pratt and Whitney Wasp engines were adapted to a host of airplanes: the Curtiss Condor; flying machines manufactured by Bellanca, Douglas, Fairchild, Waco, Beech, Grumman and Lockheed; and Cessna's renowned Airmaster, which for three successive years was named "most efficient

Star Aircraft Company of Bartlesville, Oklahoma, built this airplane for the Cities Service Company. Billy Parker, Star's owner, later joined Phillips Petroleum as its chief pilot.

airplane." Among 1937–1939 Airmaster owners were the Ungren-Frazier Drilling Co., Abilene, Texas; Service Steel Company, Detroit, Michigan; Osage Construction Company, Great Bend, Texas; and Midland Construction Company, Columbus, Ohio.

Cessna's low-wing twin engine T-50 cabin airplane quickly became a classic as the decade ended and war clouds loomed. Owners included Palmer Oil Corp., Wichita, Kansas; Air Track Manufacturing Corp., College Park, Maryland; and the fabled William P. "Bill" Lear, whose Lear Avia in Dayton, Ohio, owned two. The first was destroyed in a crash in March, 1941. Undaunted, Lear ordered a replacement and it was delivered by mid-May, proving that time was not wasted at the Cessna plant and that Lear had unquestioning faith in the T-50.[28]

Also joining the business aircraft operating community in the late 1930's and early 1940's were Pure Oil, Hal Roach Studios, General Tire and Rubber, Mayflower Transit, Finch Communications, the Detroit News, Dresser Industries, and Rexall Drug Stores. Rexall was introduced to business aviation by Justin Dart, an employee who convinced the company to purchase two Model 12 Lockheeds. A

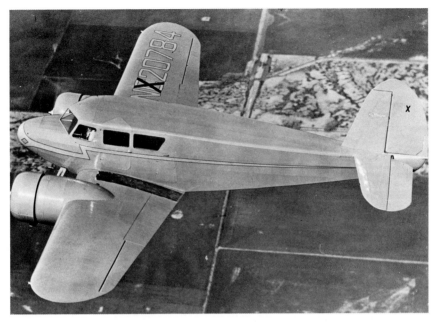

Cessna's T-50 (shown here in its prototype phase) was one of the early great airplanes that were built with business use foremost in mind. This craft helped speed the rapid growth of business air transportation as the nation shook off the great depression of the 1930's.

hard-driving yet visionary man, Dart moved on to replace Rexall's name with his own and then to broaden the company into Dart Industries years later.

   In 1937, Beech introduced its Model 18, which was to become ubiquitous both in peace and war. The first production airplane went to an Oregon insurance executive, Harry K. Coffey, who used it to visit his many branch offices throughout the northwestern United States. Testifying to the suitability of the Model 18 series to business use was the fact that some 8,000 were built from the 1930's to the 1950's.

   Other pre-World War II business aircraft owners were Tenneco, the Murchison Brothers, Brown and Root, El Paso Natural Gas, Superior Oil and Fain Drilling. Standard Oil of California was the first company to operate the Douglas DC-2, and also owned a Ford Trimotor. Lockheed's Model 18 Lodestar made its appearance, and went on to become popular for wartime transport use, for airlines and for business transportation. Redesigning the flaps systems and changing the wing tips, Lear gave his name to the aircraft, (Learstar) adding to the strong credentials he had built since 1930 in the navigation/communications field.

   The costs of owning and operating business aircraft have been of continuous interest, and on occasion of concern, to prospective or actual owners. An

Photograph courtesy of History of Aviation Collection, University of Texas

The daughter of General Fechet, chief executive of General Tire, used a time honored method of christening the "General Jim," the flagship of the company's aircraft fleet in the late 1920's.

insight into the costs associated with early business aircraft is provided by a paper written in 1931 by Jerome Lederer. The contrasts between that period and the late

Beech's ubiquitous Model 18 was introduced in 1937. By the 1950's some 8,000 had been manufactured. In peace and war the craft was one of aviation's greatest success stories and it became a staple in post-war business aviation development.

1980's are remarkable. The paper was published by Western Flying[29] and presented by the author at the 1931 National Aeronautic Meeting of the American Society of Mechanical Engineers (ASME).

Lederer gained renown in the aviation world as Director of the Safety Bureau of the Civil Aeronautics Board, later becoming President of the Flight Safety Foundation. He also was a leading aeronautical engineering executive with the National Aeronautics and Space Administration (NASA) and winner of the prestigious Wright Brothers Memorial Trophy.

In the early 1930's he was Vice President and Chief Engineer of Aero Engineering and Advisory Services, Inc., an organization which furnished safety counselling to aviation interests and worked closely with aviation insurance underwriters.

In May of 1930, the organization became one of business aviation's pioneers by purchasing two 3-place, open cockpit, biplane Travel Airs. One airplane was used west of the Mississippi River, one east, with the mission of being "used by our flying engineers to inspect aviation insurance risks; to contact our resident engineers all over the country, and occasionally to contact agents of insurance companies."

Lederer's methodically-developed data showed that pilots' salary was the largest single item of cost, running at $4,000 per year. Total fixed costs for each airplane was calculated at $8,846.20 with depreciation of the plane and other equipment pegged at 33⅓ percent a year. Running costs, including depreciation for a 400-hour period were $4,368. The average price for fuel was set at 29.5 cents a gallon and oil at about 36.5 cents per quart, with regional variations influencing both averages.

The paper, in commenting on pilot salary levels, said the item was highest of all because it was "a measure of the skill necessary to pilot present day aircraft. Therefore, with the development of safer aircraft, enabling a normal person to learn practical flying in a relatively few hours, the pilot's salary will become a minor factor," the paper optimistically concluded.

As the 1930's ended, Europe was at war and America, while not a combatant until the Japanese air strike at Pearl Harbor in December, 1941, moved inexorably toward wartime conditions. With the conversion of the nation's industrial base to programs such as the lend-lease scheme to aid the European Allies, the need for air transport increased dramatically. When the nation went to a full wartime status, rationing of critical supplies became necessary, and the government drafted many transport aircraft into service to meet military requirements. The availability of travel by airlines was drastically curtailed at the same moment as need for industrial-related transportation skyrocketed.

To balance needs, the government made aircraft available to industry and permitted existing business aircraft to continue operations which supported the war effort. Companies supplied their own air crews as one of the stipulations which permitted aircraft use.

As America emerged from the war and struggled in late 1945 and 1946 to convert a huge arsenal into a storehouse for peaceful uses, the need for civil air transportation virtually exploded.

This great expansion of requirements led in mid-1946 to a crisis which united the business aviation[30] community in an organization that was to have pervasive influence on all of aviation for the years to come.

NOTES TO "PRELUDE"

1. *Popular Aviation,* September, 1927, Editorial, p. 33.

2. *Flying Magazine,* October 192_ (date illegible) and telephone interview Richard Lampl, NBAA, with Edward Rice, Curator, History of Aviation Collection, University of Texas, Dallas, March 23, 1981.

3. Data on Hawks and Texaco's early aviation activities were supplied to the author by J.M. Groll, Chief Pilot, and L.B. Gerlach, Manager, Texaco Aviation Transport Division, February 1987. A biographical narrative written by Edith Bowie Hawks, his wife, describes Hawks' activities between World War I and his joining Texaco. No mention is made of his being in Michigan or working as a pilot for Heddon. There is a 1927 comment on friendship between Hawks and Charles Heddon of Dougiac (sic) Michigan. (E.B. Hawks, undated, typed manuscript, pp. 6 and 22, History of Aviation Collection, University of Texas.)

4. Copy of brochure titled, "Simmons Hardware Company Salesman Traveling Via Aeroplane," undated.

5. "News Report," NBAA, July, 1972, p. 7.

6. Letter, John W. Davis, Wichita, Kansas, to J.H. Winant, July 10, 1987.

7. Ibid.

8. These references to company aircraft and dates, as well as many others mentioned later in "Prelude" are drawn from a group of articles, titled, "Geneaology of Business Aviation," *Skyways,* September, 1959, p. 13ff.

9. *Aeronautics (& Popular Aviation),* November, 1929, "The Magic Carpet of Business," p. 33ff.

10. *Popular Aviation,* September, 1927, "Business Travels by Plane," p. 19ff.

11. Texaco data, Groll and Gerlach.

12. *Popular Aviation,* February, 1928, "The Washington Conference," p. 62.

13. Ibid., January, 1928, "Growth of Air Transportation, in 1927," p. 77.

14. Data on early Shell aviation activities were supplied to the author by D.L. Pease, Manager, Corporate Aviation, Shell Oil Company, April, 1987. Mr. Pease pointed out for the record that Shell Aviation Corporation has always been the owner of the aircraft, leasing them to the Shell Oil Company. This arrangement comports "with the Air Commerce Act of 1926 which provides for the requirement that a registered aircraft must be owned by an American corporation."

15. *Aeronautics (& Popular Aviation)*, June, 1929, "Business Says — You Must Fly," John C. Nulsen, p. 30ff.

16. Cole H. Morrow, McLean, Virginia, "The First Multiengine Corporate Airplane," undated paper.

17. Letter, Peter J. Fetterer, Kohler Co., to J.H. Winant, May 20, 1987 with various printed materials, 1928 to 1972.

18. *Aeronautics (& Popular Aviation)*, June, 1929, p. 30ff.

19. *Business and Commercial Aviation,* June, 1980, "Reflections," p. 39.

20. *Aeronautics (& Popular Aviation)*, June, 1929, p. 30ff.

21. Letter, H.O. Evans, General Motors Air Transport Section, to J.H. Winant, May 29, 1987 with copy of GM briefing script, "History of Air Transport Section," dated December, 1984.

22. *Skyways,* September, 1929.

23. *Business and Commercial Aviation,* June, 1980, p. 38ff; also data supplied to the author by David M. Woodrow, 3M, 1980 and 1986.

24. "The Business Aircraft: Time Machine," illustrated speech script, NBAA, Revised 1976.

25. *Popular Aviation,* September, 1932, "Modern Business Looks Up," Ora E. Graham, pp. 454-455.

26. *Popular Aviation,* August, 1932, "Why We Entered the Aviation Field," E.L. Cord, p. 397.

27. Letter, David M. Sheehan, Mobil Corporation, to J.H. Winant, May 26, 1987, with various excerpts from "Flight," 1981 newsletter of Mobil Aircraft Operations Department.

28. Letter, H. Dean Humphrey, Cessna Aircraft Company, to J.H. Winant, June 1, 1987, with data on owners of Cessna aircraft.

29. *Western Flying,* reprint May, 1931, "What It Costs to Operate a Business Plane," Jerome Lederer.

30. The term "business aviation" is used throughout "Prelude," even though it did not come into common usage until after World War II. Earlier descriptions of this segment of aviation ranged from "industrial aid flying" to "executive" flying. By the early 1950's "business aviation" received strong support as the most appropriate terminology. CAOA helped push the concept along, and Cole H. Morrow gave it added impetus in the movement which led to changing CAOA's name to NBAA in 1953.

Chapter 1

THE AWAKENING: MAY, 1946

THE COMING OF PEACE IN LATE 1945 WAS GREETED joyously. But it ushered in a long period of trial and strain in the civil aviation community of the United States. Airlines struggled to reestablish themselves and to capitalize on a huge public appetite for air transportation which had been keenly developed, and yet suppressed, by wartime conditions. In the personal-recreational flying arena there was a kind of optimistic chaos caused by the demobilization of thousands of pilots trained during the war. Many were anxious to continue flying as an avocation, others ready to accept "GI Bill" subsidies to further their education and training in aviation.

The business aviation segment felt the stirrings of a pent-up demand which was widely expected to burst into a flood of activity. Available to turn this belief into reality was a host of well-trained and highly experienced aviators who looked forward to making careers in aviation. And there was a large supply both of surplus military transport aircraft and of new models emerging from production lines converted to peacetime use. Impelling the surge in business aviation was memory of the efficiency and utility of transport aircraft during the war years. There was strong belief that these characteristics could speed the conversion of the economy to meet new civilian demands.

But the spectre of constraint, regulation, and insufficient airspace-airport capacity hung heavily over all of aviation. This posed a serious threat to the fulfillment of the many optimistic hopes and beliefs that an era of unhampered growth was ready to begin.

By March of 1946 serious problems were becoming commonplace in the nation's airway-airport system. Delays were rampant in the controlled movement of air traffic and the capacity of major airports was often strained to its limits.

Two men, one an executive of an aircraft-owning pharmaceutical company, the other president of a major aviation service and sales organization, decided the

Photograph courtesy of W. L. Patrick

Concern over growing airways-airports congestion was shared in 1946 by Sydney Nesbitt, right, and Palmer J. Lathrop (not in photograph) and led to the founding of CAOA, later renamed National Business Aircraft Association. Nesbitt was Atlantic Aviation's President, based in Teterboro, N.J. Shown with him were Cornelius Fulton, Jr., who later served on CAOA's Board as representative of Mathieson Chemical Co., and an unidentified young lady sporting bobby sox.

time had come to meet the problems head-on. There is no record as to which took the first step. But it is obvious that Palmer "Bud" Lathrop, assistant to the president of the Bristol-Myers Company, and Sydney Nesbitt, president of Atlantic Aviation Corporation, together determined there was an urgent reason for business aircraft owners to meet. Adding impetus to the need for a meeting were articles published on May 8 and 9, 1946 in major New York daily newspapers. These painted a bleak picture of "overcrowded skies" and implied that drastic limiting steps might have to be taken.

Invitations were extended to a number of business aircraft owners to attend a meeting at the Biltmore Hotel in New York on May 17, 1946. How many companies

Palmer J. "Bud" Lathrop, Vice President of Bristol-Myers, gained wartime experience in air transport operations. He was the leading force in organizing The Corporation Aircraft Owners Association in 1946.

were invited cannot be determined but it is known that 13 men assembled for the session. The Wings Club had moved its quarters from the Yale Club, next door, to the Biltmore April 1, 1946[1] and it is generally agreed that the meeting was held in the club's new rooms.

Were it not for the initiative taken by Lathrop and Nesbitt, and for the discussion and decisions reached in the May 17 meeting there might well be nothing more than a relative handful of business aircraft in use today.

Lathrop was a 1931 graduate of Princeton University and during World War II had risen to the rank of Major in the U.S. Army Air Corps. Specializing in air transportation operations in the service,[2] Lathrop learned much about the utility of aircraft and the ways in which they could greatly extend the productive use of time. Lathrop was in 1946 based at Bristol-Myers' manufacturing plant at 225 Long Avenue, Hillside, New Jersey and would, within a year, become Vice President — Production. It was he who convinced Bristol-Myers of the strong potential benefits of company-owned aircraft, and in 1946 the organization operated a twin-engine Beechcraft Model 18, naming it the "Bristoliner."

Nesbitt served as Atlantic's president from 1945 to 1952. Remembered as an outgoing individual with vision quick to focus on worthwhile causes, he was known personally to most corporate pilots in the northeast. His own healthy self-interest in the growth and well being of business aviation paralleled that of Atlantic Aviation. He was known for the vigor which he would lend to all projects which he seriously felt would help the community to grow.[3] At the time of the Biltmore meeting, Nesbitt had his offices at Atlantic Aviation's contemporary headquarters in Hangar 2, Teterboro Airport, New Jersey, then the busiest business aircraft terminal in the United States.

The others present at the May 17 meeting, which was the first formal activity leading to establishment of what would grow into the National Business Aircraft Association, Inc. (NBAA), were: L.J. Lee and C.C. Conway, Jr., both of Continental Can Company; Kenneth R. Unger, Johnson & Johnson; R.F. Bloszies, Manufacturers Trust Company; Stuart Knickerbocker (also identified in notes of the meeting as C.C. Knickerbocker or Stewart Nickerbocker), Time-Life; J.W. Dunaway (also identified as Donoway), Johns-Manville; S.S. Tyndall (also identified as Tindell), Aircraft Industries Association; John Regan, *Airports* magazine; T.J. Deegan and P.J. McDonnell, Abbott-Kimball Company; and W.J. Russell, New York State Department of Commerce.[4]

It is interesting to examine the composition of the May 17 group. In all, 11 institutions were represented by the 13 persons present. Seven were companies which owned business aircraft. The other four organizations present each had auxiliary interests in the situation: Atlantic Aviation Corporation was a major service/sales organization; *Airports* Magazine had an editorial and business stake in the crisis which led to the meeting; the New York State Commerce agency was finely tuned to actions which might impact on post-war industrial development in the state; the aircraft manufacturing industry association had pervasive interest in the orderly growth of business aviation.

There was another aspect of the group's composition that demands note. Except for Tyndall all 13 were from the greater New York area. Elsewhere, and particularly in the large and important business aviation community of the industrial Midwest, there was coolness. The need for the meeting "wasn't all that well accepted in the Midwest at the time," said one of the invitees[5] from that region. "There was a feeling that it would possibly be for business promotion" by Nesbitt, who was not well known in the Midwest then. Prominent business aviation leaders in that area discussed the forthcoming meeting but decided to "sit it out" and await the results.

But the Biltmore group, while compact geographically, was in its general character prophetically typical of gatherings which would take place over the many years to come. Organized business aviation, from its beginning point that day, has never lacked allies. Around the business aircraft there has existed a wide community of interests and institutions, including those who manufacture the products, those who maintain and service them, those who provide specialized aid, those who write about the community, and those who at various levels of government recognize the intrinsic worth of business aviation. Crisis has visited business aviation many times in many forms since 1946 and on most of these occasions the business aircraft alliance which became NBAA served as the rallying point. In good times as well as bad, NBAA provided an umbrella shielding all these diverse, yet interdependent, interests. And to their everlasting credit, all agreed that the fundamental aim of NBAA has been to represent first and foremost the interests of private-carriage business aircraft owners/operators. It has been their good health which has insured the good health of all who act in a supportive or related capacity.

The May 17 meeting was opened by Nesbitt, who used only a brief moment to introduce Lathrop. The Bristol-Myers executive moved quickly to the point. Concerns which caused the meeting were of recent origin. They had been crystallized about a week before with publication of a front page, lead column article in the *Wall Street Journal* (May 8, 1946).[6] This had been followed on May 9 by a similar story in the *New York Herald-Tribune*. Lathrop said, "I think the best introduction would be to read these articles to you." The May 8 story carried this multi-level headline:

Aerial Traffic Jams

They'll Grow Acute as New Planes Flood Sky; Are Already Serious

Airports, Swamped Now, See Sky-Liners Nearly Tripled During Next 18 Months

Traffic Control Bogs Down

The writer, Richard P. Cooke, then told in colorful language of the dimensions of the problems. "Traffic jams in the sky worry the air transport industry. They're already in evidence at big city airports and will get worse. Along the heaviest-traveled airways they'll be serious before long."

Relating how bigger airports like La Guardia Field, New York "groan and strain" to handle traffic, the story contained predictions of explosive growth in airline equipment and traffic as well as in the "independent planes" which were carrying a rapidly growing number of passengers on a non-scheduled basis.

"All this plus the host of private planes now hatching in numerous factories adds up to a prospective bee-swarm concentration of aircraft over urban areas that will simply be out of line with ability of the fields to 'bring 'em down'."

Use of "stacking" techniques to hold aircraft airborne during periods of bad weather was described, along with data on a bad day in January when only 52 of the 175 planes scheduled to leave La Guardia actually did so, and only 69 of some 175 arrivals actually landed. Some 4,000 passengers' plans were disrupted or cancelled that day, a huge disjointment in terms of passenger movements in early 1946.

The *Herald-Tribune*'s article[7] of May 9, evidently inspired by publication of bad news by the *Journal* the previous day, carried the headline, "Traffic Jams in Air Increase, Remedy Sought." Described, in addition to the woes besetting the air traffic system, was "an eight man committee formed on March 27 by the Civil Aeronautics Administration (CAA) which has come up with a series of improvements" to be recommended "for immediate action."

Among these were improved air-ground communication, revision of airline schedules to avoid simultaneous scheduling of arrivals, and changes in pilot regulations to "standardize qualifications for flying by instruments."

(The full texts of the *Wall Street Journal* and *New York Herald-Tribune* articles are printed at the conclusion of this chapter, immediately after the Notes.)

After reading these newspaper accounts of the mounting difficulties, Lathrop proceeded to lead the discussion with skill and insight, and with a specific goal in mind.

He pointed out that Bristol-Myers had vital interest in the answer to the problems, and expressed the opinion that all in the room joined him in that regard. "The success of the 'industries aid' operations" (terminology to describe business aviation which was in wide use at the time and still remains in the insurance industry lexicon) "depends on whether or not rules are made which will make it difficult for us to give the officials of our companies the services we wish," say notes of Lathrop's remarks. "Decisions are being made now which can seriously affect our operations in the future."

He concluded his opening presentation by observing "we are all in the same boat and I am of the opinion that we should organize a committee or an association and when we have these problems we at least will have a recognized group to act as our spokesman." Lathrop then paused and called for discussion of this final, decisive point.

A variety of views was brought forth. Knickerbocker, speaking as a former airline employee, stated his views on lack of professionalism in many corporate air crews. Stressing his belief that "we all look with skeptical eyes on men from the services because we know there is a great deal of difference between flying a bomber and carrying executive personnel," he went on to call for better means of complying with rules and regulations laid down by the government. He thought corporate pilots (he stated that Time-Life employed seven) "should be better qualified than the airline pilots. They can and should be if the facilities are made available to them. If they would put two or four hours a month in Link training it would be insurance."

Lathrop responded by observing that a committee could protect interests and prevent loss of freedom. It could, in other words, establish a code of practice so that "the CAA would be sure of our following the rules and regulations." Others pointed out that insurance premium savings could be one result of concerted action and conformity. Note was taken that Aero Insurance Underwriters already had such a plan in effect, using a rating system both for ground and aircrew personnel.

The Time-Life spokesman concluded his remarks by endorsing the creation of a limited organization "so that we can get together to discuss problems that confront us, but from the standpoint of bringing up a power of any extent, I don't think we should attempt it." His preference was to aim for adherence to high professional standards in business aircraft operation. Political aspects did not appeal to him.

At this point Nesbitt stated the forthright opinion that enough discussion had taken place to show the merits of organization. "We should take a vote as to whether we will have an association of appointed officers and directors and bring it along as quickly as possible," he added, an evident note of impatience in his remarks.

Considerable discussion centered on whether it was best to form a commitee along rather loose lines, or to affiliate with some already existing organization, or to "go it" alone with a new and permanently established association.

Regan (*Airports* Magazine) said that standards should be developed and a constitution "and laws of flying" written before the group approached CAA. Unger of Johnson & Johnson urged caution, saying the idea needed to be taken to other pilots and a meeting convened where there would be larger representation. Mention was made that perhaps the oil companies "should not get mixed up in such an organization because of public relations," but Unger retorted that the group "would be for the betterment of aviation and . . . the oil companies would be in full approval of the plan and that it would have nothing to do with selling gas and oil."

Dunaway (Johns-Manville) expressed an interest in becoming a part of another organization already in existence, but neither he nor others made any specific suggestions of names. (In 1946, several national aviation organizations existed. Principal were the Air Transport Association (ATA), an alliance of airlines; the Aircraft Owners and Pilots Association (AOPA), representing a broad cut of general aviation owners-pilots; the National Aviation Trades Association (NATA), an amalgam of aviation businesses and air taxi operators; and the Aircraft Industries Association (AIA), trade group of the manufacturers represented at the Biltmore meeting. (All had Washington offices.)

The AIA spokesman, who was a public relations official for his group, recommended that the aircraft operators join together immediately and separately from others. "You would increase your prestige by grouping together and better your own position," he counselled.

Finally, the discussion moved toward consensus and Lathrop brought it there by posing the remaining fundamental question: was it better to act first and then organize, or was the wiser course to organize first? Eight persons voted (one more than there were aircraft operating companies present), six favoring the "organize first" option and two favoring a program of immediate action to be followed by the process of organization.

The remainder of the meeting was devoted to discussion of many details:

Lee (Continental Can) went on at length about the variety of problems which existed in traffic control, use of "gates" for passenger access and hangar facilities. He even raised the possibility of "procuring an airport for our exclusive use."

Consensus was reached that there be only one spokesman for the group while the rest "go out and contact other pilots." Urging was made that publicity be in the name of company presidents so as to "apply more pressure without giving the appearance of doing so." One idea was to invite the aviation press to serve as an advisory board, and it was decided that publicity "be released about this meeting to the trade publications."

For the time being it was determined that the term "committee" should be used to describe the small but seemingly cohesive group, and, finally, it was decided that a letter would be written to presidents of corporations describing "what has taken place at this meeting, our objectives and asking support for the committee."

It is obvious from events which followed that Lathrop was to be the continuing leading force in moving the project along and he set to work almost immediately. The notes of the Biltmore meeting, while comprehensive and verbatim in some places, record neither the time of beginning nor adjournment of the session. It is easy, however, to conclude that the meeting was lengthy and it appears that all who attended left with a feeling of accomplishment and unity.

Given such bouyant results there must have been disappointment later that of all those present, only Lathrop and Nesbitt were among those who attended the next and decisive meeting on November 21, 1946, in Cleveland. And of the organizations present at the Biltmore, only Bristol-Myers, Atlantic Aviation, and Time-Life were represented at Cleveland.

It is also ironic that of the seven aircraft operating companies present on May 17, only Bristol-Myers became a "charter" member of the Corporation Aircraft Owners Association (CAOA). Continental Can joined the organization in 1955, after it had been renamed NBAA, Johnson & Johnson became a member in 1958, and there is no record of Manufacturers Trust Company membership until 1974, when the organization joined as Manufacturers Hanover Corporation. Time-Life joined NBAA in 1964, Johns-Manville in 1968, and there is no record that Abbott-Kimball became a member. Testifying to its strong initial support, Atlantic Aviation became the first Associate Member of CAOA, being admitted on July 16, 1947, just one month after a "charter" group of 17 regular members was listed at a special Board meeting.

Efforts made in early 1987 to establish contact with or obtain information about the careers and contemporary status of those in attendance on May 17, 1946, met with extremely limited success.[8] In a number of cases, company personnel records contained no reference to the person, indicating he had retired or left many years earlier. Others were presumed or known to have died during the 41 year interval since the Biltmore session.

Information was available only about Knickerbocker and Lathrop. The former was identified in 1945 as a 35 year old one-time commercial pilot, more recently the pilot of Time, Inc.'s Beechcraft 18S, put into service by the company in 1944. Knickerbocker was a U.S. Army Air Force Major during World War II, when he picked up 2,000 of his 4,800 hours of pilot time. Company archives say that the Beechcraft was acquired "because the production activities of this company have been expanded to so many places all over the country, presenting many problems that often require immediate attention by our production and business executives." One example cited was a middle-of-the-night trip from New York to printing headquarters in Chicago, on which pictures were carried of President Roosevelt's 1944 Navy Day speech in Central Park. The airplane made Chicago in time for the 7:30 Sunday morning printing deadline for the week's issue. Knickerbocker's 1987 whereabouts were not known.[9]

Lathrop continued to play an extremely active role in CAOA leadership in the period which followed the Biltmore meeting, but in August, 1948, he left Bristol-Myers to accept a senior position with the Cameron Machine Company of Brooklyn, New York. Cameron had no aircraft at that time and it was thus necessary for Lathrop to submit his resignation as Treasurer of CAOA. It was accepted with great regret on January 19, 1949.

Lathrop's presence, however, continued to be felt through an informal link. One prominent NBAA leader who became active just after Lathrop's official departure said that he was "constantly being quoted" in Board deliberations for several years.[10] Lathrop died at an early age in a tragic accident during the winter of 1952. His pet dog fell through thin ice into a northern New Jersey pond. Attempting to rescue the animal Lathrop also broke through the ice and into the freezing water. He drowned, a young man barely into his forties at the time of death.[11]

Nesbitt eventually retired to Florida and died there in 1985. Atlantic's President, William L. Patrick, later wrote nostalgically that, "his last project was to try to convince the State of Florida to change its State song to one he wrote. You see, he was also a song and dance man. He did not succeed."[12]

NOTES TO CHAPTER 1

1. *The First Fifty Years,* history of the Wings Club, New York.

2. *Skyways* Magazine, October, 1959 and letter, Donald Esser, Bristol-Myers, to J.H. Winant, January 31, 1987.

3. Letter, W.L. Patrick, Atlantic Aviation Corporation, to J.H. Winant, January 23, 1987.

4. "Minutes of First Meeting Held by Pilots (sic) of Corporation Owned Aircraft, May 17, 1946," five pages, typed, unsigned document, NBAA archives.

5. Walter C. Pague, Middletown, Ohio, audio tape interview with J.H. Winant, June 11, 1987.

6. *Wall Street Journal,* May 8, 1946, "lead" story, right-hand column, page 1, continued on page 6. Library of Congress periodicals archives.

7. *New York Herald-Tribune,* May 9, 1946, article, page 8. Library of Congress periodicals archives.

8. Letter, Donald Esser, Bristol-Myers; letter, Thomas M. Miller, Manville Sales Corporation, to J.H. Winant, January 29, 1987, and telephone conversation April 15, 1987; letter, E.J. Fox, Manufacturers Hanover Corporation, to J.H. Winant, February 10, 1987.

9. Time, Inc., Archives, excerpt dated November 2, 1945, M.R. Doak.

10. Cole H. Morrow, McLean, Virginia, audio tape interview with J.H. Winant, May 5, 1987.

11. W.C. Pague, audio tape statement, January 29, 1987, and telephone conversation with J.H. Winant, April 9, 1987.

12. Letter, W.L. Patrick.

Wall Street Journal, May 8, 1946, pages 1 and 6

Aerial Traffic Jams
THEY'LL GROW ACUTE AS NEW PLANES FLOOD SKY; ARE ALREADY SERIOUS

AIRPORTS, SWAMPED NOW, SEE SKY-LINERS NEARLY TRIPLED DURING NEXT 18 MONTHS

TRAFFIC CONTROL BOGS DOWN

Traffic jams in the sky worry the air transport industry.

They're already in evidence at big city airports and will get worse. Along the heaviest traveled airways, they'll be serious before long.

What's the use of trying to quadruple our traffic if the airports can't handle it? That's the sentiment of our airline officials.

Great airports like La Guardia Field already "groan and strain" to handle landings and take-offs when the weather isn't perfect. And the prospect just ahead gives traffic control men the shakes.

Flood of New Planes

Right now about 470 planes fly for the country's scheduled airlines. Before 18 months have been torn from the calendar, say the air men, there'll be nearly 1,200.

This isn't the whole story. The 1,200 figure merely represents regular, scheduled airliners. Mushrooming into being since the war, an enterprising flock of over 300 independent planes now carry passengers on non-scheduled flights.

All this plus the host of private planes now hatching in numerous factories adds up to a prospective bee-swarm concentration of aircraft over urban areas that will simply be way out of line with ability of the fields to "bring'em down."

Getting planes on and off the runways in bad weather is the airport disease that must be licked fast if the sky-jams aren't to get entirely out of hand, practical airmen declare.

Traffic Control Old-Fashioned

Present bad weather traffic control methods are old-fashioned, they say. With a restless eye on the flood of new commercial planes expected to pour into the sky in months ahead, they cite the paralysis that now grips giant airports when rain clouds sweep low.

"Take La Guardia Field in New York," they say. "With present plane traffic, it must handle 500 to 700 'movements', as take-offs and landings are called, every day to keep things rolling smoothly. As these obviously can't be spaced with precise evenness through the day's 24 hours, this means that in congested hours one plane should be zipped down the runway, landing or leaving, every 30 seconds."

Actually, when weather is bad, individual planes arriving at the port may be kept circling around an hour or more. As planes continue coming in to join the waiting list, they are "stacked" in the air over an area extending miles from the field—ordered to circle at a stated altitude until the control tower directs them to land.

Some planes are not even fortunate enough to get "stacked." On one typical bad weather day last January, only 69 planes were brought in at La Guardia, out of 175 scheduled to land. The others had to come down at other airports, some hundreds of miles from New York, or else never even took off from their departing points. Out of 175 planes scheduled to take off from La Guardia on the same day, only 52 actually made it.

Travel Plans Disrupted for 4,000 People

On that day, more than 4,000 air travelers had their plans disrupted by cancelled schedules at La Guardia alone.

Airlines suffer sharply from these bad-weather traffic muddles. They lose many potential customers who take trains because they "must be sure" of making distant appointments on time—can't "take a chance" on a plane flight cancellation.

And then, of course, there are huge losses on air tickets actually bought and then cancelled when the planes don't fly. One big carrier estimates that, in one month alone under conditions obtaining during most of 1945, an airline operating about 45 DC-3 planes loses around $250,000 due to delays and cancellations.

While the biggest air-jams are shaping up for the sky in the immediate vicinity of airports, airmen fear lesser snarls, with the threat of accidents, along the "air highways" between cities.

To the airliner pilot, the sky is not as big as it looks. Directed by a radio "beam" from the ground, the big skyliners fly along an "air highway" about ten miles wide. True, they fly at different levels; but they have to "stay on the road." And the fact that there are going to be about three times as many airliners on those roads, and flying at far greater speeds than heretofore, carries the threat of collision hazards.

New Planes Much Faster

To avoid the danger of one plane overtaking another, airliners dispatched from a given port in the same direction, and at the same altitude, even now have to be spaced at least ten minutes apart. But today's DC-3, workhorse of the lines, makes about 170 miles an hour, and the new planes will do up to 400 miles an hour.

Thus the airways, with hundreds of unscheduled passenger and freight carriers also zooming up and down them, are going to be more than comfortably crowded, say the experts.

Air transport industry concern over the sky-jam outlook is reflected in a hurly-burly scramble to get some of the big wrinkles ironed out. The Air Transport Association, which represents the scheduled airlines, has virtually reorganized itself to this end, adding new high-caliber personnel to its staff.

A committee consisting of government Civil Aeronautics Board and airline representatives has been named to rip into the New York area congestion problem. Joseph D. McGoldrick, former comptroller of New York City, is heading a $100,000 survey of conditions at half a dozen major airports, to be completed in June.

Bigger Airports Needed

The airport congestion bottleneck can and will be solved in part, but only in part, airmen insist, by the obvious step of building more and bigger airports. New York is hustling to get its new Idlewild Field ready as soon as possible. Boston and Chicago both have blueprinted new fields. So have other cities.

Many of the new fields will have "parallel runways." Where, for example, La Guardia has one runway running in one direction, Idlewild will have two running side by side.

But mere physical expansion of airfield space will not whip the number one problem of how to snap planes on and off the runways in a hurry in thick weather.

The first step in the solution of this problem, say air experts, will most likely lie in general adoption of the "glide path" and "localizer" radio beam system for bringing planes in "blind."

The "glide path" is a radio beam directed upward from a runway at about the same angle at which a plane descends. The pilot, by keeping on this beam, should be able to make his wheels touch the outer end of the runway in any weather.

Directs Plane to Runway's Center

The "localizer" is another beam which directs the plane to the exact center of the runway.

But the "glide path", "localizer" system is not yet in use at any commercial airport by scheduled airlines, and getting generally in use will take time. For one thing, before it can be employed, all planes and ground installations must be equipped with V.H.F. (very high frequency) radios. Some air carriers, however, already are installing this equipment in their planes preparatory to its regular use later on.

Another traffic control device which, it is hoped, may help smooth traffic movement at ports is a block-signal type of control, similar in many ways to that used by railroads. Under this system, a pilot waiting to come down at a port would be automatically signaled, through a light on his instrument board, when he could enter a certain "block" of air approaching the runway. Under present methods, he must await an oral invitation from the man in the airport control tower.

One device which may soon be used at big airports to help matters in bad weather is a "fog disperser." This apparatus scatters fog and makes the runways visible. While the expense of its operation is a big obstacle to its use, some of the newer types of fog dispersal apparatus are said to cost only $12 to $15 a minute to operate. With two planes brought into the port each minute, this would come to only $6 or $7 per landing.

The initial installation expense on fog dispersal equipment, however, is very high, and substantial government aid would be needed to erect it at airports.

To relieve the expected congestion on the airways between cities, it is suggested that more traffic lanes must be used. Superficially simple, this is, in fact, otherwise. Each air lane is controlled by mechanical installations on the ground along the route-installations which operate the "beams", "beacons" and "markers" along the air "highways." New lanes would mean a network of new installations.

Radar Has Handicaps

Radar, highly publicized and presenting in the layman's mind an obvious means of keeping planes from bumping fenders along the thoroughfares in the clouds, also has very serious handicaps.

One of the biggest radar drawbacks is its weight. Instruments with enough range to do much good might weigh 2,000 pounds or more. That's equal to 40% of the payload of the present DC-3's and would be an appreciable slice of the money-making capacity of the larger planes.

New York Herald-Tribune, May 9, 1946, Page 8

TRAFFIC JAMS IN AIR INCREASE, REMEDY SOUGHT

C.A.A., Army, Navy and Carriers Chart Means to Thin Crowded Routes.

Increasing traffic jams in the crowded airports and airways in the East have become such a threat to efficient operation of air transportation that government and airlines representatives have been meeting almost daily for more than a month to seek means of easing the situation, it was disclosed yesterday.

As a result, an eight-man committee formed on March 27 by the Civil Aeronautics Administration has come up with a series of improvements which it will recommend for immediate action to Theodore P. Wright, C.A.A. administrator in Washington, next week.

Better Communication Needed

The area studied is limited roughly by the cities of Boston, New York, Richmond, Pittsburgh, Cleveland, and Buffalo. Needs in this area as found by the committee include:

1. Improved communication between planes in flight and airway traffic-control centered on the ground.

2. More air routes with radio beams, thus eliminating the crowding on present beams and cutting down the danger of collisions.

3. Revision of airlines schedules to eliminate the simultaneous arrivals of planes at air terminals, a situation which now makes it necessary many times for a plane to circle a field for as much as an hour before landing.

4. Changes in civil air regulations to standardize qualifications for flying by instruments. Airline pilots now are required to be more proficient at flying in bad weather than most other pilots. Inexperienced pilots take longer to make landings by instrument and often delay other planes.

Weather Hurts Schedules

Often during unfavorable weather at La Guardia Field, according to the C.A.A. regional offices, 385 Madison Avenue, half of the scheduled flights at the field are cancelled and half of those due to come in must be turned away to land at other fields.

This, it was emphasized, represents enormous losses to the airlines. With existing facilities taxed to the limit, the C.A.A. said, worse jams are shaping up. The country's airlines, which now operate 490 transports soon will have 1,200. In addition, the number of smaller cargo lines is increasing, as well as the ownership of private planes.

One major obstacle to installation of needed equipment, the C.A.A. said, is lack of sufficient funds. Nevertheless, similar studies of traffic conditions are being made in the Dallas-Fort Worth area, in Texas, and in San Francisco, Los Angeles and Chicago.

Chapter 2

THE JOURNEY BEGINS: NOVEMBER, 1946

WORRIES ABOUT DAY-TO-DAY AFFAIRS AT BRISTOL-MYERS were extremely demanding of "Bud" Lathrop's time and effort during the summer of 1946. So was fulfillment of his promise to convene a second meeting of corporations to explore formation of an association, with aircraft ownership as the common bond.

While no records survive, the remembrances of a few persons were pieced together in 1987 to form a consistent and accurate picture of the summer's events. Lathrop sent letters to many companies, telling them of the Biltmore gathering in May and of the hope to convene a bigger and more representative meeting. On these he began to build contacts and interest.

Walter C. Pague, long a leader in CAOA and NBAA affairs, remembered Lathrop's steadfast efforts. Admitting disappointment in the results of the Biltmore meeting, Lathrop decided that the next session should be held in November in Cleveland, Ohio, where Pague felt "a well-defined business aviation community existed."[1] Many persons who were approached were "skeptical about the need for an organization" but were won over by Lathrop's "forthright, intelligent approach, which truly commanded respect."

It is obvious that Lathrop did more than send letters. Along the way, and apparently through the influence of aviation department personnel, William B. Belden, a senior Republic Steel Corporation executive, met Lathrop and a lasting friendship was established.

With Republic Steel's chief pilot, T. A. Jones, acting as catalyst, Belden and Lathrop talked during the summer and arrangements were concluded for Belden to play the leadership role if an association were formed. One who was keenly aware of the Lathrop-Belden relationship, though at a later date, recalled hearing that the two "hit it off" immediately,[2] and that while it required a bit of "arm twisting since he really didn't want to be chairman," Belden nevertheless agreed.

During the period leading up to the Cleveland meeting, Lathrop also became acquainted with K. H. Kalberer, a former Army Air Corps Colonel who is remembered principally for his activities in 1946 as "Corporation Aircraft Counselors,"[3] a New York-based consulting organization. It appears certain that Kalberer, being known to Lathrop, was prepared to become the volunteer Secretary of the incipient organization.

Arrangements were made to hold the meeting on November 21, 1946, using Parlor E of the Statler Hotel in Cleveland. Notices were sent to Lathrop's full list of potential members. The response was heartening.

But, as recalled by Pague,[4] November 21st was "a cold and dreary day" and adverse flying weather prevented a number of companies from attending. Promptly at 10:30 a.m. Lathrop called the meeting to order and an attendance roster was circulated.

The list, later typed and titled "Roster of Attendants at Organization Meeting, Corporate (sic) Aircraft Owners Association . . ."[5] reads as follows:

Representative	Company	Address
W. A. Straith	Aero Insurance Underwriters	111 John St., New York 7, NY
Walter C. Pague	American Rolling Mill Co.	Middletown, Ohio
James E. Kidd	Anchor Hocking Glass Corp.	Lancaster, Ohio
Sydney Nesbitt	Atlantic Aviation Corp.	Teterboro Air Terminal, Teterboro, NJ
John S. Gulledge	B. F. Goodrich Co.	500 Main St., S, Akron, Ohio
Palmer J. Lathrop	Bristol-Myers Co.	225 Long Avenue, Hillside, NJ
W. R. Martin	Bristol-Myers Co.	225 Long Avenue, Hillside, NJ
F. W. Nelson	Bristol-Myers Co.	225 Long Avenue, Hillside, NJ
Paul C. Craig	Champion Paper & Fibre Co.	Hamilton, Ohio
F. D. Morrison	Champion Spark Plug Co.	Toledo 1, Ohio
J. N. Reilly	Corning Glass Works	Corning, NY
Harold R. Boyer	General Motors Corp.	15-227 G.M. Bldg., Detroit 2, Mich
Harry W. Hopp	General Motors Corp.	14-254 G.M. Bldg., Detroit 2, Mich
George E. Bevins	George N. Brewster & Sons. Inc.	Fort Lee Rd., Bogota, NJ
Lawrence A. Muller	George N. Brewster & Sons, Inc.	Fort Lee Rd., Bogota, NJ
O. P. Harwood	Gillies Aviation Corp.	Hicksville, L.I., NY
J. B. Mitchell	Howes Brothers Co.	321 Summer St., Boston, Mass.
Bernard Rooten	Owens-Corning Fiber Glass Corp.	Nicholas Bldg., Toledo, Ohio
William B. Belden	Republic Steel Corp.	Republic Bldg., Cleveland, Ohio
W. S. Bixler	Sinclair Refining Co.	630-5th Avene, New York, NY
H. W. Lake	Socony-Vacuum Oil Co.	26 Broadway, New York, NY
George R. Schrock	Standard Oil Co. (Ohio)	Midland Bldg., Cleveland, OH
B. W. Chasteney, Jr.	Time, Inc.	Time & Life Bldg., New York, NY
K. H. Kalberer	United Cigar Whelan Stores Corp.	330 E. 56th Street, New York, NY
E. T. Petnagel	Wolfe Industries	62 E. Broad St., Columbus, OH

There are at least three errors in the typed roster. Its title incorrectly names the new organization by using the word "Corporate" rather than "Corporation." W. S. Bixler of Sinclair Oil was actually Donald S. Bixler, elected later in the day as a temporary director of the new group. And E. T. Petnagel was E. T. Spetnagel of Wolfe Industries, destined to become a director of the organization within a few years.

The 25 persons present represented 21 companies; of these, 18 were operators of private carriage company aircraft. The other three were Aero Insurance Underwriters, Atlantic Aviation Corporation, and Gillies Aviation.

Noting that letters and telegrams had been received from many other companies unable to attend but desiring to cooperate with any decisions reached, Lathrop, acting as temporary chairman, summarized the reasons for the gathering. Then, following appointment of Nelson of Bristol-Myers to act as temporary secretary to record the minutes, the session moved ahead quickly to the business at hand.

NBAA archives contain five slightly different versions of what took place during the next several hours. Aside from minor discrepancies which involved how many persons or companies were present and one divergence concerning election of a temporary board, all versions tell substantially the same story (See Notes 6, 7, 8, 9, and 10). The only dissimilarities are in emphasis, amount of detail, and style. None are signed or even state the name of the author.

The version which is bound into the official board minutes book of the period makes it clear that:

> *all matters of a controversial nature were settled by vote with each representative being given an equal voice in the matters under discussion. Committees were appointed by the temporary chairman to consider certain questions (no specifics given) and submit recommendations to the representatives prior to the taking of votes.*

Things went quickly and smoothly, because by the time a luncheon break was taken at 12:30 p.m., three major decisions had been made:

> 1. "After thorough discussion of the advantages both ways," said the summary, *"it was unanimously agreed that the proposed organization should be entirely independent and should not, at least for the present, affiliate itself with any existing organization or association."*

Thus, in united and frank terms was resolved one of the principal questions raised by the Biltmore meeting in May.

> 2. It was decided that the proposed organization would place a geographical limitation upon its activities by confining its operation to the United States and its possessions.

> 3. The proposed by-laws were considered in detail and controversial articles (unspecified in the summary or other remaining documents) were referred to committees appointed by the temporary chairman.

After lunch, the meeting continued for three more hours and by adjournment at 5 p.m., the by-laws questions were settled and the product was adopted "as the temporary by-laws of the newly formed Corporation Aircraft Owners Association."[11] Annual dues for Regular and Associate members were provisionally set at $100, and a temporary Board of Directors was elected.

While all five versions of the session's proceedings do not coincide, it is apparent that nine men were elected (Jennings and Kelly *in absentia*) and charged to serve until the next meeting to be called within six months:

> William B. Belden — Republic Steel Corp.
> W. S. Bixler — Sinclair Refining Co.
> Paul C. Craig — Champion Paper & Fibre Co.
> Howard L. Jennings — General Motors Corporation
> A. Kelly — B. F. Goodrich Company
> H. W. Lake — Socony-Vacuum Oil Co.
> P. J. Lathrop — Bristol-Myers Co.
> J. B. Mitchell — Howes Brothers Co.
> Walter C. Pague — American Rolling Mill Co.
> (Donald S. Bixler was again erroneously identified in this list)

The final act of the general organizing meeting was to express grateful thanks to Lathrop for his efforts of the past months and for his leadership as temporary chairman. The terse notes seem in retrospect to be meager terms in which to recognize that Lathrop had succeeded during a half year's time in skillfully steering a diverse and changing group through shoal-infested waters and safely into harbor. The new organization, during an intense five-hour session, was brought from concept to actuality, and provisionally given the tools to establish permanent status.

Immediately upon adjournment of the organizing meeting, the temporary board held its first session. Minutes record that six of the nine elected members were present.

By unanimous action Belden was named as chairman of the new association, a position which he was to fill with great distinction until the annual meeting of the members in 1951.

Lathrop was elected secretary for the purpose of taking minutes of the first board session. These structural steps completed, attention was focused on solutions to the kinds of problems which led to creation of CAOA.

Bevins, who was pilot for George M. Brewster & Son, Inc. addressed the board on steps being taken by the Civil Aeronautics Administration (CAA) to solve the pressing airways congestion situation. Plans for rerouting of airways in and around the New York-Philadelphia-Washington area had been announced just the previous evening at a meeting attended by Bevins in New York. Additionally, CAA advised that new instrument approach equipment (ILS) was being installed at many airports. Bevins reported that the New York CAA regional office lacked a good mailing list for itinerant pilots and suggested that CAOA could be helpful in filling the void. Lake, chief pilot for Socony-Vacuum, responded to Bevins' report by observing that "it will be but a matter of time before we are forced to operate under tightened standards."

At this point, Kalberer, the aircraft counselling individual, joined the meeting and was appointed to the position of "Acting Secretary without compensation." The minutes of the board meeting identify him as "representing Whelan Drug," creating a dichotomy of affiliation which is not explained in any records of the time or in memories searched in 1987.

Kalberer was directed by the board to send a membership recruitment letter to the "complete available mailing list," reporting on the great accomplishments wrought at Cleveland. Finally, authorization was given to print letterhead for CAOA with the address "330 East 56th Street, New York 22, N.Y." At the time, United Cigar-Whelan Drug operations offices were located in Oradell, N.J. and on Fourth Avenue, New York. It is believed that the East 56th Street address, a large apartment block between First and Second Avenues, was Kalberer's home.[12]

November 21, 1946 was a day of high achievement, long and arduous. From it emerged a new organization with strong purpose and a group of enthusiastic and highly motivated leaders. The board's first meeting ended in an atmosphere of optimism and hope.

But as was the case with the exploratory meeting held earlier in the year at the Biltmore, tangible, short term results were unimpressive. While eagerness for the cause was strong, less than half of the companies in attendance at Cleveland became members of CAOA during the critically important months which followed.

Only ten companies present at Cleveland were in the "charter" CAOA membership group on June 19, 1947: ARMCO, Bristol-Myers, Champion Paper, Corning Glass, B. F. Goodrich, Howes Brothers, Republic Steel, Sinclair Refining, United Cigar-Whelan, and Wolfe Industries.

Of the others attending the organizing meeting in Cleveland there is no record that Aero Insurance Underwriters ever joined the organization; Anchor Hocking waited until 1950; Atlantic Aviation became the first Associate member in July, 1947; the Brewster organization did not join until 1950; Champion Spark Plug did so in 1949; General Motors joined in 1951 but terminated the membership in 1953 for a period of several years. Gillies never joined. Owens-Corning Fiber Glass waited until 1965, Socony-Vacuum (later Mobil) until 1955, Standard of Ohio until 1951, and Time, Inc. until 1964.

Some 40 years after the fateful Cleveland meeting there were no data available on many who attended, but there were interesting facts and insights on more than half of the participants.

According to Jerome Lederer, the distinguished aviation safety engineer who worked in 1946 with Aero Insurance Underwriters, Straith was responsible for the firm's airline and business aviation safety evaluations. During the war, Straith was in charge of the "pilot training program of the Airlines War Training Institute" for which Lederer directed Air Transport Command training. While piloting an Aero

Insurance airplane, "Straith suffered a heart attack . . . over the Rocky Mountains and was killed in 1947."[13]

As noted earlier, Nesbitt remained Atlantic Aviation's president until 1952, retired to Florida and died there in 1985. While no reliable information exists concerning Gulledge he was possibly a Goodrich district manager in the tire division, with responsibility for sale of aircraft tires.[14] Reilly had a distinguished career at Corning Glass, serving as assistant to the president until his retirement in 1962, which was also the year of his death. While with Corning, he had continuing senior responsibility for corporate aviation activities.[15]

Boyer served in many management positions with General Motors during a long and remarkable career. Ancillary to his work with GM, which included supervision of aviation transportation, he was chief of the aircraft manufacturing branch of the government's War Production Board during the Korean War period. Boyer died in February, 1987. Hopp was a GMATS (General Motors Air Transportation Section) pilot in 1946 with principal assignment as the personal pilot for Charles E. Wilson, GM's president and CEO, later United States Secretary of Defense. Hopp died shortly after retiring from GM.[16]

In 1952, Spetnagel became a member of the organization's board, remaining on it through the transition of name from CAOA to NBAA. Retaining a strong interest in association affairs until his retirement in the late 1970's, Spetnagel acted continuously as Wolfe's designated NBAA representative. In February, 1987, it was reported that Spetnagel had died.[17]

Most of the persons elected to the temporary board on November 21, 1946, remained active during the association's early years. One, however, did not accept election; at the other end of the scale of service one remained a board member of CAOA and then of NBAA until 1964.

The temporary board members were a colorful and varied group. Belden, who became the driving force of the early CAOA years, was assistant counsel for Republic Steel. He is remembered as "a brilliant legal mind," a leader "who believed in going into a conference room with the responsible officials and making the decisions" there.[18] As events of the year following the Cleveland meeting would show, "his legal talents really shaped the documents which formed" CAOA. The same observer, Cole Morrow, also noted wryly that Belden at heart was not an enthusiastic flier. He would fly if he had to, "but he much preferred to take the overnight train from Cleveland to meetings in New York."

Morrow credits Belden with being "a marvelously sound person" who had "great influence on the policies to be followed, and on the integrity of the organization and its image." Always available for consultation after his period as chairman ended, he was also known "for his very dry, unusual sense of humor." Belden's service on the board of NBAA ended in 1956. In 1970, having gone into semi-retirement from Republic Steel, he died of cancer.

Bixler of Sinclair was described as "a salesman's salesman."[19] Disclaiming much knowledge of airplanes, he was nevertheless "most cooperative and helpful" and was a "marvelously personable" board member. Whether or not Bixler was alive in 1987 could not be determined.

Craig, Champion Paper, became one of the most active of the early directors who were also professional air crew members. He had "an excellent concept of how the aircraft fit into the business," viewing it as no different from "any other tool . . . (he had) a good idea of the interface between airplane operations and business operations."[20] In 1946, Craig flew Champion Paper's Twin Beech between mill sites in Canton, North Carolina and Hamilton, Ohio. In 1949, he transferred from the aviation department to the company's sales division. Champion in 1961 found it necessary to enact a vast reorganization and cost control program and all company aircraft were sold. The same year, Craig was released by the company and Champion's records show that he began to receive retirement benefits in 1969. It was thought that he died in 1981.

Jennings, based at General Motor's Washington office, was either a government relations or public relations official for the company.[21] Volunteered for board membership at Cleveland, he later declined to serve and the remaining temporary board members were so informed at their next meeting.

Lake, Socony-Vacuum, accepted appointment for a very brief period. Records show him in attendance only at the Cleveland meeting, and on the list of directors at the time of CAOA incorporation in February, 1947. There is no mention of him being present at any 1947 board meeting. Like many other pioneer oil company aviation managers, Lake had a colorful career. A member of the Early Birds, a pre-World War I pilot group, he served in the aviation department of the U.S. Signal Corps (predecessor to the Army Air Corps) in the war and piloted the first Martin bomber on its initial test flight. He joined the Vacuum organization in 1930. Retiring in 1954, he died 10 years later at age 75.

Kelly, who was B. F. Goodrich's vice president for manufacturing at the time of the Cleveland meeting, retired around 1970 as an Executive Vice President.[22] In early 1987, he was living in Akron, Ohio, but his memories of his one year term on the CAOA board, 1946–47, were dim. During his brief period of service he showed great loyalty, missing only one meeting.

Mitchell, a Harvard graduate, served for several years on the CAOA board as Howes Brothers' representative and had the distinction of being the first person elected vice chairman of the organization under the by-laws which became effective in 1947 with incorporation. It is not known when he retired from duties with the Howes organization. In the early 1980s, NBAA was informed that Mitchell, "to the best of our knowledge, is deceased." Pague remembered Mitchell's "fine background in education and as a pilot."[23] But he also recalled him as being "rather eccentric . . . we didn't know much about him, and he was generally quite critical of the activities of the organization."

Pague went on to become an NBAA legend by serving continuously on the board (and as a sometime officer also) until late 1964, a record which in 1987 stood as the second longest in the organization's history. First chairman of the first committee created by CAOA, the Technical Committee, Pague gained deserved fame as a bright and insightful professional, but no characteristic stood out more prominently than his personable manner.

Pague's flying career began in California. By 1940 he was in Canada, serving as an instructor pilot for the Royal Canadian Air Force (RCAF). In 1942 he transferred to the U.S. Navy as a pilot instructing in multi-engine aircraft at Pensacola, Florida. Later war service took him to Navy transport duties in Alaska and the Aleutians. In November, 1945 he became chief pilot for American Rolling Mill Corporation. Retired in 1981, he was from then until 1985 marketing manager for Flight Safety International in Ohio. In 1987 he was living an active and happy life in Middletown, Ohio.

Lathrop, as noted earlier, died tragically in 1952. Seven years later, Belden paid tribute to him in an editorial which looked backward to the association's beginnings:

> *It was Bud's earnest conviction that the association was vital to the survival of executive flying and his enthusiasm in presenting his position to the group made the formation of the Association possible.*[24]

The career and activities of Kalberer are not as easy to trace as those of many others who assembled at the first meeting of the temporary board in Cleveland. His role in the creation of CAOA has been described differently from what is contained in the association records.[25]

Lederer, writing to Robert A. Cooke of NBAA, said "... the concept and organization of NBAA occurred in my office at Aero Insurance Underwriters in New York about 1946–47. Colonel Karl Kalberer was my airline expert. He organized the Corporate (sic) Aircraft Owners' Association which later became NBAA." According to Lederer's letter to Winant, "while Karl was with Aero he foresaw the promise of business aviation and I gave him the nod to organize the Corporate (sic) Aircraft Owners' Association."

Lederer's memories of Kalberer were that he had served as a United Airlines captain before World War II and then rose to Colonel in the Army Air Corps. He "left Aero in late 1946 to return to an attractive position in military service."

Notwithstanding these recollections from an eminent and highly respected individual, there is no suggestion in any of the documents which relate to the Biltmore meeting (which neither Lederer nor Kalberer attended) that either played a part. The several versions of Cleveland meeting notes do not indicate that Kalberer played a founding role and aside from the attendance list there is no mention of him until he joined the board meeting to be appointed Acting Secretary.

Further, there is confusion posed by simultaneous identification of Kalberer with three organizations in late 1946: Aero Insurance Underwriters, United Cigar-Whelan Stores, and Corporation Aircraft Counselors.

Appointed as Acting Secretary of CAOA in November, 1946, Kalberer served only until May, 1947, after which Belden told the board he was not able to continue because of "'personal matters." The final reference to Kalberer in CAOA's files is in a brief letter from Lederer dated April 16, 1951, which says that he "is now in Washington at the Pentagon Building . . ."

Given the record of detailed notes or minutes of both the Biltmore and Cleveland meetings, it is clear that the genuine motivating forces which led to CAOA's founding came from Lathrop and Nesbitt, augmented by Belden in late 1946.

NOTES TO CHAPTER 2

1. Walter Pague, Middletown, Ohio, audio tape interview with J.H. Winant, June 11, 1987.

2. Cole Morrow, McLean, Virginia, audio tape interview with J.H. Winant, May 5, 1987.

3. Ibid., and Pague audio tape statement, January 29, 1987.

4. Pague tape, January 29, 1987.

5. Copy of November 21, 1946 attendance roster, NBAA archives.

6. CAOA minutes book, NBAA archives. Typed document titled, "Summary of Proceedings of Organization Meeting of Corporation Aircraft Owner's Association Held at Statler Hotel, Cleveland, Ohio, November 21, 1946." Unsigned.

7. "Summary of Proceedings at Organization of Corporate Aircraft Owners, Held at Statler Hotel, Cleveland, November 21, 1946," typed, single-space, 2-page document with pencilled notation at top of first page "Approved Jan 9 '47;" handwriting not identifiable. Unsigned.

8. "Minutes of Board of Directors Meeting, Corporation (typed word "Corporate" struck out), Aircraft Owners' Association, Cleveland, Ohio, November 21, 1946," typed, single-space, 2-page document, vertical margin lines. Unsigned.

9. "Summary Report of Cleveland Meeting of Corporation Aircraft Owners' with date of "Nov 21, 1946" added in pencil, typed, single-space, 2-page draft. Marked "File Copy" in pencil at top of first page. Handwriting similar to specimens of that of Col. K. H. Kalberer. Unsigned.

10. "Corporation Aircraft Owners' Association, Minutes of Meeting held at Hotel Statler, Cleveland, Ohio, Nov. 21, 1946," typed, single space, one page document. Contains several pencilled additions or notes in unidentifiable handwriting. Refers at one point to "Mr. Mikesell," apparent misnomer for J. B. Mitchell. Unsigned.

11. No copy of the temporary by-laws adopted November 21, 1946 is in NBAA archives. By early 1947 revisions deemed legally necessary

were made by W. B. Belden. See appendices for material on by-laws structure and content.

12. Morrow tape, May 5, 1987,

13. Letter, Jerome Lederer to J. H. Winant, January 19, 1987.

14. Letter, Raleigh E. Drennon, BFGoodrich to J. H. Winant, February 5, 1987.

15. Letter, Lee L. Robbins, Corning Glass Works, to J. H. Winant, January 20, 1987.

16. Letter, H. O. Evans, General Motors, to J. H. Winant, February 17, 1987.

17. Letter, John W. Griese, Wolfe Industries, to J. H. Winant, January 23, 1987.

18. Morrow tape, May 5, 1987.

19. Ibid.

20. Ibid., and letter, Robert W. Burke, Champion International, to J. H. Winant, March 9, 1987.

21. Evans letter, February 17, 1987.

22. Drennon letter, February 5, 1987.

23. Pague tape, June 11, 1987.

24. Editorial, *Skyways* Magazine, September 1959, p. 5.

25. Letter, Jerome Lederer to Robert A. Cooke, Vice President, Operations, NBAA, October 13, 1986; letter, Lederer to J.H. Winant, January 19, 1987.

Chapter 3

TESTING THE WINGS: 1947–1951

THE CRISIS WHICH LAUNCHED CAOA DIMINISHED BY EARLY 1947. But the new organization faced a daunting future.

The mere process of organizing did not magically produce the vigor, recognition or financial resources which CAOA required. These qualities would be difficult to capture. Dominating the association during the early years was a need to "get its act together," to find the means to carry out the CAOA mission. Grappling with external aviation issues took second place to concerns about internal problems and requirements. Recognition came grudgingly; financial resources grew at a snail's pace.

"We had some tough years getting the organization going," said one of the founding Directors in 1987,[1] "because the funds just weren't there to do the things we wanted to do. And really, in many cases, the interest wasn't there. We didn't have too many people who came forward and asked to serve ... It was tough going to make inroads ... and difficult to get the respect of government officials."

Yet, in spite of major challenges and preoccupation with looking inward, the first five years of CAOA's life witnessed remarkable events which would in time lead the association to prominence and set the tone of dignity and statesmanship which it crafted as its hallmark.

Under Belden's dynamic and occasionally impatient leadership, things became well organized and thus a solid base was laid from which CAOA later could reach out to touch and shape the major forces bearing on development of the nation's aviation system. Belden's personality was dominant and his views were strongly held. Commenting on his leadership style, Pague[2] characterized Belden as being "all business. From the moment he walked into the board or conference room it was all work. The moment the meeting was adjourned, it was back to Cleveland (for Belden) on the Ohio State Limited."

Belden held the inflexible opinion that membership in CAOA should be restricted only to companies whose aircraft were flown by full-time professional pilots. As to the belief of other Directors that companies operating only single-engine aircraft should be admitted, Belden held a strongly negative position.[3] In Morrow's opinion, Belden wanted to keep the CAOA membership very small, making of it a "country club" of exclusive nature.[4] Ralph E. Piper, an early CAOA Director, said in an April, 1988 memorandum that "Belden had a constant fight with other board members over the membership requirements. It was a friendly fight, of course, but he remained adamant ... that membership should be restricted to those companies operating multi-engine aircraft only. Most of the rest of the board members were just as adamant that membership should encompass any company that used aircraft of any kind to conduct their business." In the long run, Belden was to lose out and it is felt that his resignation from the CAOA Board in 1956 was evidence of his dissatisfaction over the broadening of membership.

Within weeks of the November, 1946 organizing meeting, Belden turned up a number of areas in which the by-laws adopted at Cleveland were deficient. He also felt compelled to move quickly to incorporate the association so as to limit the individual liability of the temporary Directors. Wasting no time, he called a Board meeting for January 9, 1947, in New York.

But things went poorly. The weather was wretched throughout the northeastern United States January 8 and 9 and only four Directors attended. Some of the others sent regrets, citing the brutal travel conditions, but no proxies were given. To make things even worse, word had been received that General Motors declined election to the Board, reducing membership to eight.

Lacking the quorum of five required in the by-laws Belden nevertheless moved firmly ahead with the business at hand, instructing the small group that they would proceed as if there were a quorum and seek ratification of all actions when the Board next met.

Urging incorporation at an early date, he asked that a map of the United States be laid on the table. On it were depicted the locations of provisionally affiliated companies, potential members and business aircraft centers. After examining the map the group unanimously picked New York State as the sensible place to incorporate.

Next Belden went through the changes required in the by-laws: provisions dealing with when members' dues would be payable, rules for proxy voting, regulations dealing with failure of Directors to attend meetings, and creation of a five-member Executive Committee which could act between Board meetings, undertake budget planning and have responsibility for annual meetings.

Kalberer distributed a paper which set forth "possible Association projects" but there was no discussion of it. Internal organizational matters were the real focal points of attention, so much so that Kalberer's paper was not even preserved with the minutes of the meeting.

Less than a month later, February 7, 1949, a Certificate of Incorporation, naming the eight remaining Directors, was submitted under New York's Membership Corporation Law; on February 13 the certificate was approved by William C.

Hecht, Jr., Justice of the state's Supreme Court, First Judicial District, New York County (Manhattan). Four days later, to demonstrate the new organization's existence, a pro forma meeting was held in Room 223, 120 Broadway, New York. The site was the office of the Corporation Trust Company which over the years was the "registered agent" of the association within New York State for legal purposes.

No record exists to identify the author of the Certificate of Incorporation. There is belief that it was a joint effort which Belden and Lathrop shared. Style and use of favorite words are clues which support this belief.

Remarkably, during the long period from 1947 to 1986 it was not found necessary to alter any substantive provision of the basic purposes and powers stated in the certificate. The few changes made during that 40 year period were required by the organization's change of name in 1953 and by change in the state law governing not-for-profit organizations.

As approved February 13, 1947, the heart of the certificate's language, testimony to the founders' vision and the fidelity of those who followed, set forth these purposes and powers:

> ... to promote the aviation interests in the U.S. and its possessions, operating aircraft as an aid to the conduct of their businesses; to foster among them the highest degree of operational efficiency and safety; to bring members into closer personal and friendly relations with each other; to interchange ideas on operational matters; to advance and maintain an enlightened understanding on the part of governmental and airport authorities of its problems; to take such steps as are proper and necessary in order to promote better relations and secure proper advantages from regulatory and other agencies, and by these means to attain wider recognition of the fact that the aviation activities of its members are of primary importance to the domestic economy of the nation.

> ... To acquire property for the corporate purposes by grant, gift, purchase, devise or bequest, and to hold and to dispose of the same, subject to such limitations as are prescribed by statute.

> To carry on all or any of its activities and to purchase or acquire, hold and dispose of ... property as may be requisite for the transaction of its business or the conduct of its affairs, in any of the states, districts, territories or colonies of the United States, and in any and all foreign countries, subject to the laws of such state, district, territory, colony or country.

Continuing the process of sorting things out, the Board on March 19, 1947 ratified the by-laws revisions as presented by Belden in January. The NBAA corporate minutes book for 1947 contains a copy of by-laws, bound in alongside the

Certificate of Incorporation, which bears all the marks of those approved in March. These are stated in full in Appendix I of this work. It is remarkable that while the by-laws were amended several times during the first 40 years of the association's life (1951, 1953, 1955, 1956, 1968, 1971 and 1976) virtually all fundamental concepts remained.

A special Board meeting called for June 19, 1947 was affected by adverse weather. Only four persons could attend but proxies telegraphed by two others enabled the group to act with authority.

Belden announced that "due to personal matters" Kalberer would no longer be able to continue as Acting Secretary. Asked in May to submit a statement of "services rendered and disbursements," Kalberer sent a bill for $735.31. The Board, however, felt that $500 "would recompense Colonel Kalberer adequately for his services and disbursements" and thus the matter was settled. Recalling Kalberer's connection with CAOA, Pague[5] said it probably began because "he was a friend of Bud Lathrop." During his period as Acting Secretary the Board received "only a very limited amount of correspondence . . . He was so inactive that the Board felt there was no need to continue with him."

With great reluctance, but with his strong loyalty prevailing, Lathrop consented to being elected Secretary to replace Kalberer and held the post for the succeeding 17 months. During that period the address of the association reverted to Bristol-Myers' plant at 225 Long Avenue, Hillside, New Jersey. Commenting on the unsuitable situation in early 1948, Lathrop wrote ". . . I am neither qualified nor able for long to continue the job of Secretary of the CAOA. I simply took the job over because I didn't want to see the thing fold up after the Kalberer episode which I see now had its unfortunate implications."[6]

During the summer of 1947 the Board devoted considerable attention to discussing the need for more members. Efforts made during the year had brought the total to only 17 by June, so the group decided to seek outside advice. Fred Betz, Executive Secretary of the Chamber of Commerce of Eastern Union County, New Jersey, twice made presentations, recommending that membership cards be issued along with plaques and that a monthly newsletter be distributed. The name "In The Air" might be suitable, said Betz, who at the same time offered himself as editor. While the Board evidenced approval of the Betz proposals, nothing came of them and for the next year CAOA went along on its own limited volunteer efforts.

By July it had become evident through his continuing absence that Lake, elected to the Board in Cleveland, would not serve. No further mention of his name is made beginning with the July 16, 1947 Board meeting; his company, Socony-Vacuum (later Mobil) did not become a member of the organization until 1955. The "original" Board of nine was now reduced to seven.

September 24, 1947 witnessed the first annual meeting of the association, with the location Room 101 of the Biltmore Hotel in New York. The roster of member companies had grown to 19 and they were listed as follows (dates shown parenthetically are those recorded in NBAA archives as either of application or of admission):

Bristol-Myers Company *(May 7, 1947)*
Champion Paper and Fiber Company *(April 28, 1947)*
Howes Bros. Company *(April 16, 1947)*
The B.F. Goodrich Company *(May 2, 1947)*
Republic Steel Corporation *(April 22, 1947)*
Sinclair Refining Co. *(May —, 1947)*
American Rolling Mill Co. *(May 12, 1947)*
National Dairy Products Corp. *(May —, 1947)*
United Cigar-Whelan Stores Corp. *(May —, 1947)*
Wolfe Industries *(May 2, 1947)*
Reynolds Metals Company *(May 2, 1947)*
Corning Glass Works *(May 1, 1947)*
General Electric Co. *(April 22, 1947)*
Goodyear Tire and Rubber Co. *(May 16, 1947)*
L.B. Smith Inc. *(June 19, 1947)*
Burlington Mills Corp. *(June 12, 1947)*
Al Buchanan Drilling Co. *(May —, 1947)*
Hanes Hosiery Mills Co. *(July 19, 1947)*
Atlantic Aviation Corporation *(July 19, 1947)*

The annual meeting heard a brief financial report which gave the news that revenues for the year were $1,900. The only expenditures were $160 in incorporation expenses and the $500 settlement with Kalberer. As required by the by-laws, the membership elected its first institutional group of Directors, terminating the temporary Board which had served since the organizing meeting the previous November.

Three year terms were given to Belden, Bixler and Lathrop. Craig and Mitchell were elected to two year terms, as was J.G "Jimmy" Guess of Burlington Mills. One year terms were voted for Pague as well as for T. Wilson "Will" Hotze of Reynolds Metals Company and J.R. Dunham, United Cigar-Whelan Stores.

Kelly of B.F. Goodrich, who had attended every Directors' meeting from January to July, 1947, did not stand for election to the permanent Board; the other six remaining "original" Directors all were elected to staggered terms. Guess served until 1949 and remained active in NBAA affairs until his retirement. NBAA received word that he died March 24, 1982. Hotze remained with Reynolds Metals until retirement in 1980. Living an active retirement in 1987 in Richmond, Virginia, he wrote[7] to comment on the great technological advances made since World War II: "Just think of the equipment we used from 1945 to 1952–55 and what is . . . in aircraft now . . . I would certainly like to be young again and use all that good stuff!" Upon Hotze's retirement he was succeeded by his son, Curtis, in the position of Aviation Manager for Reynolds Metals, giving distinction to what may be the only father-to-son transition in the recorded history of professional business aviation management.

Dunham's life ended in 1954 in the crash of a converted bomber in central Ohio. His several passengers and co-pilot, all United Cigar-Whelan employees, also were killed in the accident. The accident had "tremendous impact" on business aviation[8] because of Dunham's prominence in CAOA-NBAA. Pague's personal remembrances of Dunham were that he was "a reserved kind of individual." Morrow remembered him as "happy-go-lucky."[9] Both recall that the demands of piloting the United Cigar-Whelan aircraft prevented Dunham from attending many Board meetings.

It is noteworthy that the seven men who persevered through the trying organizational period from November, 1946 to September, 1947 gained temporary group distinction for a period thereafter. CAOA letterhead as late as 1949 bore the title "Founding Members" under which were listed the names of Belden, Bixler, Craig, Kelly, Lathrop, Mitchell and Pague.

After the 1947 annual meeting of members adjourned, the Board elected Belden as Chairman of the association, Mitchell as Vice Chairman and Lathrop as Secretary and Treasurer.

Then, as it ended its first official year of existence, and in what seemed to be a routine action, CAOA took a major forward step. At Belden's suggestion and reflecting the directorate's general feeling that it was time to "get moving" a Technical Committee was created "to advise on all technical matters that may come before the association." Named to serve on this first of all association standing committees were Craig, Dunham and Pague, with Pague to serve as Chairman. To insure continuity and good communication, Belden was careful to point out that the new committee would "act in conjunction with the Secretary." So was born an activity which over the first 40 years became central to NBAA's purposes and which would provide a major bridge of communication between operators of business aircraft and the suppliers of products and services. From the Technical Committee, its successive chairmen and staff liaison personnel evolved a working relationship for the exchange of ideas, and the solution of problems and complaints, which has few equals in the world of aviation.

As 1947 drew to a close CAOA's Directors appeared to share a common opinion, coupled to a growing sense of unease, that the time had come for CAOA to begin proving its worth through action. Needed was the means for reaching outward, to target issues and programs, to promote "enlightened understanding" in government. The agenda was clear. Still required was the vehicle for dealing effectively with the many items on the "menu" of needs.

A tenuous start was made by year's end. The first association newsletter was published in November and a Legislative Committee was created. Belden and Dunham were named to this activity with the aim that they "take necessary action to insure CAOA is kept informed of legislative proposals in Washington."[10] Neither initiative survived for long and by the end of the next year other means were in place to get the same jobs done.

Yet, standing as one of those uncommon periods which in retrospect is seen as a turning-point in the course of events, the year 1948 became a "watershed" for CAOA. Before the year ended CAOA forged a long-standing but controversial liaison with a major aviation magazine, conducted its first public forum on aviation issues and hired its first salaried employee. The end of the year also brought the resignation of Lathrop, who had left Bristol-Myers in August. And the year had the peculiar significance of witnessing no annual meeting of the members.

Negotiations begun in February, obviously based on lengthy informal discussion, led on March 17 to a contractual arrangement which named *Skyways* magazine the "official publication" of CAOA. The five-year contract called for considerable effort on *Skyways*' part. Its regular monthly issue would have one page devoted to CAOA news. Further, CAOA members would receive a specialized version of each issue containing a four-page insert devoted to CAOA affairs. Safeguards were built into the agreement, some of which would disappear as the relationship ripened. Content of the inserts would be subject to approval of the CAOA Chairman. The association also had the right to terminate if any "independent article were published" which CAOA judged to be derogatory or harmful. A financial *quid pro quo* called on CAOA to pay $10 a year on behalf of each member company. The driving force in the arrangement was J. Fred Henry, head of the multi-magazine Henry Publishing Company, remembered by Morrow[11] as a great benefactor to CAOA. He felt the young association "owed its existence to Fred Henry . . . he gave us a home address, telephone, and secretarial services," none of which CAOA could afford on its own. Describing Henry as "a movie actor type, handsome, very charming, brilliant," Morrow cited him as the first in the media to recognize that "corporate flying was a factor to be dealt with." Pague[12] recalled Henry as "an entrepreneur, a well travelled man, large and heavy-set." Victim of slowly advancing cancer, Henry had lost one leg by the time the CAOA contract was drafted. By the early 1950's his health was rapidly failing and Bennett "Ben" Horchler, assistant publisher, assumed CAOA responsibilities.[13] After Henry's death in September, 1952 his widow, Lois, a diminutive, pretty and highly intelligent woman, took over "lock, stock and barrel."[14] In Pague's opinion she was even more dedicated to the association than her husband and less interested in the other Henry Company magazines. Lois Henry's warm relationship with CAOA-NBAA continued until 1961, when the magazine was sold. The *Skyways* link continued for only two more years thereafter.

While there is no doubt the Henry link provided a rich and far-reaching means for publicizing CAOA, it is a fact that other magazines shied away from voluntarily or eagerly providing comment on CAOA-NBAA. And as the relationship grew in the late 1940's Henry himself played what could be judged as too dominant a role in the actual day-to-day operation of the association. On balance, and particularly in the late years of the agreement's life, the link with *Skyways* was without doubt more damaging than helpful to NBAA.

The first "official publication" appeared in June, 1948, after CAOA members had been told the arrangement "had many attractive features and none of the disadvantages of other types of affiliation"[15] to which CAOA had given consideration. Yet Board minutes and archival material make no mention of any other "affiliation" being given thought. When the June *Skyways* appeared, Lathrop moved and the Directors agreed that Henry should be an "ex officio" member of the Board. This unusual designation was listed in minutes for four meetings only. After that, Henry was recorded simply as "also present."

At the same June, 1948, Board meeting a guest appeared at his own request and made a proposal which, without intention, resulted in evolution of an aviation event of world rank, the NBAA Annual Meeting and Convention. Shelby Maxwell of Burlington Mills, an outspoken and abrupt, yet warmly attractive man, was the guest. He made a strong case that the time had come for CAOA to "go public" by holding a special conference or "Open Forum" in Washington at which major issues and problems could be threshed out with government officials and manufacturers. Henry and Lathrop were given responsibility to look into the proposal and the Executive Committee was given authority to go ahead with it. With all the detailed arrangements provided by *Skyways* staff, the Forum took place August 11, 1948 at the Statler Hotel (later renamed the Capital Hilton). The attendance roster lists 73 names apart from the government speakers. Fifty attendees came from 33 companies operating business aircraft; 16 industry representatives were present and seven persons from other associations. The list is close to a *Who's Who* of early business aviation. Ten of those present would be Directors or Associate Advisors to the Board, and three would be elected as the association's chief executive officer. Others would become firmly established players on the business aviation stage. (The attendance list as printed in the November, 1948 *Skyways* insert is printed at the conclusion of this chapter, after the notes.)

Among speakers were Fred B. Lee, then Deputy Administrator of the Civil Aeronautics Administration, Beverly Howard, President of the National Aviation Trades Association, Joseph T. Gueting, Jr., Manager of the Personal Aircraft Council, and Gill Robb Wilson, aviation editor of the *New York Herald Tribune*. Maxwell was fiery during a "Pilots' Forum," complaining of communications problems with control towers and range stations. Hotze expressed the great need for a "purpose built" aircraft designed especially for business use: 10 to 12 passenger capacity, speed well in excess of 200 miles per hour, and range sufficient to need only one stop in transcontinental flight. The *Skyways* report of the forum said the manufacturers present agreed on the need but felt "cost of developing such a ship today would necessitate there being a dual and even a triple market for it."

The forum was judged an outstanding success and did much to advance CAOA's name and credibility. Pague recalls it as the first issues-oriented CAOA deployment, a "real meeting place for members and others to come and voice their opinions."[16] Unlike NBAA conventions of distant future years there were no industry exhibits at the Statler in 1948. But manufacturers didn't neglect an opportunity. Sample goods "simply came out of suitcases" in industry attendees' hotel rooms.[17] And while the annual meeting of the members and the "open forum" were not fused until 1950, and a long evolutionary process followed, the launching of a faintly-outlined concept in 1948 would turn out to be one of the most important decisions in the association's annals. Shelby Maxwell's place in NBAA history was secured.

Contrasting with the benefits of the forum was the gaping hole it exposed in CAOA's management capabilities. The need for placing the arrangements in *Skyways* hands focused attention on the desirability for CAOA to have its own professional staff. This was keenly felt by Lathrop, who found it increasingly difficult to balance CAOA demands with his own heavy job responsibilities at Bristol-Myers. The stress may even have caused him to lower his sights. In early 1948 he replied to an inquiry for information from the American Petroleum Institute, saying that CAOA had few members but adding without apparent enthusiasm that "ultimately we hope to have 50 or more."[18]

Soon, through referral by Nesbitt of Atlantic Aviation, Lathrop was contacted by Jean H. DuBuque, an aviation marketing and promotion figure. DuBuque had moved his consulting business from Dallas to Washington and in February, 1948, he sought to interest Lathrop in naming him to represent CAOA in Federal rules making and regulatory affairs in the capital city.[19] Nothing came of the exchange of letters. But DuBuque's inquiry sped consideration of need for staff help and raised the thought of a Washington base. DuBuque obviously retained interest in CAOA, for in August, 1952 he would contact Morrow and be brought aboard as full-time Executive Director of the association.

In August of 1948 Lathrop made the move from Bristol-Myers to Cameron Machine Company and gave notice to Belden that he must soon resign from CAOA duties. Responding, Belden wrote on September 29: "Fred Henry has written me about the question of obtaining a paid secretary and I hope to see him in New York within the next week or two to discuss this matter with him."

Before year's end CAOA's Directors "bit the bullet" and hired the association's first employee. He was C.B. Colby, a well known journalist, employed in the understanding he would be "Executive Secretary" and would give "at least" two days to a week to CAOA. Colby was given a cramped office, not much more than eight by ten feet, at the Henry Publishing suite, 444 Madison Avenue, New York. A New Hampshire native, Colby had been a pilot since 1930, wrote for *Air Trails* and *Air Progress* magazines and from 1943 to 1946 was aviation editor of *Popular Science Monthly*. He was also a founding member of the Aviation Writers Association. Pague[20] recalled him as being "a technical writer, a known writer, whose credentials looked good." There also had been long standing friendship between Colby and Henry. A surprising aspect of the arrangement was Belden's written instruction to Colby that he was to "work under the general supervision of Mr. J. Fred Henry,"[21] who in fact held no managerial position in CAOA.

CAOA's year 1948 closed with cautious optimism. The group had proved its ability to serve as the rallying point for airing of issues and it now had sorely-needed staff capability. But, with the resignation of Lathrop as Secretary, it suffered the loss of a towering leadership figure.

And somehow, the year ended without an annual meeting of members being held as specified in by-laws. Need for the meeting was talked about during the

Much of the post-war business aircraft fleet consisted of surplus military transports and bombers. In the early 1950's Tennessee Gas Transmission Co. (later Tenneco) acquired a B-26 bomber and placed it in service after extensive conversion and flight testing. One of the contemporary attractions of the B-26 was its speed.

February Board session, and the June *Skyways* insert said it was planned for Cleveland at air show time in September. That was the final word.

The business aircraft community, meanwhile, was growing. *Planes*, the AIA publication, said that in August "sales of executive type aircraft actually exceed(ed) sales of two-place or trainer types by a substantial margin."

And Gill Robb Wilson wrote in the *Herald Tribune* that "if the Executive Fleet continues to grow . . . the development could be the biggest thing in civil aviation. The planes . . . are now used chiefly to transport top officials, but I gather that company sales and promotion departments"[22] are getting more and more use. Wilson also took note "that from a national security angle the Executive Fleet even now is worth its weight in gold."

Starting his new duties, Colby tried to establish working connections in official Washington but was largely unsuccessful. Distance and lack of travel funds made it difficult to establish CAOA's credentials. Attempts to gain membership on the important Air Navigation Development Board of the Commerce Department were exemplary. These resulted in an exchange of letters[23] which amounted to a polite brush-off. The Board noted that the only associations involved, all without vote, were the Air Line Pilots Association (ALPA), ATA and AOPA; no hint was given that expansion was planned or wanted. This kind of frustrating experience would in two years turn into one of the catalysts in the decision to move CAOA's office to Washington.

Lathrop's departure resulted in election of William R. Martin, Assistant to the President of Bristol-Myers, to the Board and as Treasurer. Head of the company's

Photo courtesy of History of Aviation Collection, University of Texas

Sam Keener, right, was a visionary businessman who believed that use of an aircraft could open the door to worldwide construction contracts for his Salem (Ohio) Engineering Company. He launched the first round-the-world business aircraft flight in 1949. Nelson U. Rokes, left, was chief pilot on the successful 50,000 mile journey.

flight department since 1946, Martin held academic degrees from St. Lawrence University and the New York University School of Banking. During the war he amassed 2,000 hours as pilot in the Alaskan Air Transport Command.

In April, 1949, Martin reported that a cash balance of $3,547 existed, up from the $1,200 reported two years earlier. An annual meeting was held on May 25 at Bristol-Myers' 630 Fifth Avenue, New York offices. Guess, Hotze and Mitchell chose not to run for re-election. Taking their places were J.C. Jones, of R.M. Hollingshead Corporation, Howard Maurhoff, National Dairies Corporation, and Cole H. Morrow, J.I. Case Co., Martin's interim election by the Board was confirmed by membership vote.

Reporting for the Technical Committee, Pague gave an endorsement to a newly developed "crosswind landing gear," and the members were told that the association had grown to 50 members, the "ultimate" expressed by Lathrop a year earlier.

Morrow's election, in particular, was a significant event, as he soon rose to positions of strong leadership. He would replace Belden as Chairman, act as a force in promoting the move to Washington, and would devote tremendous energy to firmly establishing CAOA's credentials after the move was completed.

While the annual meeting of members went smoothly, the Directors meeting which came after it ran into turbulence. Belden, on the edge of being re-elected Chairman, pointed out that a major error of omission had been committed. A "corrective" amendment to by-laws, planned for action, had not been brought before the members. Lacking the correction, no Chairman could serve for more than two years. Bixler was then elected as Chairman on a temporary basis, Martin was redesignated Treasurer and Colby named Secretary. At a special hurried-up proxy meeting of the members held June 29, the needed by-laws change was made and Belden was again seated in the Chair.

Much against Belden's grain, 1949 witnessed the beginnings of concern voiced by Morrow and then several other Board members over lack of status in CAOA for companies which owned only single-engine aircraft. Mitchell brought the matter before the annual meeting, but no action was taken. His idea was that thought be given to admitting such companies, even when the piloting was done by holders of private licenses alone. Further discussion took place at Board level later in the year and the Technical Committee was asked to prepare recommendations on the subject. Soon Craig, an original member of the committee, resigned from the Board and his place in the technical panel was taken by Morrow.

Summer, 1949, turned into a season for resignations. First, Bristol-Myers sold its aircraft as an economy move and Martin, after only a few months' Board service, left as of July 20. At almost the same time Colby submitted his resignation to be effective August 15, only eight months after his appointment as Executive Secretary. Pague could recall no dissatisfaction with Colby. "We were quite surprised when (he) submitted his letter of resignation. What he really wanted was to spend more time with his writing."[24]

With a large number of government officials making appearances, the 1949 Forum, held at the Statler in Washington, August 3, was another success. William P. Odom, the noted aviator who had recently completed yet another record-setting solo flight, was made the first Honorary Member of CAOA. Cited was his non-stop Honolulu to Teterboro flight in a Beech Bonanza, described as "a small executive airplane." A national hero to the end, Odom died soon after the CAOA Forum, crashing in his P-51 aircraft at the Cleveland Air Races September 5.

Belden, meanwhile, lost no time in replacing Colby. Effective September 1, 1949, Nathaniel F. Silsbee became Executive Secretary on the same part-time basis as Colby. Also an aviation writer and editor, Silsbee (known as Neil or Nat) in 1940 had been author of a nationally-syndicated column, "Wings Over America." He next served four years in the Army Air Corps, rising to Lieutenant Colonel in technical

Nathaniel F. Silsbee, center, was the second person employed as CAOA staff chief. He shared a convivial moment in 1950 with Henry W. Boggess, left, Sinclair Refining Company, CAOA/NBAA Director and later chief executive, and C. F. Zimmerman, Continental Oil, Director 1958–1964. Reflected in the mirror is the face of Scott E. Miller, Airesearch Aviation Services Company, stalwart association supporter over the years, and, as depicted above, host at the first hospitality suite.

research, public relations and intelligence staff work. The period 1946–1949 saw him as technical editor of *Skyways* and managing editor of *Aero Digest*. Like Colby, he was a close friend of Henry. In Morrow's opinion Silsbee "became the first real Executive Secretary the organization had, . . . a fine gentleman, dedicated, who did a marvellous job."[25] Pague shared this admiration, describing Silsbee as a "very conscientious individual."[26] Joseph B. Burns, a Director from 1950, described Silsbee as a "quiet, dignified sort of fellow, a good man for the organization. He didn't try to tell people how to do things. He told them what needed doing and then allowed them to use some sense."[27] Using the same limited quarters at 444 Madison Avenue, Silsbee by December of 1949 established an auxiliary "operations office" in the Mallard Aviation facility at Teterboro. There he and volunteers from the membership would for the next year meet on a weekly basis with itinerant pilots. The employment agreement with Silsbee was similar to Colby's but there was a noteworthy difference. It called on Silsbee to "work under the general supervision of *the Chairman of CAOA* and Mr. J. Fred Henry." (Emphasis added)[28] CAOA appeared to be moving toward closer day-to-day control of its staff.

Early 1950 brought the recommendations from the Technical Committee on single-engine aircraft, setting out criteria for size, instrumentation and radio equipment. The committee also felt that such aircraft should be flown by full-time professional pilots with commercial ratings. The Board failed to act, probably because of the deeply divided and emotional beliefs held by key members. But by the mid-1950's major by-laws revisions and procedures would finally settle the matter in favor of single-engine owners, not at all to the satisfaction of some Directors, notably Belden.

Dun's Review carried a long article written by Silsbee in February, 1950, "The Airplane As A Business Tool." He estimated that there were about "8,000 (business) aircraft, (counting) only four-place and larger craft. Three years before, there were probably fewer than 2,000 business aircraft." Saying there were now 1,500 multi-engine airplanes in such use, Silsbee reflected on the past: business aviation "started in a very small way in the mid-1930's. Actually, up to 1935 there were only four multi-engine executive planes in the entire United States, and a Dallas oilman bought the fifth that year." Silsbee gave no source for these calculations.

Silsbee's story did not mention an achievement completed in late 1949, the first around-the-world flight of a business aircraft. The journey logged 50,000 miles and included stops in more than 30 cities and 24 countries. Used to solicit business for Salem Engineering Company of Ohio, a major construction firm, the trip was the brain child of company president Sam Keener. It was the follow-on of a successful air tour of Europe in 1948. Nelson U. Rokes, prominent in NBAA affairs, was pilot of the DC-4 Skymaster (N4K) which made the journey, with Delmar Flickner crew chief. "Travelling by private plane to see the potential customer and surveying his problems and needs right on the spot is the only way to do business in this field," wrote Keener. Undaunted by prospecting half a world away, he felt that "strangers are friends you have never met before." Leaving Akron-Canton airport August 7, 1949, the Skymaster returned home December 17, precisely 46 years after the Wright brothers made their first successful powered flights at Kitty Hawk. Rokes soon left Salem to head Procter and Gamble's flight department, staying there until retirement in the late 1970's.[29]

The 1950 annual meeting witnessed election of John C. Yost, Armstrong Cork Company, Cornelius Fulton, Jr., Mathieson Chemical, and Burns, Fuller Brush Company, as Directors. These men filled vacancies caused by Martin's mid-1949 resignation and those of Jones and Craig in November. Yost and Fulton served relatively brief periods but Burns, Vice President and General Counsel for Fuller Brush, remained and became a distinguished association executive, serving with great intelligence and flair as elected president and Chief Executive Officer in the late 1950's. Belden was elected to his fourth term as Chairman and Maurhoff was named Treasurer. Silsbee was designated Secretary.

The year also brought the annual meeting and the forum into tandem, spreading them for the first time over two days, May 18 and 19, 1950, at the Statler in Washington. An innovation was made by moving the members' meeting out of New York, an event not favored by Belden, who preferred the intimacy and control which came with a small conference room to that inherent in an open hotel environment.

A prestigious group of speakers at the Forum included Donald W. Nyrop, Deputy CAA Administrator (later Northwest Airlines Chairman) and Lederer, then

Director of the Flight Safety Foundation. Members heard that CAOA failed its goal of having 100 members and that the cash balance increased to $5,521. A highlight of the Forum was presentation to Arthur Godfrey of a citation noting his "outstanding contribution to use of aircraft as an aid to business during 1949 ... and by promoting the idea on his radio and television programs." While the presentation bore no name other than "citation" the idea behind it eventually grew without plan or purpose into the annual NBAA Award for Meritorious Service to Aviation, one of the industry's greatest honors. (See Appendix for complete list of award recipients.)

The hospitality suite, an attraction which abounded at later annual meetings, was born at the 1950 gathering. Airesearch Aviation Service Company sponsored the first suite, with its principal host Scott E. Miller, one of the best liked and most congenial figures in business aviation. CAOA had no suite of its own in 1950, and Miller with typical grace volunteered Airesearch's suite as a place to receive Godfrey after the award presentation. Present at every annual meeting from 1950 through 1986, and committee Chairman of five, Miller's attendance record was arguably one of the best of the association's first 40 years.

Glimmers of international affiliation sparkled briefly on December 5, 1950 with receipt of a letter from John R. Martin of Canadian Brewers, Ltd. He explained that Canadian corporate aircraft operators were thinking of organizing, being inspired by the CAOA example. Would there be possibility of affiliating with CAOA? The Board's response was not encouraging. Enthusiam and assistance were offered but Martin was told CAOA had no means for direct affiliation. It would be nine years before the Canadians created an organization and eleven before it became an independent entity. But the brief encounter of 1950 nevertheless marked an important moment of aviation history and planted a seed which finally bore bloom in 1981 with creation of the International Business Aviation Council, Ltd. (IBAC).

By late 1950 the Korean War gave business aviation a major challenge, possibly its greatest yet. CAOA found itself at a crossroads. The tiny New York office was becoming ever more confining as were the many direct operational ties to *Skyways*. The lure of Washington was growing more tempting. But harsh facts put a damper on temptation. CAOA had little money, only modest prospects and an emotionally-charged division of opinion on moving, even within New York.

In early 1951 Nyrop, now Civil Aeronautics Board chairman, wrote (whether voluntarily or in response to finely-crafted prompting is not shown in archives) to suggest a move to Washington. He made a strong case that the government would be looking to CAOA for information and help in handling priorities for aircraft parts, supplies and equipment during the war period. He touched as well on the subject of possible deferment from military service of company pilots. Nyrop's appeal was strong: come to Washington so you can work closely with us. Neither Pague nor Morrow recall that the war-related aspects were large factors in the decision to move.[30] But the CAOA Board asked Morrow to include "liberal" quotations from Nyrop's communication in a letter which Morrow was preparing for circulation to members on the topic of a possible relocation. In

Radio celebrity Arthur M. Godfrey was an avid pilot as well. He received CAOA's first "Citation" from association Chairman William B. Belden, right, at CAOA's 1950 Forum in Washington. In later years Godfrey was a supportive NBAA member, serving as principal speaker at its 25th anniversary banquet and as a member of the Energy Committee created by the fuel crisis of the early 1970's.

general the membership was aware that CAOA, through Silsbee's and Morrow's efforts, was already deeply involved in Washington meetings of the Emergency Aviation Council on quotas, allocations and possible rationing.

Pague remembers the issue of relocation as extremely difficult.[31] The New York office was tiny but economical. The Henrys were good friends who felt the "official" *Skyways* label might be lost in a move. Alternative New York space was expensive. Yet the Board felt it was easy to operate out of New York, then still the nation's association capital. Lack of money was the principal negative consideration, in Morrow's opinion.[32] Belden is remembered as opposed to Washington; Pague, Morrow and Hotze were among those recalled as favoring it.

The dam broke on January 26, 1951. In quick succession, an offer of office space in Washington was disclosed, the Board determined bravely to mount an intense membership drive and vowed to increase annual dues. The Executive Committee, plus Morrow, who the minutes note "has been in close touch with the developing Washington situation," were left to conclude the details.

Starting March 1, 1951 the Washington office was occupied on a sublease from the Aeronautical Training Society, whose Secretary Wayne Weishaar had found himself with more space than needed. CAOA was given a furnished office 21 by 12 feet, designated as Room 404 of the Stoneleigh Court building, 1025 Connecticut Avenue, N.W., just north of K Street, (later torn down and replaced by The Blake Building). A 10 by 4 foot storage area was included, Weishaar would supply limited secretarial service, and the cost would be $80 a month. Silsbee and his wife, Elizabeth, who would assist him with CAOA work, quickly moved house from Merrick, Long Island, N.Y., and eagerly settled into the new routine. "Paperwork was stacked all over the room" in New York, recalled Pague,[33] and the Washington space gave needed relief. But most important it put Silsbee where he needed to be, close to a government which was more and more tightly regulating the aviation world.

CAOA's Board increased membership dues from $100 to $150, and set into motion plans for the next Annual Meeting and Forum at the Statler. To celebrate the move to Washington the Board decided to hold its March 21 meeting in the new office but only Belden and Morrow appeared. The governing body thus diminished the occasion and at the same time called attention to a nagging problem: its poor attendance record. From December, 1948 to December, 1950, an actual quorum could be counted only at 10 of the 17 Board meetings. Perhaps a fresh start, provided by the move to Washington, was the medicine needed to perk up the slightly run down patient.

NOTES TO CHAPTER 3

1. Walter Pague, Middletown, Ohio, audio tape interview with J.H. Winant, June 11, 1987.

2. Ibid.

3. Ibid. and Cole H. Morrow, McLean, Va., audio tape interview with J.H. Winant, May 5, 1987.

4. Morrow tape, May 5, 1987.

5. Pague tape, June 11, 1987.

6. Letter, Palmer J. Lathrop to Sydney Nesbitt, January 29, 1947.

7. Letter, T. Wilson Hotze to J.H. Winant, January 30, 1987.

8. Pague tape, June 11, 1987.

9. Morrow tape, May 5, 1987

10. CAOA Board meeting minutes, November 5, 1947.

11. Morrow tape, May 5, 1987.

12. Pague tape, June 11, 1987.

13. Morrow tape, May 5, 1987.

14. Pague tape, June 11, 1987.

15. CAOA Newsletter, March 1948.

16. Pague tape, June 11, 1987.

17. Ibid.

18. Letter, Palmer J. Lathrop to E.E. Lothrop, American Petroleum Institute, January 6, 1948.

19. Letter, Jean H. DuBuque to Palmer J. Lathrop, February 17, 1948.

20. Pague tape, June 11, 1987

21. Letter, employment proposal, W.B. Belden to C.B. Colby, November 9, 1948.

22. Gill Robb Wilson, "The Air World" column, *New York Herald Tribune*, August 18, 1948.

23. Exchange of letters, CAOA and Air Navigation Development Board, U.S. Department of Commerce, December 6–15, 1948.

24. Pague tape, June 11, 1987

25. Morrow tape, May 5, 1987

26. Pague tape, June 11, 1987

27. Joseph B. Burns, West Hartford, Connecticut, audio tape interview with J.H. Winant, April 8, 1988.

28. Letter, employment proposal, W.B. Belden to N.F. Silsbee, August 18, 1949.

29. News Release, "Flying Ohio Businessman . . .," Salem Engineering Company, July 10, 1949, Rokes archives, History of Aviation Collection, University of Texas.

30. Morrow tape, May 5, 1987 and Pague tape, June 11, 1987.

31. Pague tape, June 11, 1987.

32. Morrow tape, May 5, 1987

33. Pague tape, June 11, 1987.

CAOA FORUM ATTENDANCE

(Statler Hotel, Washington, D.C., August 11, 1948)

Aircraft Industry Representatives:

Aircraft Radio Corp	H.S. Christensen
Atlantic Aviation Service	Stewart M. Ayton
Beech Aviation Corp.	Leddy Greever
Bendix Aviation Corp.	J.M. Hadley
Consolidated-Vultee Aircraft Corp.	A.E. Lombard, Jr.
	Wm. C. Wold
Irving Air Chute	I.B. Hartzog
Lear, Inc.	Richard T. Cowden
Glen L. Martin Co.	F.S. Cross
	Wm. F. Druckenbrod
	Geo. B. Shaw
Piper Aircraft Corp.	W.T. Piper
Pratt & Whitney Aircraft Div.	L.L. Snow
J.D. Reed Co.	J.D. Reed
Ryan Aeronautical Corp.	J. W. Miller
Spartan Aero Repair	M.D. Wilson

Industrial Companies:

Armco Steel Corp.	Walter C. Pague
	James M. Banker
Bethlehem Steel Co.	A.J. Green
	Robert Jeffrey
	A.E. Junker
	John Somerville
Bristol-Myers Co.	Palmer J. Lathrop
	Wm. R. Martin
	W.T. Dawson
Burlington Mills Corp.	S. M. Maxwell
	James G. Guess
J. I. Case Co.	Cole H. Morrow
Champion Paper & Fibre Co.	Raymond T. Rickards
	Richard W. Smith
Deere & Co.	Joseph R. James
Eastman Kodak Co.	J.W. Clemow
	Edw. W. Knitter
General Electric Co.	Andrew Boyajian

B. F. Goodrich Co.
Grand Central Airport Co.

S. J. Groves & Sons Co.

Gulf Oil Co.
Howes Leather Co.

Koppers Co., Inc.
L. B. Smith, Inc.
Lever Brothers Co.
Minneapolis-Honeywell Co.
Modern Welding Co.
National Dairy Products Corp.
National Gypsum Co.
North American Companies
Republic Steel Corp.

Reynolds Metals Co.

Riss & Co.
Royal-Liverpool Group
Salem Engineering Co.
Shell Oil Co.

Sinclair Refining Co.
Socony-Vacuum Oil Co.
United Cigar-Whelan Stores, Inc.
Universal Moulded Products Corp.
Virginia Coal & Iron Co.

R.H. Witney
Charkes Kidder
R. Fox
Alan C. Fletcher
N.L. Mitchell
Al Williams
James P. Moran
Charles H. Scott
James F. Haley
R.V. Bate
John L. Minihan
J.M. Brandt
O.R. Armstrong
J.P. Hellebrand
Richard J. Notebaert
F. Lieber
Wm. B. Belden
T. Arthur Jones
T. Wilson Hotze
Hugh H. Hardwicke, Jr.
J.B. Redwine
Rolland C. Swanson
C.F. Cobourn
W.D. Turner
G. Hughes
M. Hamon
A. P. Hynes
Kenneth F. Horton
A. Billgren
John R. Dunham
L.D. Kirby
Major C.F. Sowa

Aviation Associations:

Aeronautical Training Society
Aircraft Industries Assn.

Aircraft Owners & Pilots Assn.
American Petroleum Ind.
National Aviation Trades Assn.

Wayne M. Weishaar
M. Brown
Don Mockler
Joseph T. Geuting, Jr.
J.B. Hartranft, Jr.
E.E. Lothrop
H. Meixell
B. Howard

Chapter 4

CHARTING THE COURSE: 1951–1955

THE MEDICINE WORKED. MOVING OF CAOA HEADQUARTERS to Washington soon produced benefits, among them new leadership, greater involvement in aviation industry affairs and new awareness of direction and purpose. Growth of membership and the annual meeting and forum quickly followed.

In the spring of 1951 CAOA accepted an invitation to become a dues-paying member of the Executive Committee of the Radio Technical Commission for Aeronautics (RTCA), a prominent organization which had since 1936 acted as the principal advisor to the Federal government on aerial communication and navigation standards. Starting July 1 Silsbee was the CAOA designee, becoming involved in the ongoing implementation of RTCA's benchmark 1948 statement of requirements for a "common (military and civil) system of all-weather navigation, landing aids and air traffic control." The massive upgrading required to build the new system was expected to go on into the 1960's.[1]

A Washington presence also brought membership on the Air Coordinating Committee, from 1945 to 1958 the key industry advisory group helping to shape Federal policy on aviation. Morrow was named to serve, with Silsbee as his alternate. Appointment of Morrow highlighted Belden's reputed avoidance of outside involvements. He "didn't like to go out and give speeches and would pass these off to others," said Morrow.[2] "He didn't like the Washington representative role," and preferred that Morrow take on such obligations.

June's annual meeting and forum at the Statler was the scene for presentation of the "CAOA Merit Award" to Colonel J. Francis "Jack" Taylor, USAF, for major contributions to development of all weather navigation aids and instruments. Speakers included Nyrop of CAB, Charles F. Horne, CAA Administrator, Emory S. Land, ATA President and Delos W. Rentzel, Undersecretary of Commerce for Transportation. Two years later Rentzel, having become a senior executive with Auto Transports, Inc., was elected to the NBAA Board.

Cole H. Morrow, J. I. Case Company and CAOA/NBAA chief executive 1951–1954, presented the "1950 Merit Award" to Air Force Colonel J. Francis Taylor, Jr., at the 1951 Forum.

A comprehensive directory of CAOA members, much expanded from an initial effort made in January, 1950, was issued mid-1951. In addition to its name, each member could list its official in charge of aviation, chief pilot, co-pilots, scheduling personnel, CAOA representative's name, aircraft by type and registration number, and equipment carried such as transmitters, receivers, frequencies and VOR, ILS and ADF aids. The main idea behind the directory was to hand a working tool to air traffic control personnel so that they could easily identify member aircraft and, it was hoped, give them expeditious handling. The 1951 edition listed 236 aircraft, 175 of which were multi-engine. Operating this "fleet" were 128 regular member companies. And while its usefulness was occasionally brought into question and it risked being eliminated in a cost reduction drive only four years later, the directory gained importance over the years; while its original purpose was soon outgrown and its format was changed to meet contemporary needs, the *NBAA Directory of Member Companies and Aircraft* became a coveted publication, much protected by the association from distribution or use outside the membership and selected government personnel.

June brought a major change in leadership, with Morrow, Chief Plant Engineer of the Case Company, Racine, Wisconsin, being elected Chairman in place of Belden. Morrow, a stocky, high-keyed man who spoke in earnestly deliberate fashion, would lead CAOA for three years, giving to it an enormous amount of effort and dedication. His engineering background showed through in his personal bluntness but there was no question of his devotion. Walter C. Pague described him as "a very energetic, ambitious person" who "devoted an infinite amount of time to the organization." He was "a very outspoken individual, controversial in the eyes of some persons," but his efforts "were all directed at the best interests of the organization."[3] Joseph B. Burns, another contemporary Director, described Morrow as "very opinionated . . . and a little abrasive, but in life you've got to do things like that some times." Morrow, he added, "wanted good things for business aviation and did what he thought was right . . . He made substantial contributions, injecting technical aspects and operational matters, all very practical ideas. It was in Cole's time we changed the association's name to NBAA. We were trying hard to inject a business element into the organization."[4] Morrow's service as Chairman included some rough going. In 1987 he recalled personally loaning money to CAOA[5] to meet payroll needs for a two month period when cash flow was negative. An experienced pilot, Morrow took his engineering degree at Vanderbilt University and joined Case in 1937. Leaving it in 1961, he served until retirement in 1979 in several positions with FAA: Director of Airports Service, Chief of Planning Research and as a Chief in the Systems Research and Development Service. In 1987 he lived in McLean, Virginia, active in several aviation groups.

During the 1951 meeting Maurhoff was elected Treasurer and Silsbee Secretary. Dunham, Morrow and Pague were re-elected by the members to three-year terms as Directors. Sadly, the B-26 tragedy in 1954 ended Dunham's term prematurely.

The July 1951 Board meeting adopted a resolution, drafted by Burns, which gave deserved praise to Belden for his four years in the chair: Because of his work a sound foundation had been built and "there is practically no limit to be set to the future growth and usefulness of the Corporation Aircraft Owners Association. This success has been achieved by the unselfish effort and firm determination of William (Burlingame) Belden."

A different context, also framed without perceptible limit, was used by Silsbee to describe business aviation in a September *Skyways* article. "A recent survey" conducted by CAOA showed "that there are more than 8,000 aircraft operated by businesses," Silsbee wrote, "and nearly 1,400 of them are multi-engine planes." Silsbee's data showed there were 222 DC-3's in the "fleet," 146 Lodestars, 65 converted bombers, 165 amphibians, 604 Twin Beechcrafts and 178 "older models" of Lockheed 12A and Twin Cessna type. Noted was the evolutionary change in character of business aircraft. The small fleet which existed 10 years before was "largely for advertising and publicity value;" now transportation was the moving force, growing rapidly.

As 1951 ended Silsbee's health began to fail, but he carried on with his duties despite growing difficulty. In January, 1952, the Board heard that an impending rent increase had sent him on a search for new office space. Room 206 of the Medical Science Building, 1029 Vermont Avenue, N.W. (close by the junction with L Street) had been made available at $110 a month until January, 1954. The move had been authorized in December by the Executive Committee. Principal among features was that the new quarters offered two separate rooms. And in the move, CAOA had at last found its own, independent home.

At the same January meeting Morrow proposed a novel idea: that the 1952 annual meeting and forum be held in Chicago, breaking the pattern of meeting in Washington. Morrow's thinking was that the move to mid-America would attract a larger attendance from a much broader cut of the membership. He was correct. And as was the case with so many other CAOA decisions, the change would prove to have great unanticipated future impact. This one gave CAOA the freedom to use the best of a variety of meeting sites extending eventually from coast to coast.

By the next month Silsbee was seriously ill, first housebound and finally, trying unsuccessfully to work from his bed. On February 15 he died. The Board received the news with great sadness and asked his widow to stay on temporarily. Silsbee's 16 months as staff chief were extraordinarily productive, and demanding as well. He would be long remembered for excellence and statesmanship; his early death would be lastingly regretted.

On March 23, 1952 Herbert O. Fisher reported for duty as Silsbee's replacement. The most notable quality of Fisher's service was its brevity, for he resigned, giving minimum notice, effective August 7 to take on duties with the Port of New York Authority. Fisher had no time to leave an imprint on CAOA; his term was the briefest of all staff chiefs during NBAA's first 40 years. Chief test pilot for Curtiss-Wright before joining CAOA, he had been Director of Aviation for Indianapolis from 1930 to 1938 and was "hump" transport pilot in the China-Burma-India (CBI) theater of war. Designated as the first Executive Director of CAOA, he left to become Chief of Aviation Development with the port authority, duties he would retain with various titles until his retirement in the late 1970's. A decade later he was living an active retirement in Kinellon, New Jersey. Morrow saw Fisher as "a 'gung ho' guy who saw the potentialities of CAOA." While self-promotional, he "did a good job but left quickly." Fred Glass, Port Authority aviation director, "stole him away," said Morrow, adding that CAOA "couldn't pay him the salary the port authority could."[6]

After Fisher's leaving, Morrow conscientiously spent two weeks in Washington keeping things going while he and others searched for a new Executive Director. Morrow's time was freely given. By mid-August, a new staff chief was in place.

He was DuBuque, the consultant who had written to Lathrop in early 1948, when thoughts of employing CAOA staff were dreams only. DuBuque's career was extremely varied, perhaps too much so, consisting for the most part of an extraordinary number of very brief affiliations. He worked for a few months in 1941–42 with Aero Insurance Underwriters, and was known both to Kalberer and to Lederer. During the war, he served under Lederer for a time in the Airlines War Training Institute. Later he worked very briefly with Beech in Wichita and for a few months with Lear, Inc., in Michigan. Director of Aviation for Dallas for five months, he left to set up his consulting business, first in Dallas and then in Washington.

Another full-time employee joined CAOA staff in 1952. She was Corda Mae "C.M." Cearnal, an Arkansas native who assumed the association's secretarial-accounting-administrative duties after Mrs. Silsbee departed in late June. "C.M.," a popular, outgoing woman, remained on staff until the early 1960's, acquiring an enviable reputation for loyalty, integrity and hard work.

Silsbee's death, coupled to Fisher's all too brief service, resulted in postponement of the Chicago general meeting. Put off from June, it was postponed a second time because dates conflicted with the dairy industry's convention and was finally held October 2–3 at the Blackstone Hotel. Morrow remembers the session as an eventful breakthrough, with record attendance, industry hospitality suites, and for the first time an aircraft display at Meigs Field.[7] C.R. Smith, the legendary American Airlines president, was a speaker, and Harvey Gaylord of the Helicopter Council, AIA, accurately predicted a strong future for helicopter use by corporations. Nyrop, still CAB chairman, debunked two fears which he said had tainted corporate flying since the 1940's. Firstly, he said, high utility had exploded the myth that companies bought aircraft only "based on tax reductions." Secondly, "the fear that private company planes would siphon off business from regular airline operations has been proven false." It was unfortunate that 35 years after Nyrop's talk and despite hundreds of similar statements, both fears were widely held. Even Nyrop, speaking as Northwest Airlines' chief executive in later years, would take a dimmer view of the business aircraft's role.

The 1952 members' meeting was notable for a "first," a contested election for Director positions. In addition to the slate presented by Pague, Chairman of the Nominating Committee, three persons were nominated from the floor: Scott E. Miller, Airesearch Aviation Service Co.; Ralph Matthews, Sawhill Manufacturing Co.; and Fisher, late of CAOA staff. Miller and Matthews withdrew their names. Fisher did not. Consisting of proxies and the 31 persons present, the vote was: Maurhoff, 108; Ralph E. Piper, Monsanto Chemical Co., 105; Spetnagel, 107; Anthony Zuma, Tennessee Gas Transmission Co., 101; and Fisher, 11. An apparent "coup" had failed.

The association's officers were re-elected at Chicago but a month later Bixler, one of the 1946 "originals," found it necessary to leave the Board. He was replaced by Henry W. Boggess, Personnel Director of the Sinclair Refining Co., who became a literally and figuratively towering figure in the association. In January, 1953, Maurhoff resigned but agreed to remain as Treasurer until replacement could be made.

By early 1953 the Board brought to fruition a long-debated idea that CAOA's name should be changed. A leader in the movement, Morrow felt that the "corporation" connotation had negative public overtones and that the word "business" needed emphasis.[8] Several suggestions were made for a better name, including Association of Business Aircraft (ABA), Business Aircraft Operators (BAO), Business Operators of Aircraft (BOA), Association of Aircraft for Business (AAB) and Business Air Transportation Association (BATA). The origin of the chosen new name, National Business Aircraft Association, is obscure but those involved recall it was essentially a shared idea born in spirited discussion. The idea led to a special membership meeting at the Wings Club, New York, June 26, 1953. The notice said that "the present name . . . is awkward and does not fairly describe the segment of the aviation industry represented by our membership." Agreement was expressed by 143 votes. Seven were opposed. Making the case for the loyal opposition was J. Sheldon "Torch" Lewis of Thatcher Glass Co., one of business aviation's most colorful, durable and popular figures, later internationally known for his monthly "Greenhouse Patter" magazine column. In a pointedly-worded telegram, Lewis said the change would lessen the status of corporate operators and "associate us with dusters, non skeds and all the other riff-raff of aviation." This, he contended, would cause the corporate segment to lose its identity.[9]

At the same meeting, and by a 139 to 11 vote, another change was enacted to better describe the association's identity. This change in by-laws required that a majority of Board members must be "business representatives not regularly employed as pilots." Aim of the new requirement would be to correct erroneous beliefs that the organization spoke primarily for pilots. Later the same year at St. Louis, Piper said "NBAA is essentially an organization of corporations . . . It is by no means a union, or trust, or a pilots organization."[10]

The year 1953 brought other changes. An Awards Committee, chaired by Boggess, was created, as were membership and legislative committees. The latter two, as in the past, foundered. The awards committee, however, made a major contribution to association history and prestige before the year was out.

Skyways' contract was renewed for an additional five years, but the association also struck out on its own in 1953. In addition to producing "Special Reports" on topical issues, staff launched "Air Dispatch," a newsletter containing information from the *Skyways* insert along with other material. The letter was prominently but ineffectively labelled "Confidential."

Piper in 1953 became Chairman of the Technical Committee and soon broadened its membership base. The idea was to go beyond the Board for members and set up regional listening posts. Named as members were Richard Lane, Food Machinery and Chemical Corporation, California; Don Richardson, Minnesota Mining and Manufacturing, Minnesota; Orlin W. Sorenson, Signal Oil and Gas Company, California; Zuma, of Tennessee Gas Transmission, Houston; Pague of ARMCO, Ohio; and Lee Dorrance, Gaylord Container Corp., Missouri.

Zuma's service was short lived. He resigned from the Board under "pressure of business" May 27, 1953, having served less than eight months. In August, Spetnagel took Maurhoff's place as Treasurer, completing a long series of unexpected Board changes made since the Chicago meeting.

St. Louis was the 1953 Annual Meeting and Forum site. In an attempt to expand the scope the Board decided that "members will be invited to exhibit (at the October 29–30 event) but placing on them the responsibility of making direct arrangements with the (Park Plaza) hotel." Nine companies exhibited in booth space set aside in the mezzanine, setting a precedent which, with vastly different ground rules, grew into one of aviation's major world forums. The first group of exhibitors who took the bold step in 1953 were Aviation Age, New York; Barber-Coleman Company, Rockford, Illinois; Bendix Radio, Baltimore, Maryland; Champion Spark Plug Co., Toledo, Ohio; Collins Radio Company, Cedar Rapids, Iowa; The Jeppesen Company, Denver, Colorado; Lear, Inc., Los Angeles, California; Temco Aircraft Corporation, Greenville, Texas; and Wilcox Electric, Kansas City, Missouri.[11] As at previous meetings there were other suppliers present at St. Louis, using hospitality suites, but their names were not recorded; it was creation of the mezzanine exhibition cluster that marked the important turning point. Aircraft were on display at Lambert Field, and three helicopters, one Hiller and two Bells, provided transportation from airfield to hotel. And for the first time a local arrangements committee of member company personnel looked after the planning of the meeting. Piper served as Chairman, setting a precedent difficult to match. Attendance at the meeting was 223, larger than ever before. But that wasn't all. Still another notable breakthrough took place in St. Louis.

Under Boggess' skillful hand, the NBAA Flying Safety Awards program was crafted during the summer months and the Awards Committee, working at an intense pace, breathed life into it the annual meeting, creating a means of gaining wide international recognition for business aviation's safety record and extensive publicity for NBAA.

Certificates for a million or more miles of accident-free business aircraft operations were given to 16 companies at St. Louis. Ohio Oil Company (later renamed Marathon Oil) led with 5,261,328 miles. Half million miler pilot awards went to 42 persons, among whom were such fixtures as Pague, C.F. Zimmerman, Conoco; Carl J. Lund, International Paper; A.L. Ueltschi, Pan Am World Airways; George W. Vaughan, H.H. Phillips Drilling Co.; Nelson U. Rokes, Procter and Gamble; and Lewis, Thatcher Glass.

The meeting saw adoption of two pragmatic amendments to by-laws. One eliminated the requirement that Associate members operate aircraft, properly judged as an objectionable inhibitor, not essential to a sound supplier-operator relationship. The other lowered the Directors' quorum from five to three, a tacit way of acknowledging there was a continuing problem with attendance at meetings.

Morrow was re-elected Chairman and Boggess named Vice Chairman. Spetnagel continued as Treasurer, and the members elected Belden, Burns and Boggess to three-year terms. Rentzel was elected to a term expiring in 1955 and Stetler B. Young, Rynel Corporation, was given a one-year term.

And even though he was not present to receive it the NBAA Merit Award appropriately was given to Charles A. Lindbergh in St. Louis. It was presented symbolically at the meeting to E. Lansing Ray, publisher of the *St. Louis Globe-Democrat*, which had been a backer of the epic transatlantic flight. The actual award was later presented to Lindbergh at his Darien, Connecticut, home by a delegation headed by Morrow.

In 1954 Chairman Cole H. Morrow, standing, right, presented certificates of merit to aircraft manufacturers whose products fulfilled business use requirements. Among those present at the head table at the awards banquet in Dallas were, from left, Dwane L. Wallace, Cessna, William T. Piper (standing), Piper Aircraft, William P. Lear, Lear, Inc., and Leddy L. Greever, Beech. Wallace, Piper and Lear would in later years each be the recipient of the NBAA Award for Meritorious Service to Aviation.

In the afterglow of a highly-successful annual meeting, attention was directed by Morrow to setting up an NBAA "Business Aircraft Design Committee," a means which he had earlier described as "trying to determine what is required in aircraft specifications to do the job properly for corporations . . . we are not trying to find out what some of the operators say they want, because I believe that what they want and what they require might be two different things."[12] While an effective committee was not formed, Morrow gave a large amount of personal time to the idea, even sketching the design of a prototypical airplane. NBAA soon held two forums on conversion or design of aircraft, one at St. Louis and another at the Wings Club. And at the 1954 annual meeting in Dallas citations were presented to four companies for producing aircraft "designed primarily to meet the requirements of business aircraft operators." They were Beech for the Twin Bonanza; Aero Design and Engineering for the Aero Commander; Cessna for the Model 310; and Piper for the Apache.

January 1954 saw the NBAA offices move once again, this time to Suite 204, 1701 K Street, N.W. (at the junction with Connecticut Avenue). Members were told that "continued growth . . . requires expansion of National Headquarters and enlargement of staff," the latter reference apparently made to "C.M." Cearnal.

In June Young resigned from the Board, having served only seven months. Gerald J. Eger, Secretary of the International Harvester Co., who would give much managerial strength to NBAA, took his place.

The year also witnessed establishment of an NBAA Flight Safety Committee which, while short-lived, paved the way for development late in the decade of the NBAA Recommended Standards Manual, an internationally-recognized, frequently updated reference and guidance work. "Rip" Strong, Chief Pilot of National Dairy Products Corporation, was Chairman. Subgroups had responsibility for such matters as pilot standards and proficiency, aircraft maintenance and standards, aircraft equipment minima, and emergency preparedness. Among participants were distinguished names: Dave Peterson, Sinclair Refining; Owen Mayfield, Hercules Powder; Neville Watson, C.V. Starr; Fulton of Mathieson; Donald Baldwin, Texaco; Howard Pember, Texaco; and several "consultants:" Bill Person, Flight Safety Foundation; Bill Hall, U.S. Aviation Insurance Group; Bill Walter, Associated Aviation Underwriters, and Ueltschi, founder of Flight Safety, Inc.

By 1954 NBAA data showed significant growth in aircraft since Silsbee's analysis of 1951. A partial breakout of the business multi-engine "fleet," according to a staff paper, was "approximately as follows:"

Civil Types		Converted Military Types	
Douglas DC-3	275	Lockheed Ventura	17
Douglas DC-4	2	Martin B-26	6
Aero Commander	86	Douglas B-23	15
De Havilland Dove	55	North American B-25	25
Beechcraft Model 18	675	Boeing B-17	3
Lockheed Lodestar	210	Convair B-24	4
Lockheed Model 10	3	Douglas A-26	25
Lockheed Model 12	2		
Grumman Mallard	53		
Grumman Widgeon	140		
Convair 240	2		
Convair 340	2		
Beechcraft Twin Bonanza	3		
Ryan Twin Navion	5		

These new data were conclusive evidence that the mix of business aircraft was changing rapidly from World War II conversions to aircraft purpose built for civil use.

The annual meeting at Dallas spread activities over three days, October 27-29, giving a form to the event which was still in use in the late 1980's. Attendance soared to 432. George E. Haddaway, editor of *Flight* magazine, and Al Harting, Dallas Airmotive, co-chaired the meeting with the kind of irrepressible enthusiasm

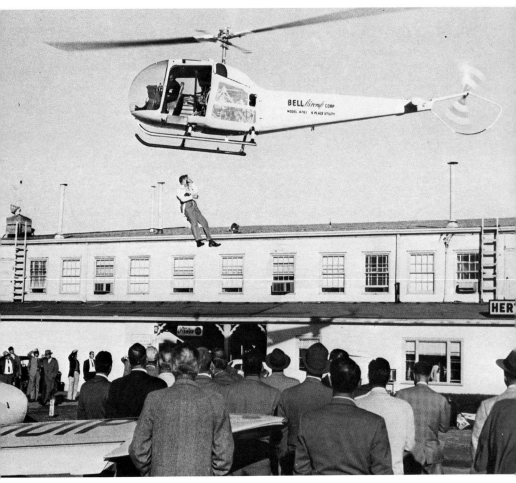

An irrepressible George E. Haddaway, editor-publisher of Flight *magazine, was winched up to a hovering Bell helicopter during flight line demonstrations at the 1954 annual meeting in Dallas. Co-chaired by Haddaway, the Dallas event was a landmark, firmly establishing NBAA's credentials as the focal point for business aviation. The great success of the Dallas gathering set the pattern which led to recognition of the annual meeting as one of aviation's premier events.*

which marked both personalities. Haddaway described the meeting as "the first trade show ever connected with the convention."[13] Seventy-five aircraft were displayed at Love Field, there was an expanded indoor exhibition area at the Adolphus Hotel, and the three days ended in a mammoth Texan barbecue which would long be remembered and often recalled by those who took part.

Morrow remembers the meeting as "the first really major"[14] one and Pague recalls it for a different reason. "That was truly the first (time we had) a Maintenance and Operations meeting,"[15] he said. Pague, who chaired the session, said that prior attempts had missed the mark or were not properly organized in advance. "The operators wanted to debate issues with the manufacturers. For example, why this, and why that? Why can't we get service? It was a good sounding board for people to stand up and express themselves."

Burns recalls Dallas as "the first place where business aviation really flexed its muscle. The suppliers began to see the potential. The management people realized that this was not a pilots' organization but was an operational organization which could help them. And the pilots ... recognized it as a business organization."[16]

The example of Dallas led to a tradition to which a full day eventually was devoted at NBAA annual meetings, with a dozen or more maintenance and operations meetings scheduled, each for a specific aircraft model or type. The meetings grew into one of the most important, and occasionally turbulent, of all links of understanding between manufacturers and owners.

At Dallas Morrow stepped down as Chairman, having indicated earlier in the year that "personal and business reasons" might preclude him from serving further. Boggess, a tall, thin-as-a-rail man of great intelligence, a vast vocabulary, and warm personal charm, was elected to succeed Morrow. Piper was named Vice Chairman and Eger Treasurer. Eger, Morrow and Pague were elected by members to three year terms as Directors; nomination from the floor of Harvey Glass, Texas Illinois Natural Gas Company, gave him 22 votes to 142 each for those elected.

Morrow was cited in a Board resolution for his leadership. Highlighted was doubling of membership; further, "the prestige of the association increased immeasurably both in Washington and throughout the nation."

Very soon after taking the chair Boggess made it clear he would personally take on important NBAA activities. He told the December, 1954, meeting he would be the "principal on various government boards, and panels," and the "Executive Director would be alternate." Lying beneath this declaration was the growing feeling that DuBuque was taking for himself more authority than was proper. Morrow described DuBuque as "effective" and said he "worked hard."[17] But, Morrow added, he had "problems with Jean because he began going off on his own and in effect made statements which were policy statements, things which should have been cleared with the Board or at least the Chairman."

According to Morrow, Boggess wanted to try in his own way to harness and channel DuBuque's efforts to good effect. But in the long run the attempt did not succeed and in August of 1956, just before the end of his second term, Boggess decided that "DuBuque had to go."[18]

Meanwhile, by early 1955 Boggess, with Burns' strong help, was leading the Board through a searching examination of NBAA with a view toward a reorganization plan on which the membership could soon act. Principal aims were

Shown in a mid-1950's setting was a quartet which gained great prominence in NBAA affairs. From left, Leddy L. Greever, later Vice President, Beech Aircraft, Mrs. Olive Ann Beech, and Michael C. Murphy and Earle W. Bauer, both of Ohio Oil (later Marathon Oil Company). Greever was Associate Advisor to the NBAA Board 1978–1980 and, with Scott E. Miller, vied for the best annual meeting attendance record of NBAA's first 40 years. Mrs. Beech and Murphy were recipients (1969 and 1971, respectively) of the Award for Meritorious Service to Aviation. Murphy also was an NBAA Director 1967–1970. Bauer was a Director 1971–1983 and Board Chairman 1979–1981.

to regionalize the association's efforts, give new titles to its officers and increase their number, and to create a sliding dues scale.

A committee chaired by Burns soon completed the job, wrote by-laws revisions and cleared them with the Board. A special meeting of members was held March 28, 1955 in the East Room of the Mayflower Hotel, Washington, to act on the changes.

After minimal debate the reorganization plan was adopted, with 12 persons attending the meeting and 166 members represented by proxy. The vote was 167 to 11.

The amendments established a vehicle for setting up regional units of NBAA, each to be chartered by the Board. Also set up was a framework to accommodate election of various Vice Presidents for regional representation or to take charge of specific activities such as membership development or public relations. Further, an Executive Council was established, which it was hoped would be populated by senior executives. The purpose was to obtain high level advice on "the policies and practices of the Association." The by-laws changes also eliminated the title of Chairman and replaced it with President, an arrangement which would last until 1971.

On a purely practical scale, a by-laws change was also enacted which set up a democratic means by which candidates for Director, other than those named through the Nominating Committee and Board, could stand for election. The new means barred the kind of unexpected floor nomination situations which took place in 1952 and 1954, and guaranteed that members would know the names of all candidates well in advance of the annual meeting itself.

A month after the special meeting the Board elected Boggess as President, redesignated Piper as National Vice President, left unfilled the new post of Executive Vice President, and continued Eger's service as Treasurer. DuBuque continued as Secretary. So once again, this time through the medium of an ambitiously revised structure, the association set a stage on which it hoped change, growth and new ways of fulfilling its mission would be acted out.

NOTES TO CHAPTER 4

1. CAOA *Report, Skyways,* September, 1951.

2. Cole H. Morrow, McLean, Virginia, audio tape interview with J. H. Winant, May 5, 1987.

3. Walter C. Pague, Middletown, Ohio, audio tape interview with J. H. Winant, June 11, 1987.

4. Joseph B. Burns, West Hartford, Connecticut, audio tape interview with J. H. Winant, April 8. 1988.

5. Morrow tape, May 5, 1987.

6. Ibid.

7. Ibid.

8. Ibid.

9. Telegram, J. S. Lewis, Elmira, N.Y., to CAOA Headquarters, June 23, 1953.

10. NBAA, "Special Bulletin" December 11, 1953, "Report on Sixth Annual Meeting and Forum."

11. Ibid.

12. *American Aviation,* June 25, 1952, interview with Cole H. Morrow.

13. Letter, George E. Haddaway to R. Lampl, NBAA, November 27, 1982.

14. Morrow tape, May 5, 1987.

15. Pague tape, June 11, 1987.

16. Burns tape, April 8. 1988.

17. Morrow tape, May 5, 1987.

18. Ibid.

Chapter 5

WINDS OF CHANGE: 1955–1962

S OME OF THE ATTRACTIVE POSSIBILITIES CREATED BY
the 1955 reorganization were realized; some never came into being or were
short lived. But the wisdom of restructuring NBAA to deal successfully with new
challenges was an undiluted benefit. While not aware of all that was to come in the
years just ahead, the leadership nevertheless prepared NBAA for times of
unprecedented change. The remainder of the decade and the years just beyond
brought major events: the dawn of the turbine power era, growing constraint
imposed by aging airways facilities, enormous progress in the avionics art, and a
massive overhaul of government regulatory authority brought on by a horrific in-
flight airliner collision.

Continuing the aircraft design efforts begun by Morrow in 1953, NBAA in
late 1955 all but issued a challenge to airplane manufacturers. Following the annual
meeting held in Detroit, October, 5–7, Boggess accused the industry of foot
dragging and said NBAA was thinking of underwriting development of a high speed
transport especially designed to fill executive needs. The idea was to be brought to
the new senior level Executive Advisory Council, a creature of the recent by-laws
changes, at its first meeting in December. Boggess said the group "would have no
difficulty in raising the large sums needed to subsidize the development of a
transport prototype."[1]

But there were signs among the exhibits shown at the Sheraton-Cadillac in
Detroit that manufacturers were beginning to look ahead, examining the prospects
of a market for turbine powered business aircraft. Based largely on recent military
experience gained in the Korean War, the government in 1953 organized efforts to
adapt jet power to civil transport use. Application in business aircraft was inevitable.
In Detroit, North American Aviation, Inc. and Fairchild Airplane Division displayed
their preliminary plans.[2] The North American presentation showed both turboprop
and turbojet designs with common features, including eight-passenger normal

seating capacity, 1,500 statute mile range, and operating altitude of 43,400 feet with cabin pressurization equal to 8,000 feet. A large placard said aircraft would be available 30 months after the firm received a production go-ahead. Fairchild's display was for a larger airplane with three turbine engines located in the tail. Observers noted that North American was negotiating a jet trainer contract with the U.S. Air Force and this could put plans for the business airplane on the back burner, at least temporarily.

While not showing a prototype at Detroit, Lockheed was also known to be developing a medium sized jet aircraft for military training use. Later named the JetStar, this new craft made its maiden flight in 1957,[3] a year before North American's military version of the famed Sabreliner performed its first flight.

The 1955 meeting set a new record attendance of 517 "despite unfavorable flying weather."[4] There was mention of a "Miss NBAA," Florence Gallagher of Chicago,[5] first in a line of ladies (sometimes also named "Miss Business Aviation") who were selected to reign over meetings during the next decade. While archives do not show precisely when this custom was discontinued, J.S. "Torch" Lewis years later noted in his "Greenhouse Patter" column that the death blow was given when "Miss NBAA" turned out to be a "Mrs."

Another annual meeting innovation appeared at about the same time. There was frequent difficulty in getting attendees into symposium rooms. Scott E. "Scotty" Miller, of AirResearch Aviation Service Company, drew on his own Rotary Club experiences and proposed that "on timer" awards be given. Persons arriving in the symposium hall prior to the stated startup time were given numbered tickets. At the end of the session, a drawing was held and the winners received handsome prizes, usually the donated products of member companies. Miller's suggestion paid off, attendance soared at meetings, and the practice was still in existence in 1986.

Boggess was re-elected as President, dependable Pague was named National Vice President and Eger was re-elected Treasurer. Voted three year terms as Directors were Curtis G. Talbot, General Electric Co., Schenectady, New York, and Robert C. Sprague, Jr., Sprague Electric Company, North Adams, Massachusetts. Spetnagel was re-elected to a three year term. Then, in an unusual but planned move, Sprague resigned the next month, paving the way for Ralph E. Piper of Monsanto, who had not stood for re-election at Detroit, to come back to the Board for another term.

Detroit was also scene of the first presentation of NBAA million miler pilot safety awards, testimony not only to the skill of those honored but to the maturity of business aviation. The initial recipient group included true aviation pioneers (mileage stated in parentheses):[6]

Harold J. Bowen of Corning Glass (1,021,625), Raoul Castro (1,040,000), Wilfred R. Dotter (1,107,000), and Thomas J. Schuetz (1,008,900) of International Harvester, W.P. Hobson (1,109,580) and B. Owen Mayfield (1,318,900) of Hercules Powder, Carl J. Lund of International Paper

(1,014,800), John A. Lyon of Malco Refineries (1,400,000), S.M. Maxwell of Burlington Industries (1,020,744), George E. Meyers (1,120,000), Ralph E. Piper (1,038,000) and Richard N. Thurston (1,094,878) of Monsanto Chemical, Norman Mitchell of the Minneapolis Star and Tribune (1,055,250), George C. Pomeroy of Swiflite (1,050,000), and topping them all, Nelson U. Rokes of Procter & Gamble (2,779,548 miles).

Discussing the coming onset of the million miler safe flying era, the Board had decided that a "clock or barometer" would be a suitable award provided the cost did "not exceed $25, including engraving." Rising costs granted only a short life to this award scheme and alternatives were soon put to use.

At the same September Board meeting and "after full discussion," details of which were not stated in the minutes, the Board voted not to make a special merit award for 1955. But as it turned out, a "special citation for distinguished service" was given to Frederick B. Lee at the awards luncheon, praising him for "outstanding individual initiative and leadership as Federal Administrator of Civil Aviation."

Responding, Lee spoke of doubling of air traffic within 10 years' time and Federal plans to handle the increase. "The important thing is to have a concerted, continuous program for updating our airways," he said, adding that if all elements of aviation could agree on needs and how to meet them "there's not a doubt in the world we can lick the traffic problems."[7]

Unknown to him or his audience, Lee's remarks were ironically prophetic. They echoed down through the succeeding three decades as, time and time again, detailed plans were announced, only to be later thwarted, to improve and expand aviation system capacity to meet user demand.

Continued growth of NBAA, meanwhile, resulted in need for more office space by the beginning of 1956. Interest focused on the new Pennsylvania Building at the corner of Pennsylvania Avenue and 13th Street, N.W. The location was favored by the Board because it "was close to the Commerce Department, CAA, ANDB, RTCA and CAB." A lease was concluded for 810 square feet known as Suite 344 (third floor) at $310 a month for five years. By March 1, the move was completed and $2,750 was allocated for an "automatic typewriter," carpet, drapes and other needs.

Boggess reported in early 1956 that the new Executive Advisory Council had its first meeting December 9, 1955 in New York. He stressed the "value of the constructive suggestions offered by the Council members." One matter apparently discussed was a sliding dues scale. But the issues of financing development of an aircraft evidently did not surface. Many months later a letter from Boggess to the eight-man council took a different tack.[8] In it he referred to Morrow as chairman of the NBAA New Airplane Committee (there is no archival record of its other members) and told of his attempts to encourage a manufacturer to build "a modern, high performance, fast, pressurized airplane for business use."

Boggess said surveys of member companies had helped Morrow define the specifications of an airplane. "Several major aircraft manufacturers are interested in

Members of NBAA's Board of Directors in late 1955: Front row, from left, Cole H. Morrow, J. I. Case Company; Henry W. Boggess, Sinclair Refining and association President; Joseph B. Burns, Fuller Brush Company; E. T. Spetnagel, Wolfe Industries. Standing, from left, Gerard J. Eger, International Harvester and NBAA Treasurer; Walter C. Pague, ARMCO Steel and NBAA National Vice President; Curt G. Talbot, General Electric, and Robert C. Sprague, Jr., Sprague Electric Company. (Absent: Delos M. Rentzel, Auto Transports, Inc.)

such a project," he added. The letter concluded by suggesting that "chief executive officers of member companies and of aircraft manufacturers" meet "in a closed executive session" at the forthcoming annual meeting in Miami to try "to finalize a definite program."

The eight council members to whom the letter was sent were William V. Fisher, President, Anchor Hocking Glass Corporation; General Lucius D. Clay, Chairman, Continental Can Company; F.F. Elliott, President, Crane Company; Theodore H. Belling, President, Fram Corporation; Roy A. Freuhauf, President, Freuhauf Trailers; Herbert P. Buetow, President, Minnesota Mining and Manufacturing Company; J.C. Donnell, II, President, Ohio Oil Company; and P.C. Spencer, President, Sinclair Oil Company.

There is no evidence that the proposed Miami discussion was held, either on a formal or person-to-person contact basis. And soon, in early 1957, Boggess resigned as President and Morrow left the Board, diminishing much of the drive to sustain the executive advisory process. As he left the presidency Boggess wrote to Joseph B. Burns, his successor,[9] saying, "I am most hopeful we do not let the Advisory Council idea die." He urged Burns to appoint a group "for the balance of this year," adding that "after all, we are an organization representative of the owners of business aircraft and . . . it seems obvious that policy matters . . . should have the understanding support of executives." Three months later Burns announced that five of the original eight council members, Fisher, Belling, Freuhauf, Buetow and Donnell had accepted reappointment. But that seemed to be the end of it. Despite enthusiasm shown by NBAA leaders, the task of marshalling the company presidents was simply too daunting. There is no further written record of the council's activities, nor is there recollection of any in the memories of persons active in NBAA at the time.

While these events were being played out, Belden submitted his resignation from the Board. Responding, the Board in April, 1956 approved "a lifetime individual honorary membership" to be presented to him at the October annual meeting in Miami.

The new sliding dues scale which had been discussed with the executive advisory group was adopted. Under it, annual dues for aircraft operating (Regular) members ranged from $100 to $250, depending on number of aircraft flown. Those for Associates were a flat $150.

In April, Sprague was again elected to the Board, filling the vacancy left by Belden. And the Directors, sensing that things could not work out satisfactorily with DuBuque, began to take a long look at William K. Lawton, public relations official for L.B. Smith Aviation Corp., in Miami. Lawton's contemporary work as local chairman of the 1956 annual meeting at the McAllister and Columbus Hotels was impressive.

Without his knowing it, Lawton was interviewed by Morrow while driving him from a Board meeting to the airport.[10] A favorable report went back by telephone to the Board and on July 20, 1956 Lawton agreed to become NBAA's Executive Director. DuBuque's resignation was accepted to take effect August 1. Lawton was a seasoned journalist, graduate of New York University, World War II naval aviator and public relations practitioner. An Associated Press stringer on Long Island in 1938, he made national bylines for his dominant coverage of "Wrong Way" Corrigan's astonishing non-stop flight to Ireland.

DuBuque's career after leaving NBAA was obscure. It is recalled that he went to Taiwan to work with China National Airways, died there and was cremated. A container of his ashes was shipped to NBAA headquarters, probably as no other address was known.[11]

Burns' memories of DuBuque's NBAA service were typical of others'. "He seemed to be an itinerant flyer looking for a place to roost. I don't think he devoted the time required to get the job done. Also, (and no fault of his) the policies were not well defined, and he didn't have any real mandate to follow." Burns added that the DuBuque experience resulted in Boggess' giving special care to the appointment of

Lawton. "Henry was very careful to set the ground rules for Bill. So, Lawton knew just what was expected of him."[11]

The 1956 annual meeting in Miami took note of NBAA's growing strength: there were 270 voting members, more than ever before. The by-laws were once again amended. Board size was increased from 9 to 11 persons; a new provision required that not less than 6 Directors be management employees of their companies; and Associate membership was broadened to include those "with interest in business aviation."

On October 23, the members elected Piper to an additional two-year term. Boggess, Burns and Sprague were given three year terms as Directors. Boggess was re-elected to a third year as President, but gave indication he would prefer not to finish the term. Burns became Vice President and Eger was re-elected Treasurer.

A month later James Ketner, Jr., Texas Eastern Transmission Company, Shreveport, Louisiana, and James M. Grogan, Pillsbury Mills, Minneapolis, Minnesota, were elected by the Board to fill the two new chairs. Grogan did not accept election; Ketner did and could boast on his retirement in 1963 that he had never missed a meeting of the Board.

As 1956 closed NBAA staff was growing. In addition to Lawton, "C.M." Cearnal and her sister, Kathryn, there was a new young face. Richard W. Groux, a Fordham University graduate who later ranked second of 588 in Squadron Officers School, Maxwell Field, joined staff November 26, as Assistant to the Executive Director. And authority was given to hire one additional person, a secretary-typist.

One of the first assignments given to Groux was a directive from Boggess "to come up with the best way to organize the association" along the lines drawn in the 1955 by-laws changes. Groux said that Boggess was "very complimentary on what I outlined . . . Basically it envisioned a strong central Washington based office with about four or five area offices which would interface directly with members for representation and problem solving. My role would be to organize and supervise these activities which would be more operational and technically oriented."

But, as with other hoped-for innovations of the time, "The offices were never developed. I always felt," said Groux, "that it left a hole in the intelligence gathering and support that could have been engendered." But resources available to NBAA were not a match for the requirements which full-blown regionalization imposed. Instead, as Groux observed, NBAA put its effort into one headquarters office basket. "What we were striving for initially in Washington was credibility. The ATA had a strong . . . organization on one side of the spectrum. And AOPA was . . . at the other end of things. NBAA took more of a middle ground and probably became the unblessed mediator between the two extremes."[12] The aura of change drifted beyond staff.

It was also in the air among NBAA's elected leadership. Boggess, hoping to leave the President's chair, proposed that the position be given to James (Jim) Donnell, II, member of the executive advisory group and President of Ohio Oil (later Marathon Oil Company). The offer was to be discussed with him at a December 14, 1956 meeting in New York.

Earle W. Bauer, later a Director and Chairman of NBAA and an Ohio Oil employee from 1946, remembers that event.[13] "Jim (Donnell) stopped by to discuss the prospect with both Mike Murphy (the company's Aviation Director) and me. . . . Mike did not encourage him to take the job. He felt it might interfere with his important job of managing and directing a rapidly growing oil company." Donnell turned the offer down. Burns was immediately moved up to Executive Vice President, Boggess soon vacated the President's chair, and at the March 29, 1957 Board meeting, Burns was seated in that chair.

At that same meeting Morrow gave his resignation as a Director. Burns immediately proposed that an honorary membership be given to Morrow at the forthcoming annual meeting in Denver. The Board agreed unanimously, passing a resolution giving him "hearty appreciation for the efforts and the invaluable service rendered to the association." Morrow thus joined Belden in the coterie of living honorary members. Reportedly there was one other: Seaborn P. Collins, National Commander of the American Legion. *Skyways,* in December, 1954, told of Collins' speaking at the annual meeting. On the spot he, "was elected Honorary Member No. 1 of NBAA." Gone from the small group was William P. Odom, the sole honorary member of CAOA, and that for only a few weeks prior to his death in 1949.

Mid-1956 brought renewed contact from Canadians who were still trying to organize a business aircraft association. First raised in 1950, the matter was officially aired again by the NBAA Board in December, 1956. The minutes record a recommendation that NBAA "take an international affiliation concept into consideration in its expansion plans." Further, it was requested that "the matter come back to the Board . . . at a later time." As it worked out, nothing tangible came back to the Board. But the Canadian Business Aircraft Association was organized before the end of the 1950's with John R. Martin of Canadian Brewers as first CBAA President. Established initially as a part of the Canadian aircraft owners and pilots group, CBAA cut those ties in 1961 and became a wholly independent association. While direct affiliation to NBAA had been mentioned as a possibility 11 years earlier, the idea was never again raised.

But NBAA, commenting on the founding of CBAA, said in June, 1959 that this might lead to "formation of an international business aviation organization, recognized to participate in international aviation meetings." This, it was felt, "could provide red-tape cutting now hampering many phases of international flight by business aircraft of all countries." The dream persisted, though it would be many years before it turned into reality.

Much of NBAA's strength in the mid- to late-1950's was applied to vexing operational problems. None was more trying than the lengthy battle to select a new common airways navigation system which could satisfy and be shared by civil and military users alike.

The military was dedicated to its TACAN system, of which some 225 of 450 planned installations were in place by 1955. The Air Transport Association, voice of the airlines, urged delay in the selection process pending evaluation of TACAN.

Other civil aviation groups, NBAA included, favored the VOR-DME (Visual Omni Range, Distance Measuring Equipment) system which was being put into place at the same time. NBAA said at House of Representatives hearings that the military should not be permitted to force use of a system "developed in secret and thereby destroy the common system which has been properly coordinated and accepted" by virtually all civil user elements.

In 1956 the government adopted the VORTAC design configuration (VOR for bearing information, TACAN/DME for distance measuring). Boggess told the Board in September that a telegram had been sent to the Air Coordinating Committee (ACC) congratulating the government but making it clear "this was not an endorsement but a means of telling the government (that) NBAA would support the decision now that it had been made." While a battle was thus ended the war was not: the International Civil Aviation Organization (ICAO) would soon need to address the issue and select a preferred navigation system for world-wide use.

Just as the navigation system selection turbulence was smoothing another event of cataclysmic size shook the aviation world. It was the most horrifying event in civil aviation history, the in-flight collision of two airliners over the Grand Canyon in Arizona. The crash took place June 30, 1956. One hundred twenty-eight persons, all the passengers and crew of TWA flight 2, a Super Constellation, and United flight 718, a DC-7, were killed. It was the worst death toll of any aircraft accident to date.

Investigation of the tragedy turned up major gaps in the tracking of aircraft and in communications. One certainty was that airliners frequently detoured over the canyon in good weather because of the spectacular views afforded from the air. When last reported, the two aircraft, which had departed from Los Angeles three minutes apart, were on converging tracks, 80 miles from each other, with vertical separation of 2,000 feet.[14]

Soon after, *Aviation Week* magazine commented that this "worst of all civil air disasters . . . lends considerable strength to campaigns to bring air traffic control up to date and prepare it for the jet era."[15] And there were strong Congressional reactions. The House Commerce Committee began a probe of "legislative responsibilities in the handling of air traffic." *Aviation Week*, adding to a growing clamor of concern over crowded skies, reported that a "massive airways traffic jam snarls the East," and told of a day when there were 12 hour delays in New York and 14 hour waits in Washington, forcing 30,000 passengers to cancel travel plans.[16]

Two years later, the Grand Canyon crash and the growing traffic snarl produced a new and independent Federal Aviation Agency, in which were vested responsibilities for certification, safety, and air traffic control, as well as the historic mission of promoting air commerce.

During this period of flux general aviation organizations were banded together for the first time on an institutional basis, forming under government sponsorship the General Aviation Facilities Planning Group (GAFPG). The purpose was to state clearly general aviation's future requirements as part of a special planning effort being led by Edward P. "Ted" Curtis, Special Assistant to the

President (Eisenhower) for Aviation Facilities Planning. NBAA and the 10 other GAFPG organizations each put $1,500 into funding a survey of needs and by May, 1957 a report[17] was given to Curtis and CAA Administrator James T. Pyle.

The estimates called for a doubling of general aviation aircraft by 1975 but the report said "this is hardly a measure of the impact . . . on facilities. Flying habits of the pilot and user" of these aircraft "will force operational peak loads far beyond those generated by scheduled and military flying. These general aviation peaks may well become the major consideration in our facilities planning." The GAFPG report added that "the use of aircraft for business purposes will continue to increase dramatically . . . and once again this will bring an impact far more than that indicated by the simple increases in hours flown and members of aircraft." Cited as an example were the "high performance characteristics" expected in future business aircraft and the increased use of instrument flight rules (IFR). The government planners were urged to meet general aviation's needs, thus guaranteeing it "will continue to contribute ever more greatly to the country's economic advancement and to the lives and working habits of individuals."

The Curtis report itself[18] not only looked for massive increases in aircraft and traffic by 1975. It deplored the inability of the aviation system to handle even the 1957 levels, particularly at major airports and under poor weather conditions. To make matters right, it concluded that several major steps would have to be taken. The report urged creation of an Airways Modernization Board and use of the existing two cent aviation gasoline tax and possible new user levies as financing tools. Further, it urged that "an independent Federal Aviation Agency" should be created to consolidate functions, support common needs and take responsibility for all regulations. Envisioned were stringent new measures which would create zones of airspace where positive control could be employed.

Various tests were employed to find ways of separating aircraft reliably during this period of turmoil. Attention swung also to the invasion of navigable air space by tall towers, signs that the radio and television broadcasting industry was growing rapidly. During the period of turbulence which shook aviation in 1957, NBAA turned its attention more seriously than ever before to promoting efficiency and safety among business aircraft operators.

The early 1950's had witnessed preliminary work on developing codified recommendations for management, operation and maintenance of aircraft. A Flight Operations Committee headed by Piper (Donald Baldwin, Texas Company; William B. Watt, Hoover Company; Robert Sheriff, Thompson Products) had pushed it along in late 1955. Then, following discussion with Randall H. Carpenter, Flight Safety Foundation, the Board in 1957 decided that definitive action was needed. Piper and Buril Barclay of CAA were asked to contact Harley D. Kysor, Eastern Air Lines pilot and aviation consultant, to see if he would develop a training-operations manual for $1,500. Anticipated was a reference guide which companies could use to develop their own self-tailored manuals.

Kysor agreed. The project, however, moved along only an inch at a time for a range of reasons, mostly the inability of Board members to agree on specifics. Yet the final product, issued after the turn of the decade, was truly a benchmark work. It was the result of Piper's editing and it bore the title *NBAA Recommended Standards Manual.* Updated periodically in later years by staff member John A. Pope, it became one of NBAA's premier publications, world renowned as a reference tool.

June of 1957 brought news of forthcoming changes in the Board. Talbot said he would reluctantly have to resign and suggested that his place be taken by Eugene M. Beattie, GE's air transport manager and an American Airlines pioneer. Sprague told the Board he would spend most of 1958 and 1959 as a Sloan Fellow in industrial management at Massachusetts Institute of Technology. He planned to resign before year's end and suggested that John H. Winant, Director of Employee and Community Relations at Sprague Electric, would be a good replacement. At the same meeting B.J. Bergesen, manager of Ford Motor Company's air transport activity, was elected to fill the second Board opening created by the 1956 by-laws change.

So, at the annual meeting held in Denver, September 5–7, 1957, institutional change was in the wind. Eger, Bergesen, Ketner and Pague were elected to three year Director terms. Eger was elected both Executive Vice President and Treasurer in the knowledge that the double-barreled arrangement would be brief. Burns was elected to his first full term as President.

A slightly-balding, quick witted man with a radiant smile, Burns brought impressive personal credentials to the Presidency. Originally an attorney working with the Connecticut National Guard, he later served for some 25 years as senior labor counsel for the Fuller Brush Company. From there he rose to the position of Secretary of the corporation and was its General Counsel when elected NBAA President. Later he became Executive Vice President and President of Fuller. Not wanting to outlive his usefulness to NBAA, he resigned from the association Board in 1965. Subsequently, at the Governor's request, he established the lottery system in Connecticut and served as the state's Commissioner of Transportation. Active in Republican politics, he chaired the Ford for President Committee in 1976 and brought in a 26,000 vote plurality in the state. In 1987 he was an independent attorney in West Hartford, dealing principally in estate planning.

The transition from Boggess' leadership to Burns' was smooth. Both men are remembered fondly and with admiration. Boggess "was the type of person you would not forget," said Bauer,[19] a close friend. "He was a courtly gentleman, tall, skinny, yet impressive. He was also very serious in his approach to things . . . Henry was strong minded. When he took a position it was very difficult for him to move from it. Some times this caused ruffled feathers but he did much to stretch the scope of NBAA."

Burns, in Bauer's reflection[20] was the consummate "Fuller Brush Man. He did a really good job, with a lot of style, a lot of exuberance. He was a great wit, marvelous at heading a meeting or organizational function." Bauer felt there was some concern in NBAA ranks that Burns was more drawn to institutional aspects and this "made it appear he was not as sensitive as some others to the pilot side of

NBAA." But Bauer, like all others who observed Burns closely, felt that his leadership qualities were superb and his judgment of high quality.

The Denver meeting attracted about 800 attendees. Corbin Douglass was local chairman, watching over the main events at the Cosmopolitan Hotel and the small spillover of maintenance/operations seminars at the Brown Palace. Passersby were startled to see a single engine, pontoon-fitted aircraft floating in an outdoor pool at the office complex next door to the Cosmopolitan and attendees agreed there were more hospitality suites than ever before. An evidence of the growing importance of business aviation was the presence at Denver of a small group, headed by William Maass and David Ewald, who were evaluating whether or not to begin publication of a new magazine. A positive decision was made early the next year and *Business and Commercial Aviation's* first issue appeared in late 1958, the first journal to put virtually all its eggs into the business aviation basket.

November saw the Board elect Beattie of GE to an interim term. In December Sprague resigned and at a Wright Day Board meeting on the 17th Winant was elected as an interim term Director and then appointed Treasurer, leaving Eger to continue occupying the Executive Vice President chair.

In March of 1958 Spetnagel resigned and C.F. Zimmerman of Continental Oil was named to an interim Board term. "Zim" Zimmerman (whose first name was Cletus, a fact as little known as he was widely respected) brought first rate credentials to the Board. But as important, he was based in Houston, an area of fast growing influence, well meriting representation on the association's Board.

September 22-24, 1958 saw the annual meeting take place in Philadelphia with the Bellevue-Stratford the headquarters and Robert Morrision, Insurance Company of North America, local chairman. While the scope and size of the exhibition area was growing, it could still be accommodated in the same building as other events. At the Bellevue-Stratford the rooftop public function areas were turned over to NBAA, with the exhibits ringing the central ballroom where forums were held. While space was ample, many attendees complained of the long delays and inconveniences imposed by the inadequate number of elevators.

Piper left the Board at Philadelphia and was praised for his "untiring, energetic and selfless devotion to the service of NBAA." Three year Director terms were voted for Beattie, Winant and Zimmerman, as well as for a new Board member, John P. Meyers of the Hubinger Company, Keokuk, Iowa.

Writing in March, 1988 about his years of service on the Board, Piper was moved to say "the value of NBAA membership is unlimited. It has proven itself in many ways, and the results have made the membership fee look small in comparison to the benefits. The hitch has always been that any effort by the NBAA benefits all business aircraft operators whether they are members or not. It is difficult to see why there is an operator anywhere who does not support the organization."

The Board re-elected Burns as President, named Bergesen Executive Vice President, and re-elected Winant Treasurer.

The association was still on the move. The Pennsylvania Building offices were expanded by breaking through a wall to create an additional room. Association

Present at the 1957 annual meeting in Denver to receive million miler safe pilot awards was a distinguished group. From left, front row, C. J. Lund, International Paper, Richard Ranaldi, Petan Co., G. P. Rider, Delta Drilling, George W. Sherwood, Briggs Manufacturing, Ralph W. Prock, Cabot Carbon, J. Ralph Seidner, Goodyear Tire, and Norman L. Mitchell, Minneapolis Star and Tribune; middle row, Philip Van Treuren, Dairypak, Shelby M. Maxwell, Burlington Industries, Don M. Teel, U.S. Steel, Nelson U. Rokes, Procter & Gamble, J. Sheldon Lewis, Thatcher Glass, A. C. Korb, Westinghouse, and Wilfred R. Dotter, International Harvester; top row, Roy L. Coyle, Parker Pen, Richard N. Thurston, Monsanto Chemical, John A. Bouteller, Jr., Service Pipeline, Robert L. Hansen, Kroehler Manufacturing, Ralph E. Piper, Monsanto Chemical, Robert J. Kusse, Fruehauf Trailer, and William P. Hobson, Hercules Powder.

finances were sound. With a voting membership of 291, expenses for the fiscal year were $67,524 and receipts $73,755. The year's surplus, added to earlier accumulations, produced a reserve of $89,738, a safety net which was was only a dream just a few years earlier.

NBAA sent its greetings to E. L. Quesada, named in late 1958 as first Administrator of the Federal Aviation Agency, a product of the Curtis report and the Grand Canyon tragedy. The association also pledged its support of the formidable work required to rebuild public confidence and expedite the modernization of the airports-airways system.

But NBAA satisfactions with the new FAA concept were tempered by some misgivings. Groux, looking back on the closeup vantage point of his contemporary staff position, felt the 1958 act had "repercussions and failings still being felt in 1988."[21] His reaction was that the new agency made dealings between government

The NBAA Board of Directors posed for a photographic portrait in August, 1958. From left, seated, Henry W. Boggess, Sinclair Refining Co., Gerard J. Eger, International Harvester Co., Joseph B. Burns, Fuller Brush Co. and NBAA President, and John H. Winant, Sprague Electric Co. and NBAA Treasurer; standing, John P. Meyers, The Hubinger Co., E. M. Beattie, General Electric, Jim Ketner, Jr., Texas Eastern Transmission Corp., Walter C. Pague, ARMCO Steel, B. J. Bergesen, Ford Motor Co. and NBAA Executive Vice President, and C. F. Zimmerman, Continental Oil.

and industry too legalistic, too stiff, sweeping away the kind of give and take which characterized the Air Coordinating Committee (ACC) which was abolished as one of Quesada's first official acts. In short, he felt the new arrangement created a "we" and "they" situation in which inflexible power resided with the Administrator.

Two major government-industry undertakings were soon launched, however, with NBAA playing active roles until their completion in the early 1960's. Project Horizon set out to establish national aviation goals. The other, Project Beacon, sought long term navigational solutions to air traffic problems, principally through growth of the traffic control system.

GAFPG was disassembled after it made its 1957 report, but in January, 1959, its core group came together again with a new name. It was General Aviation Council (GAC), composed of most of the 11 GAFPG organizations. Burns was named its 1959 chairman, as Winant would be for 1962 when he was NBAA President. GAC aimed at cutting across traditional parochial lines and giving unified positions to the FAA Administrator on major issues. But achievement of unity was elusive during GAC's life. The early goal of presenting only unanimously held positions was finally

In Philadelphia, 1958, exhibits at the annual meeting were still unelaborate, with cloth or drapes serving as background for simple display boards. Beech's presentation, shown against the confining background of the Bellevue Stratford's rooftop ballroom, was as sophisticated as any other.

abandoned, scrapped for a more pragmatic but awkward agreement to present both majority and dissenting opinions. Eventually and to its discredit, GAC foundered on this shoal and by the mid-1960's it sank. More than half a decade passed before another attempt was made to create general aviation unity on an institutional basis.

In February, 1959, NBAA took active part for the first time in an official international activity when Lawton became one of the advisors to the U.S. government delegation to ICAO in Montreal. At issue was the acceptance of VORTAC, a move bitterly opposed by the British, who had developed a competitor system, DECCA. While a mighty battle followed, VORTAC won the war in April when ICAO adopted it as the designated global system.

NBAA felt a need in 1959 to go beyond *Skyways'* coverage and began publication of its own *NBAA News Report,* using it to give "a concise roundup of current activities" involving the association and its staff. The new publication did not take the place of the periodic bulletins which the association sent to its membership on specific items of topical interest such as Federal rule making action. The report was created as a digest, highlighting events which did not lend themselves to the normal information channels. It was also intended that the news report would be distributed widely outside the membership and thus serve both as a recruitment device and as a means of gaining wider recognition of the organization's work. With a shortening of title to *NBAA Report* in the early 1970's, the digest continued to play an important role through 1986.

From the 1950's until the late 1960's the final day of each annual meeting featured aircraft demonstration flights and a hangar luncheon near the aircraft display line. The 1958 version of the catered buffet lunch was typical.

In some ways the 1959 annual meeting in Minneapolis was a mixed success. While attended by more than 750, forum participation was adversely affected by conflict with the baseball World Series and severe weather forced cancellation of the final day's airport program, at which dozens of aircraft fly-bys were to be featured.

But there was excitement over advances in turbine powered aircraft. The Grumman 159 (better known later as the G-1) had made its debut flight in August, 1958. Deliveries began in June, 1959. Its presence in the display line at Wold-Chamberlin Field was electrifying. North American said [22] it would make a decision in November on whether to manufacture a business version of the military Sabreliner. (The decision was favorable, leading to a six-place turbojet with 500 miles per hour cruise and 1,720 mile range). Lockheed announced that the Air Force had selected its JetStar, first flown in 1957, as a navigation trainer. The civil version was forthcoming. Fairchild proudly showed that its F-27 high wing turboprop was in actual service with ships owned by Kimberly-Clark and Westinghouse parked on the ramp.

Targeting birth of the airline-jet era for 1959, the Jet Age Planning Group which was created by CAA Administrator Charles J. Lowen in 1956 was witnessing on-time fulfillment of its central task. In establishing the group, Lowen said "we mean to do everything within our power to get ready in three years.... In cooperation with the aviation industry we look forward to new highs of safety and service with jets."

The October 6–8 annual meeting, headquartered at the Leamington Hotel, saw Bergesen elected to succeed Burns as President. Winant became Executive Vice

President and Beattie Treasurer. Burns and Boggess were elected to three-year Director terms.

Burns' years of leadership drew an accolade from one of the staff members of the period. Groux hailed him "as the catalyst of the time who probably proved most beneficial to NBAA. He had a broader vision and more enthusiasm than the others who were involved then. He was a class act and helped impart that sense of worth to the NBAA and the undertakings going on then."[23] Burns' own stated principal goal was "to interest top management in the utilization of the aircraft as a business tool for the benefit of industry. Additionally, we had to secure our right to use airports . . . As it turned out, business use actually helped to develop airports."

Another major Burns goal was to leave a management-oriented imprint on NBAA. "There was an undercurrent in all the years that I was with NBAA that pilots should be able to manage the organization. But the management people didn't want to see it turned into a pilots' labor organization . . . And I think that's one of the reasons they asked me to go on the Board. I had background in things like that. But there were always good people, pilots like Walt Pague and Ralph Piper, who recognized the fact that managerial control had to be there in order to make it an effective organization."[24]

Piper, commenting independently on the flavor of NBAA deliberations in the 1950's, said that "Participation was a prominent item of discussion at every meeting. 'We must get executives involved if the organization is to grow,' we said. 'Otherwise, it will just be another pilots organization with not enough clout.' How right the founding fathers were! A look at the stature of the presidents over the years is an indication that the organization indeed had clout."[25]

Burns had lively opinions of his predecessor and successor in the NBAA Presidency. He and Boggess "became very close personal friends. He was a true gentleman in all senses of the word. He was a management person and knew what had to be done. He wanted to work with government in constructive ways, and he was masterful and diplomatic in that field. You couldn't be with him without liking him." Bergesen also earned high marks with Burns. "He was basically a pilot with a very, very good background. He represented Ford Motor Company and that was extremely important (to the stature of NBAA). His work in getting the Detroit group, a very large business aviation segment, into the organization was very important. He was a real businessman."

Developed principally by Winant and Burns, a staff retirement plan was adopted effective January 1, 1960. Winant also presented a codified description of staff practices and policies for the first time. These actions mirrored stronger organizational stability and growth of staff, which by late 1959 had seven full time employees.

March 1, 1960, brought addition of another promising young talent to NBAA staff. He was Bruce N. Whitman, a graduate of Kent School and Trinity College in Connecticut, with triple ratings as pilot, bombardier and navigator in the U.S. Air Force. He joined NBAA after a year's service with the U.S. Attorney's office in

Washington, where he doubled in brass as a student at the George Washington University school of law. Whitman was first an Executive Assistant with the NBAA staff, then moved up to the post of Senior Executive Assistant. In mid-1961 he received an extremely promising offer to become Assistant to the President, A.L. Ueltschi, Flight Safety, Inc. Leaving NBAA at the end of August, 1961, he went on to become a major figure in business aviation, serving as Vice President and then Executive Vice President of the company, a world leader in flight simulation training.

Meanwhile, it was recognized in 1960 that the Technical Committee, for many years a special source of association strength, had fallen into disuse. Bergesen felt strongly that remedial action was needed and plans were made to use the annual meeting, to be held in Los Angeles, as a forum for public reactivation. R.J. "Bob" Hixson, Ford's Chief Pilot, took the chair. Plans were developed for sending a bi-monthly report to the membership on discrepancies experienced in various makes and models of aircraft. The data would come from FAA and from reports sent to NBAA headquarters by member companies. Soon an *NBAA Maintenance Bulletin* began to appear on a regular basis. One measure of its success was its eventual distribution on a world wide basis. Another was expansion in the 1970's to the *Maintenance and Operations Bulletin.* And while the rejuvenated Technical Committee took responsibility in 1960 for monitoring procedural air traffic problems and issues, these matters were turned over to a new Airspace/Air Traffic Control Committee, chaired by E.E. Dunsworth of Trunkline Gas Company.

The 1960 meeting, not without risk, marked NBAA's first venture on the West Coast. Selection of Los Angeles as meeting site recognized the tremendous growth of business flying in the region and the knowledge that the jet engine would soon shrink the nation's size by almost one half. But NBAA had never before dared to go so far from home. The choice proved wise.

Selected to be chairman of the meeting was "Scotty" Miller, Airesearch Aviation Services Company, already an institution in business aviation and a long-time participant in NBAA affairs. Held at the Ambassador Hotel, September 20–22, the gathering was the largest yet, with attendance exceeding 1,000 for the first time. Three hotel ballroom areas held 114 exhibit booths. Perched on the broad lawn in front of the Ambassador was a Bell 204B turbine powered helicopter, first such presentation in NBAA history. The final evening's dinner event was the most memorable ever. Miller took over the entire Coconut Grove night club and treated the packed house to an after-dinner show which featured Gordon and Sheila Macrae along with an aspiring new young singer, Wayne Newton, and a host of Tahitian hula dancers.

Featured speaker at the principal convention banquet was A. Scott Crossfield, at the time chief test pilot for North American Aviation, and many years later, in 1984, recipient of the NBAA Award for Meritorious Service to Aviation. Crossfield urged business aviation leaders to take the initiative in development of turbojet airplanes tailored to business needs. Reliance on spinoff from military applications would not do the trick, he said. Business aviation had a tremendously promising future, and it must carve out its own niche to serve its own specific, custom-built needs. Within two years, the jet age arrived, bringing the inspiration to accomplish what Crossfield proposed.

Bergesen, Winant and Beattie were re-elected to the officer posts and three year Director terms were voted for Bergesen, Eger, Ketner and Pague.

The huge success of the Los Angeles' meeting was one evidence of the camaraderie which permeated NBAA during its years of rapid growth to maturity. There were reunion aspects which must be recognized for their importance to the solidarity of the association. Bauer was permanently impressed by this side of the annual event.[26] "Because of its dignity and high sense of professionalism," he said, "NBAA was a magnet to attract a broad cut . . . of distinguished aviation people . . . to its annual meeting."

This group included many persons whose activities involved other segments of aviation but who "went to NBAA perhaps to see a bit of what was going on but mostly to visit old friends whom time and circumstances had separated on a day-to-day basis." Named by Bauer as exemplary: "Len J. Povey, 'Skeets' Coleman, George Haddaway, E. Tilson Peabody, Landis Carr, Walter Beech and Roscoe Turner."[27]

In early 1960, only a month after Maass of *B/CA* told the Board that the *Skyways* connection was counterproductive, Mrs. Henry made it known that Wayne Parrish, principal of the American Aviation Publications group, had given her a purchase/sale offer. She and Leonard Eiserer of the Parrish group appeared at a Board meeting to give details. Heavy emphasis was laid by both on the fact that the "official publication" designation was a primary condition of the arrangement. Within a few weeks' time NBAA was deluged with offers: an expansion of preliminary *B/CA* ideas voiced by Maass, an exploratory offer from AOPA *Pilot* magazine and strong interest from *Flying*. At the end of a trying two day session in New York, the Board concluded it would give NBAA's blessing to the Parrish purchase offer, but some members voiced grave concern over a stipulation which gave the new publisher final say on editorial content. Two months later the Board was informed that Groux had resigned from staff to become editor of *Skyways*. While this piece of news was welcomed, the arrangement proved to be doomed and within two years the long relationship, born in the tiny CAOA office on Madison Avenue in 1948, was voided by mutual agreement.

In May, 1961, the Board elected John G. Kruse, Assistant Secretary, Minnesota Mining and Manufacuturing Company, as interim Director and in June, Lawton reported that the search for a successor to Groux was narrowing to a very short list. He tilted toward John A. Pope and soon the decision was made. Pope, a New Yorker, Pace Institute graduate and World War II Air Corps pilot, joined the organization August 17, 1961, as Executive Assistant. He became a well known fixture on staff, serving in senior capacities until his retirement at the end of 1984. Shortly after Pope's accession, Ann T. Miletich joined the organization as staff accounting chief. Her period of service stretched from November 6, 1961 until retirement May 1, 1986, a total of 24½ years, the longest of any staff person in NBAA's history. Miletich, a World War II Army nurse, and a close associate of every NBAA Treasurer, was known for conscientious and loyal attitudes both to her peers and to the institution.

Some 898 attendees were at the 1961 annual meeting headquartered at the Mayo Hotel, Tulsa, September 26–28. There, for the first and only time, the exhibition area was an art deco motion picture palace, built in city center as a great theater, long since abandoned. All the orchestra level seats had been removed. Exhibit booths crowded the sloping floor and spilled up into positions on the stage. Association leadership changed hands during the meeting, with Winant elected President, Beattie Executive Vice President and Kruse Treasurer. Three year Board terms were given to Beattie, Kruse, Meyer, Winant and Zimmerman.

Reflecting on Bergesen's two years as President, Bauer remarked[28] "he ran a good organization and worked hard and conscientiously with NBAA. He was . . . a gracious man, accommodating, and fostered the work of the Technical Committee. It blossomed under his leadership." Bergesen had an impressive background of international airline piloting, having worked for several years with American Overseas Airlines prior to and during World War II. Transferring to American Airlines, he joined the Ford organization at war's end. Bauer questioned whether Bergesen "was really effective in tying together some of the loose ends between the operating and the Federal (FAA) areas . . . I believe he had more of a leaning toward his airline associations than in the other direction."

Winant was in his mid-30's when he took the helm of NBAA and was the final person to assume chief executive officer responsibilities at so young an age. A Williams College graduate, he was at 21 a Marine Corps infantry platoon leader in World War II, decorated for heroism in combat. Later years saw him as a news editor with Associated Press and involved in family-owned businesses before joining Sprague Electric in 1953. When he became NBAA President he was Director of Industrial Relations and Director of Aviation for Sprague. Active in electronic industry affairs, he had just concluded two years as Chairman of the Electronic Industries Association's (EIA) national industrial relations council. Years later EIA recognized his pioneering work by making him an honorary life member of the industrial (human) relations group.

Winant's relationship with NBAA was long and remarkable. In many ways it was without precedent. Joining the Board in 1957 he served in all elective officer positions and remained a Director continuously until August, 1971. Then, after a three-week break in Board service, he became NBAA's staff Chief, serving in that post and as a Director until November 30, 1986. His total service as a Director was just two weeks short of 29 years, a record which likely will never be equalled.

Early 1962 brought Boggess' resignation from the Board, along with news of his impending retirement from Sinclair Oil. Retired first to a newly-built house near Lakeland, Florida, he is known to have moved subsequently to an apartment in the St. Petersburg area. Mail addressed to him there in the late 1970's was returned to NBAA and attempts to reach him were futile. It was assumed Boggess had died.

In February of 1962 contact came from the newly organized Business Aircraft Users Association of the United Kingdom. Its Chief Executive, Ross R. Stephenson wrote to extend BAUA's good offices, a courtesy which Winant reported to the NBAA Board. Staff was asked to give every support it could to this new sister organization whose aims matched those of NBAA. A ripening of the relationships between NBAA and BAUA, encouraged by the Canadian CBAA, eventually led in 1981 to the foundation of the International Business Aviation Council, Ltd. (IBAC) a global network of organizations dedicated to the promotion of business aircraft operations.

With the approach of 1962 all signs pointed to full emergence of the jet age in business aviation, but there was skepticism in some quarters. *Skyways* based an article on Project Horizon's conclusion that there would be 200 corporate jets in use by 1970 and concluded "this kind of a market will not support production of the many . . . jets now being offered or planned by U.S. and foreign plane builders."[29] Cited were the JetStar, already in production at $1.2 million, the Aero Commander 1121, planned for 1963 introduction, North American's NA265 Sabreliner, expected in 1962, the Piaggio–Douglas PD-108 Vespa and the De Havilland 125, expected in 1963. Several other models were planned for offshore production. Already in the market was the four-place Morane-Saulnier M.S. 760, available since 1955 under a marketing arrangement with Beech. The ship owned by Louise and Henry Timken had the distinction of being the first business-use jet to be shown at an NBAA meeting. Also decribed briefly by *Skyways* was the SAAC-23 (Swiss American Aviation Corporation) which was being developed by the colorful industrial risk taker and inventor genius William P. Lear. Scheduled for flight test in 1962, the airplane was renamed the Learjet and had its first flight a year later. Its name soon became a synonym for business turbojets, just as its design marked an historic breakthrough.

Skyways believed "it is highly improbable that 12 manufacturers can hope to produce planes of this type at a profit." Noting that Beech, Cessna and Piper, the largest U.S. manufacturers "have not shown much interest in the business jet field," the magazine concluded that "relatively few executive jets will actually go into production" but nevertheless they "will be a part of the general aviation picture."

Neither the Project Horizon nor the *Skyways'* conclusions were even close to the mark. The decade witnessed a virtual explosion in business aviation growth. By 1972 there were 1,000 (rather than 200) business jets in use, along with some 1,500 turboprop aircraft.

Relationships between NBAA and *Skyways* began to experience bumpy going starting in June, 1962 with publication of a "Torch" Lewis column which suggested formation of "a guild of business pilots" which could deal with "salary standards and contractual relationships." The Board had never taken such a position and felt it was inconsistent with the magazine's "Official Publication of

NBAA" designation. The sticking point was that the contract gave Parrish's associates final editorial choice. Winant convened a special Board meeting June 20 in Washington to talk directly with Parrish and as a result the column was not published. Problems related to advertising shortfalls were aired by Parrish. The parties agreed "the relationship should be reviewed during the next several months." Although unsaid at the time, it was apparent to both that the interests of each were becoming overly strained and the parting soon would come.

Pittsburgh's William Penn Hotel was site of the 1962 annual meeting, which attracted 873 registrants October 2–4. Burns and Kruse were voted three year terms as Director, as was Aubrey Keif, senior Texaco aviation marketing official. Winant, Beattie and Kruse were voted second terms as principal officers of the burgeoning association.

Beattie, in line to succeed Winant as President the next year, never achieved the position. Burns, as did many others, lamented this. In his opinion, Beattie "had the knowledge, the ability to recognize that each aviation element, airlines, private flying, the government, all had a distinct place. Putting them all into proper place was very important. Gene could do that. He was a very sharp person."[30]

By the end of 1962 NBAA was recognized as a mature organization characterized by dignity and statesmanship, kindling respect in government and industry alike. Its annual meeting was becoming acknowledged as the global meeting place for many elements of the general aviation community and as the world showcase for product and service innovations.

While some of its hopes, such as the regionalization planned in 1955 and the continuing use of an executive advisory group, failed to materialize, it achieved durability, a true sense of purpose, and a lasting place of prominence in aviation. Fifteen years after its incorporation NBAA had located and carved out its permanent niche.

NOTES TO CHAPTER 5

1. *Aviation Week,* October 17, 1955.

2. Ibid.

3. *A Study of Business Aviation in 1985,* NBAA/Colgate Darden Graduate Business School Sponsors, October, 1985.

4. *Aviation Week,* October 17, 1955.

5. *Skyways,* November, 1955.

6. *Flight,* November, 1955.

7. Ibid.

8. Letter, H.W. Boggess to Executive Advisory Council, August 16, 1956.

9. Letter, H.W. Boggess to J.B. Burns, February 25, 1957.

10. Cole H. Morrow, McLean, Virginia, audio tape interview with J.H. Winant, May 5, 1987.

11. Joseph B. Burns, West Hartford, Connecticut, audio tape interview with J.H. Winant, April 8, 1988.

12. Letter, Richard W. Groux, Reston, Virginia, to J.H. Winant, April 24, 1988.

13. Earle W. Bauer, Findlay, Ohio, audio tape interview with J.H. Winant, October 22, 1987.

14. Clayton and Knight, *Plane Crash,* New York, 1958, pp. 75–78 and 84.

15. *Aviation Week* magazine, July 9, 1956.

16. Ibid., July 16, 1988.

17. "Background Memorandum on the Future of General Aviation," W.K. Lawton to the NBAA membership, May 22, 1957.

18. "Curtis Report on Aviation Facilities," sent to NBAA members May 17, 1957.

19. Bauer tape, October 22, 1987.

20. Ibid.

21. Groux letter, April 24, 1988.

22. *Business/Commercial Aviation,* October, 1959.

23. Groux letter, April 24, 1988.

24. Burns tape, April 8, 1988.

25. Ralph E. Piper, St. Louis, Missouri, memorandum to J.H. Winant, March, 1988.

26. Bauer tape, October 22, 1987.

27. Ibid.

28. Ibid.

29. *Skyways,* November, 1961.

30. Burns tape, April 8, 1988.

Chapter 6

THE JET AGE — TRIAL BY TRANSITION: 1963–1969

THE YEAR 1963 HAD SCARCELY BEGUN WHEN TRAGEDY
struck NBAA's leadership. Gene Beattie, 53, was expected to move into the
President's chair late in the year. But on a Sunday night in February, after returning
home to Greenwich, Connecticut, from a weekend of skiing in Vermont he was the
victim of a heart attack. Taken to the local hospital, he weakened rapidly and was
dead within a few days. Trying to sort out the saddening consequences, the Board
decided to leave the Executive Vice President position unfilled, perhaps until the
annual meeting, and Winant removed himself from the Nominating Committee. An
air of gloom pervaded the association as the impact of Beattie's death struck home.

Meanwhile, and as the leadership was slowly restoring a sense of
equilibrium, the attempts being made by NBAA and *Skyways* to patch up their
relationship were failing. On April 30 they agreed to terminate the contract and the
Parrish organization went ahead with plans to merge *Skyways* and *Airlift*
magazines into a new journal, *American Aviation*. Reporting to the Board, Winant
said that Parrish and he had many telephone and personal contacts in the months
since summer of 1962 and that the termination of the 15-year relationship "was done
in good spirit."

Feelers quickly came from others interested in publishing a magazine for
NBAA but the Board took a decision not to affiliate or to enter the publishing field
independently. The best interests of NBAA would be served by independence and
the opportunities it created for better coverage by all aviation journals.

Looking back on the *Skyways* relationship, John A. Pope, a senior staff
member for 23 years, considered the divorce decision a benefit. What happened from
that point onward, he said, "was a gradual increase in the amount of editorial
content NBAA received in the existing aviation publications. NBAA was no longer a

competitor but now a *bona fide* newsmaker and worthy of ink. That ink, unusually favorable to NBAA, spread the word about association activities and programs . . . Editorial content was and is the best advertising that NBAA could have obtained and all of that was of great assistance in recruiting new members." [1] Pope's opinion seemed almost to echo what Robert H. Wood, *Aviation Week* editor, had written to NBAA back in 1953: ". . . I must confess that we have not had much information from you and your association, and your affiliation with *Skyways*, I believe it is, can hardly endear you to other magazines." [2]

Steady improvement was felt in association fiscal affairs. The 1963 period (which ended August 31, rather than the June 30 date adopted in the 1970's) was the first in which the budget exceeded $100,000. Receipts were estimated at $101,781, and expenses set $5,000 higher to permit heavy funding of new membership recruitment efforts and additional services. While membership had grown to 493, it was apparent that substantial further potential existed.

The Shamrock Hilton in Houston was the scene of the 1963 annual meeting, with C. C. Holt of A.I.M. Instruments Chairman. Attendance was well over 1,000 and for the first time the display booths occupied a designated "Hall of Exhibits," a 30,000 square foot, high-ceilinged building attached to the hotel. Hobby Field, then Houston's principal airport, was used as the aircraft display area. "Turbine Take-Over" was how *Flight* [3] headlined the meeting. "The new jets and turboprops so dominated the . . . display," the magazine reported, "that only one new production piston-engine airplane . . . took part in the fly-by." Among the displays were mockups of the "Lear Jet, Hawker-Siddeley DH-125, Dassault-Pan American Airways Mystere 20 (later renamed Falcon), the HFB Hansa 320 and the Mooney-Mitsubishi MU-2." Another new project, described from the speakers' rostrum, was the Beech King Air. More than passing note was made that of these six new models only two were of American origin. The challenge from offshore manufacture, of such great concern to the U.S. manufacturing industry in the early 1980's, was already a budding reality in the early 1960's.

Winant was elected unanimously to a third term as President and noted sadly at the opening night banquet that this unusual situation resulted from Beattie's death. Zimmerman was named Vice President and Kruse Treasurer. The Executive Vice President position remained unfilled as the Board continued to review options for officer succession.

Pague was elected to a one-year Director term, his last, to fill out the vacancy left behind by Beattie. Three-year terms were voted for William L. Robinson, General Traffic Manager for Sears Roebuck, Dill M. "Don" Teel, Chief of U.S. Steel's aviation division, Horace E. Wood, Chief Pilot for the Gillette Company, and Bergesen.

Harry Wallingford of Texas Eastern Transmission, Chairman of the Air Space/Air Traffic Control Committee, was reappointed, with William Dameron of Sears Roebuck named Vice Chairman. Frank Thera of Minnesota Mining and Manufacturing Company was redesignated as Technical Committee Chairman, with Owen Mayfield, Hercules Powder, Vice Chairman.

FAA Administrator Najeeb Halaby spoke at the opening banquet and Morrow, now Director of Airports Services for FAA, led a discussion on better utilization of VFR (visual flight rules) airports by aircraft equipped with VOR-DME gear. Morrow's appearance was in part a followup to NBAA's submission to Halaby of a list of 497 airports. If these airports could be equipped with radio navigation aids giving transponder bearings and distances, then properly equipped aircraft could make use of them for non-precision approaches with 300 to 2,000 foot ceiling conditions.

From the highly successful Houston meeting came several major innovations. In November, the Board decided to establish a joint committee with the National Aviation Trades Association (NATA) to develop standards and procedures to improve vendor-customer satisfactions. Winant headed the NBAA delegation and "Sime" Bertolet, Reading Aviation and NATA president, was captain of the other team. David L. Flannery of ALCOA and Donald G. MacDonald of the Burroughs Corporation were NBAA representatives, as was Lawton. From this effort emerged the NBAA Support and Service Committee, an active force until the early 1970's.

Convinced there was a need to give more recognition and a real voice to associate members, Winant proposed at the November, 1963 meeting that a new position be created, Associate Advisor to the Board. The idea came from growing feeling on Winant's part, first expressed by him in Los Angeles in 1960, that the strongly supported associate segment often felt like outsiders in respect to NBAA policies. The proposed position would have Board stature without the privilege of vote. The incumbent would take part in all Board deliberations. To do this effectively he would be expected to assay associate sentiments and to see to it that the Board considered them. Agreement was quickly reached and "Scotty" Miller of Airesearch, who had ably and enthusiastically chaired the 1960 meeting, was contacted by Winant and asked to serve until the 1964 annual meeting. Miller, widely known and affectionately respected, accepted and is recorded as attending his first Board meeting March 19, 1964.

Miller in 1988 recalled his early days on the job as Associate Advisor: "The first thing I did was to mail a form to all associate members asking them to state any problems they would like to have presented to the Board, and to suggest what they would do to solve these problems. I also told them they would hear back from the NBAA office within 30 days . . . It worked like a charm as most were simple problems . . . It was just a little matter of communication between the two parties. It turned out to be great public relations for NBAA."[4]

Another decision taken at the November meeting was that the time had come for NBAA to conduct annual spring seminars of one or two days length on major technical issues which could not be adequately covered in the time available at annual meetings. It was planned that the first of the seminars would be held at or near one of FAA's prime research facilities and would focus on development of all-weather landing systems. The session was held in May of 1964 at the Chalfonte-Haddon Hall Hotel in Atlantic City with more than 150 in attendance. With a change in format the seminar series continued until the end of the 1960's and was judged a first rank service to business aviation during that period.

Meyers submitted his resignation from the Board at Atlantic City and Charles W. Summers, President of Security (grain) Elevator Company, Hutchinson, Kansas, was named to take his place.

The same meeting also served as the terminal point of an ill-fated attempt at membership service which had existed on an on-again, off-again basis for almost a decade. Announcement was made to the Board that Gore, Youngberg and Carlson, insurance brokers, were throwing in the towel and cancelling the NBAA pilot disability (loss of license) insurance program. Low participation was the reason. Mentioned at Board meetings as early as 1950, the program was the product of a study initiated in 1955 by a three-man committee consisting of Grogan of Pillsbury, Bob Kusse of Freuhauf Trailers and William Dotter, International Harvester. Their work attempted to respond to a desire expressed by pilots for some type of financial protection against the kinds of disability which would result in loss of FAA airman certificates. After several false starts the insurance program was finally put into motion in 1956, with William Vance, representative of Chicago brokers, the principal architect. Between 1956 and 1964 the program was underwritten by a series of somewhat skeptical insurance carriers and had been cancelled by at least three of them. Vance performed feats of brinkmanship in rescuing the program each time, but the final try, with Continental Casualty the insurer, was ended by notice to NBAA that all policies would be cancelled June 1, 1964. Reviewing the unsettling history, the Board decided in May that "NBAA henceforth would refrain from participation in insurance programs." But that did not turn out to be the case. Perhaps a glutton for punishment in this regard, NBAA later acted twice as sponsor of loss-of-license programs. In 1986 it was still laboring away at the subject, hoping somehow to find the right formula of coverage and premium to attract and hold a pool sufficient to carry a program.

January, 1964 brought election of Aubrey Keif as Executive Vice President, which in effect designated him to succeed Winant and paved the way for orderly progression of officers through the various chairs. But by early spring tragedy struck again, with Kruse victim of a heart attack, the second principal officer to die of that cause within little more than a year. Thera of Minnesota Mining and Manufacturing was named to succeed Kruse on the Board and Teel of U.S. Steel was elected as the new Treasurer.

April 1, 1964 brought addition to NBAA staff of another key player, Frederick B. McIntosh, designated originally as Executive Assistant. An Oakland, California native, he was an Army Air Corps veteran of World War II, serving in a number of capacities until 1961. A fighter pilot and instructor in the war years, he was also posted to intelligence duties and was among the select group chosen to fly captured German bombers across the Atlantic for piece-by-piece analysis in the United States. McIntosh remained with NBAA for 19 years, bringing it great distinction, while earning for himself a reputation for resourcefulness and for

William J. Schulte, right, FAA's Assistant Administrator for General Aviation, received the 1964 Award for Meritorious Service to Aviation. With obvious relish, John H. Winant, left, NBAA President, and William K. Lawton, Executive Director, rehearsed the presentation ceremony in the association's suite at the Americana Hotel, Bal Harbour (Miami), Florida.

greatly strengthening the association's standing with FAA technical personnel. By late 1964, five senior staff aides were serving with William K. Lawton, the Executive Director.

Mostly at the urging of Summers, the Board in July spelled out in detail its interpretation of by-laws that Regular (voting) membership was available to the "serious businessman pilot who held a minimum of commercial and instrument ratings." The idea was to dispel any mistaken belief that only companies using full time professional air crews were welcome. The 1964 action was ultimate resolution of a schism which had gnawed at NBAA since its earliest years and which had seemingly been clarified after the transition of leadership from Belden to Morrow 10 years earlier. Well publicized, the Board's action put the subject to rest permanently. It had the further benefit of attracting outstanding persons to leadership positions as the years passed.

NBAA's 1964 annual meeting in Miami was held late in the year, taking place November 5–7 so as to avoid the height of the hurricane season. The choice was wise. Sunny, low humidity weather blessed the event, which centered on the Americana Hotel, Bal Harbour, with Frank Hart of Miami Aviation acting as Chairman. With some 1,700 persons registered, the previous attendance record was broken.

Business/Commercial Aviation (B/CA) proclaimed "Jets Steal Show at Successful NBAA Meeting,"[5] and noted that "five of the seven new biz jets appeared." There was a trio of British-made DH-125's (also marketed as HS-125) three Sabreliners, two Learjets, two JetStars and a Jet Commander. In lustrous prose a British journalist reported to his readers back home that the sight of the 125's "was stimulating . . . alongside the seething mass of American business aircraft."[6] Unable to appear were the Fan Jet Falcon and Hansa 320. Good sense caused NBAA to eliminate its usual program of devoting an entire afternoon to airport fly-by demonstrations as the advent of turbine power had turned it into a virtual aerobatic contest. But there was massive evasion and *B/CA* observed that NBAA's action "had little influence on the Biz Jet boys," adding that observers witnessed numerous jets "making shotgun takeoffs, roller-coaster climbs and abrupt short field landings." The airport demonstration afternoon custom was subsequently reinstated and existed for two more years, but it vanished thereafter from the NBAA's program of regular events, supplanted by a more conservative approach to showing aircraft performance characteristics.

There was no question that a wholesale transition from piston to turbine power was irreversible. The shift came midway in Bauer's career and he remembers the period for its trauma as well as its position as a unique advance.[7] "The transition period was very difficult," he recalled. Economic considerations were one reason. "When the jet age came, prices went up like a sky rocket. Companies had a difficult time accepting this new price range and justifying that kind of outlay . . . there was also concern over safety and passenger acceptance." But the advent of jet airline travel in 1959 and its rapid growth helped to settle things down, "and was a big influencing factor" in the acceptance of turbine powered business aircraft. Soon, Bauer recalled, "it became apparent that the additional speed and time saving factors meant you could transport people at an acceptable price."

Business aviation began doing things in different ways, Bauer concluded, "and NBAA's way of doing things also changed" in fundamental character. There were other great demands imposed by the transition. Former World War II pilots who had started a company's aircraft operation with a piston powered transport or converted bomber suddenly found themselves managers with responsibility for a number of employees and in many cases millions of dollars worth of aircraft. NBAA recognized the need for increased managerial skill and educationally-oriented programs began to take shape.

Other serious concerns required action. Looming on the horizon like a distant storm cloud for many years, the issue of airways user charges hovered darkly

The 1964 aircraft display line at the Opa Locka, Florida, airport showed a mixture of piston and turbine powered aircraft, evidence of the growing sophistication of business aviation, as well as the requirement for enhanced professionalism. A trio of British made DH-125's, partially visible at top right, comprised the largest single grouping of turbojets.

overhead in 1964. Bringing it into close range were Administration proposals made in late 1963, prior to the assassination of President Kennedy, for imposition of a tax specifically on aviation fuels, to take the place of the two cents a gallon general fuels levy enacted in 1956 in the interstate highway bill. At its Miami meeting NBAA took a bold step by conducting a symposium which for the first time presented a representative of the Bureau of the Budget, government's leading advocate of the argument that users should pay the costs of Federally-provided services. Several other aviation associations were invited to participate in the NBAA symposium, but the Air Transport Association (ATA) airline spokesman, declined, and it was soon learned that it was attempting to persuade others to do so. The symposium nevertheless was conducted with a distinguished group of panelists: Roger W. Jones of the Budget Bureau; Max Karant, Vice President of the Aircraft Owners and Pilots

Association (AOPA); Walter R. Laudenslager, President, NATA; Keif of NBAA; and A. Paul Vance, President of the National Pilots Association. Winant served as moderator and pace setter. There was agreement among the association spokesmen that the government proposals failed utterly to recognize aviation's benefits for the general public; further, there was concensus that some of the types of charges which had been given consideration were virtually impossible to administer except at costs which would exceed potential revenues. B/CA called the session "highly significant" and said it "could well mark the start of (an) era of closer cooperation among all four groups for the good of the entire general aviation community."[8] But as the decade lengthened the issue grew into one of aviation's most contentious problems. At times it was a devastating source of division between segments of aviation and at times it tore at the fabric of general aviation unity. Resolution, unhappily received in parts of the aviation world, did not come until 1970 when the Congress finally created a series of taxes on users, a trust fund in which to place them, and a plan to spend the revenues on needed improvements.

As expected, Keif was elected NBAA President at Miami, Wood became Vice President and Teel was named Treasurer. Thera was elected to a one-year Director term and three-year terms were given to Dunsworth, Trunkline Gas Company, Jack J. O'Brien of the Garrett Corporation, Summers and Winant. Pague, closing out 18 years of continuous service, left the Board with the lasting thanks of hundreds of colleagues extended gratefully to him. His departure was cause for poignancy. The last of the association's true pioneers had finally stepped down from its leadership.

Miller completed his term as Associate Advisor at Houston and Robert B. War, public relation chief for Atlantic Aviation, took his place. Mayfield retained the Technical Committee chair and Wallingford was named Air Space/Air Traffic Control Chairman for another year.

Commenting on Winant's three years as President, Bauer said[9] that NBAA "achieved a much better relationship with the industry and government under his leadership . . . a crucial point was passed (in terms of) coordination by NBAA with FAA and with the Congress. . . . This was the truly important thing accomplished in that period." As he stepped down Winant was helping to plan another major move of NBAA offices. Staff were bursting Suite 344 of the Pennsylvania Building at its seams. Negotiations for larger quarters were under way and by March of 1965 a move upstairs to Suite 401 was completed. It had potential for expansion, potential which would soon materialize.

Keif, senior aviation marketing official for Texaco, brought an impressive background to the NBAA Presidency. A Colorado native, he learned flying in the British Royal Flying Corps in World War I and was pilot of Jennies, Sopwith Camels and Bristol fighters. Interviewed as he prepared for his new NBAA duties[10] Keif displayed his international background. "I'd like to see a close liaison between NBAA and ICAO in Montreal (because) modern business aircraft . . . are impeded by the same political barriers that have been lifted or eased for the international air

Many of NBAA's leaders were true aviation pioneers. Aubrey Kief, chief executive officer 1964-1965 was a splendid example. His flying career began prior to 1916, included service with the Royal Air Force in World War I, and eventually led him to Texaco's senior aviation fuels marketing position.

carriers," he explained. An urbane, smartly tailored, white-maned and somewhat portly person, Keif on occasion left the impression that he was rather stand-offish. Bauer considered him "rather aloof."[11] Others thought he tilted toward airline concepts and did not have his full attention focussed on business aviation requirements. But Keif was an extremely well known aviation personality and his term, while briefer than the norm, brought distinction to NBAA.

His international tendencies soon resulted in another brief round of exploration of a world federation of business aviation. Bergesen was asked by the Board to look into the matter and reported in January, 1965, that a meeting was planned with David Nelson, U.S. representative to ICAO in Montreal. A letter was sent to CBAA and BAUA inviting them to participate. So, on April 6 and 7, 1965, a tripartite meeting took place at the Queen Elizabeth Hotel in Montreal, with Fred Hotson, CBAA President, Kenneth McAlpine, BAUA Council member, and Lawton attending. The result, reported to the NBAA Board in May, was that the "three organizational representatives were to agree to a plan of action which would set up an international business aviation group composed of the three (associations). They would then seek to interest other nations." The Board passed a motion urging that NBAA "continue active participation in these steps." But that was all. The matter went back into hibernation again and little was heard about it for the next several years.

Meeting at 3M's corporate conference center, Wonewock Lodge in Minnesota, on May 6, 1966, the NBAA Board received saddening news of the death of B. J. "Bob" Bergesen, who died at his home in Birmingham Hills, Michigan of a long-existing heart condition. A message was communicated immediately to Bergesen's widow, Gladys, telling of his qualities of "vision, counsel, strength, courage and leadership" during his years at a Director and elected officer.

While NBAA's stature was growing in the mid-1960's it was not exempt from criticism. Writing in the 1965 pre-annual meeting issue of *B/CA*, Editor James Holaham took the association to task[12] on several counts.

It "hasn't the weight of numbers so important to bureaucrats," he wrote. "Many feel that a large increase in the NBAA's membership would provide it with the big stick it needs to compete for fair treatment" by government agencies. Further, Holahan said, some of the most prestigious business aircraft operators "have chosen to fly outside the association." And finally, he wrote that among air crews "The greatest criticism . . . is probably that its (NBAA's) efforts for the line pilots leave much to be desired." The editorial concluded that "NBAA indeed has come a long way since that pioneering meeting in May of 1946. It still has a long way to go."

The annual meeting in Los Angeles was extremely successful, with the irrepressible "Scotty" Miller taking his second turn as local Chairman. More than 1,800 attended and the ballrooms of the Ambassador were filled with displays of 82 exhibiting companies. Forty-three aircraft were on the display line. For the first time airliners tailored to business aviation configuration were shown, including the Boeing 737E, Douglas DC-9 and BAC-111. Grumman promised that its eagerly awaited turbojet Gulfstream II would soon appear in the flesh.

And for the first time there was heavy accent on helicopters. Many attendees shared the opinion that helicopters were just about where turbine fixed wing aircraft stood five years earlier; that is, on the threshold of a major marketing boom. Bell, Fairchild-Hiller and Hughes all exhibited aircraft or mockups with turbine power. Great interest was seen in the near future use of rotor wing aircraft for direct connection between company facilities, between plant lawn and airport and in central city or crosstown connections. The important role of helicopters was starting to be defined. Within a few years' time the role would be firmly established.

The Los Angeles meeting was the first time 100 companies received million-miler safe flying awards; 267 pilot million-miler certificates were awarded, as well as 150 half-million mile pilot awards.

After only one year in the chair, Keif relinquished the Presidency at Los Angeles and Wood was named to succeed him. Summers was elected Vice President and Teel re-elected Treasurer. Ward was named to a second year as Associate Advisor.

Three-year Board terms were voted by the membership for Keif, Mayfield of Hercules Powder, and Thera. Then, in a surprising move and not without debate, the Board determined to create a title outside by-laws scope and named Keif Chairman for the the next 12 months.

In accepting the Presidency Wood described himself "the first operational business pilot" to occupy the chief executive position. He laid great emphasis on finding actual solutions in operational problem areas and pledged strong efforts to increase membership.

A golf tournament sponsored by Grumman (later Gulfstream Aerospace) was a prominent related event at each year's NBAA annual meeting. Two association veterans examined the souvenir glassware at a mid-1950's tournament luncheon. Don M. Teel, left, of U.S. Steel, was the only person to serve as association Treasurer for five years. Walter C. Pague, ARMCO Steel, was a founding Director of CAOA and continued his board service for an 18 year period ending in 1964.

And because he had attended no meetings since his election, Robinson of Sears Roebuck was declared to have ceased service on the Board. Within a month his place was taken by Donald Gex of W.R. Grace, elected to a one-year term.

The fast-paced events of recent years, the rapid advances in technology and aircraft performance, and the emergence into real life of major anticipated issues such as user taxes and jet noise caused NBAA in 1965 to become more forward looking than ever before. Often reactive to the ebb and flow of outside forces, the organization reached the point where it was necessary to take better control of such forces. In addition, the annual meeting had grown beyond any expectations and this raised unanticipated problems of communication, planning and execution. Regulatory and political problems were becoming ever more complex. The operational aspects of the rapidly blossoming turbine era were daunting.

NBAA's prudent response began at the December, 1965 Board meeting. A Policy Committee was created and charged with drafting a set of objectives, each dealing with a defined area. Emphasis was placed on the need "to adopt the sound planning practices used by business and industry and apply them to the association." Ward was named Chairman of the committee, to serve with Dunsworth, Mayfield, O'Brien and Winant. This group, not knowing it at the time,

Members of the Technical Committee assembled at the 1965 annual meeting in Los Angeles. Seated, M. L. Nicholson, Mine Safety Appliances, and B. Owen Mayfield, Hercules Powder; standing, from left, Ralph E. Piper, Monstanto Chemical, Robert F. Nagel, Westinghouse Electric, C. B. Dickinson, Square D Electric, Carl J. Lund, International Paper, and Arthur Lippa, Jr., U.S. Steel.

began an ongoing activity in which long range planning became the focus, and which continued for two decades.

Late 1965 and early 1966 witnessed two remarkable innovations in membership services, both of which gained worldwide recognition. On a practical scale they also placed extremely useful tools into the hands of business aircraft operators. Principal credit for them went to Donald A. Baldwin, chief of Texaco's aviation division, and Vice Chairman of the NBAA Technical Committee.

Always a source of ideas inspired by future possibilities, Baldwin keenly felt the need for a means by which operating cost and range data, particularly for turbine powered aircraft, could be reliably collected and made widely available. Manufacturers' figures were disparate. There were no real common denominators. Advertised performance data were frequently based on differing norms. Here was an opportunity for NBAA to create order out of confusion, just the kind of challenge Baldwin cherished.

So, with Mayfield's blessing and strong help, and with great assistance from NBAA's staff, formats were put together. By late 1965, 100 reports on operating costs were available. The jet range format was instituted in February, 1966. Among other characteristics called for was 45 minutes reserve fuel load after diversion to an alternate airport. From that time onward advertisements for business jets routinely carried information on achieveable range followed by the words, "including NBAA reserves." Because of Technical Committee efforts a new phrase entered the lexicon of business aviation.

Gaining in prominence, meanwhile, the spring symposium program rolled onward. The second was held at Atlantic City in April, 1966, with the theme "Air Traffic Control, 1966–1969." And while presentations were acclaimed for technical content there was no cautionary flag raised by speakers to warn that an ugly period of air traffic and airport congestion would soon begin, brought on by the combination of burgeoning turbine powered air travel and a control system which was beginning to creak under the load. This new period of congestion made pale the post World War II crisis which launched CAOA/NBAA.

At the same time, the government put forth the proposal that a new Department of Transportation should be created, bringing together in one family diverse agencies in the transport field. Along with FAA, these included highways administration, highway safety, urban mass transit and the U.S. Coast Guard, the last having responsibility for many Federal waterways. NBAA and others expressed fears, with the association stating its reservations that the scheme would "submerge the independent FAA." But the bill figuratively sailed through the Congress and by the end of 1966 Alan R. Boyd was named first U.S. Secretary of Transportation. The need for NBAA to monitor Federal policies for their impact on business aviation took on increased importance.

While government restructuring was being carried out there was churning at the NBAA staff level. Dissatisfaction was growing with Lawton's approach to issues. As they became more complex he tended to become more strident. Morrow, observing from his position in FAA, thought Lawton was influenced too much by other associations.[13] Bauer had similar emotions.[14] "At the time I thought that NBAA did not (maintain) enough solid rapport with the government agencies . . . there were a lot of areas which were not clarified." The relationship between Wood and Lawton became so strained that in late May Lawton summarily resigned.[15] The details were given to the Board at its next meeting, along with news that Lawton had taken a position as Director of Marketing and Information with Flight Safety Inc., in New York.

Wood proposed that Ward, the Associate Advisor, would be an ideal candidate to lead staff. An offer was made to him and on August 8, 1966 he became the association's seventh staff chief.

To take over Ward's vacated Associate Advisor position the Board designated pioneer aviator Len J. Povey, Vice President, Mackey Aviation Services, Fort Lauderdale, Florida, one of the most colorful and popular men in the aviation world.

Ward was a Naval Air Transport pilot in World War II, serving in the Caribbean, Honolulu and Guam. The war over, he attended the University of

Spring seminars were a highlight of NBAA's membership services during most of the 1960's. Ohio State University and Purdue University were the settings for intensive two-day courses aimed at sharpening the managerial skills of chief pilots and aviation department managers.

Pennsylvania and Villanova, put in a short hitch with Capital Airlines (later merged into United) and then decided to put his journalism degree to work. This led him to Atlantic Aviation and his contacts with NBAA.

The 1966 annual meeting was a return appearance in St. Louis, scene of many breakthroughs in 1953. The year 1966 was as significant. Attendance jumped to 2,347 and there were 105 exhibitors at the Chase-Park Plaza. Lambert Field's display line contained 75 aircraft.

Symposiums laid heavy emphasis on pilot transition to turbine aircraft and the FAA's spokesman, Edward King, stressed deficiencies noted by type-rating inspectors. These included "inability to understand the aircraft performance manual, unfamiliarity with little used cockpit switches, and neglect of the check list."[16] Those who had attended specialized transition programs had a much better record than those who attempted to go it alone, King added.

Three year Board terms were voted for Wood, Teel, Gex and Henry H. Timken, Jr., of the Timken Ball Bearing Company, Akron, Ohio. The Board reelected Wood President, Summers Vice President and Teel Treasurer.

E. Tilson Peabody, General Motors aviation chief, was named to chair a new Corporate Aviation Management Committee; Harold Curtis, National Distillers, was designated as chairman of another newly created group, the International Operations Committee; and Povey was named as head of a third innovation, the Support and Service Committee. All of these groups were products of the Policy Committee's efforts to set objectives. Five areas of heavy long range involvement were singled out for particular stress in the coming years: Corporate aviation management, aircraft and equipment, support services, regulations and control, and international operations. The new committees, along with the two standing committees already in existence, were given specific mandates with which to work. Shortly after the St. Louis meeting, the Policy Committee's results were published in a pamphlet which served as a challenging road map for staff planning and membership action for years to come. In addition to the new committee designations, Mayfield was named to retain the chair of the Technical Committee and William F. Gilbert of the Weyerhaeuser Company, Tacoma, Washington, was appointed to head the Airspace/Air Traffic Control panel.

Shortly after the St. Louis meeting, the long-awaited Gulfstream II made its maiden flight, adding a top of the line product to the growing inventory of purpose built turbine business aircraft.

Holahan, the *B/CA* editor who raised serious questions about NBAA in 1965, saw things in a much brighter light in late 1966. In an editorial titled "Our Kind of Association,"[17] he referred to interviews of aviation managers and chief pilots. "To a man, every one had a good word to say about it (NBAA) . . . It is our kind of association . . . We laud the work it has done and encourage it to continue that work in the challenging years that are sure to follow."

Within months, major challenges appeared.

As the number of turbine powered aircraft in the civil fleet increased, a public outcry began over the noise they generated. Exemplary was a ban on business aircraft use at New York's LaGuardia Airport in 1963 and 1964. Lengthy negotiations, led by John Powers of Lockheed-Georgia, lifted that ban, but the threat of others existed. In an attempt to counteract adverse public attitudes, NBAA's Technical Committee undertook a bold program. With Mayfield and Baldwin the prime movers, action started to develop noise abatement procedures by which pilots could reduce the amount of noise generated on takeoff and landing. Angle of attack, power setting and optimal altitudes were the key ingredients. Proposals were tested and put into final form before 1966 ended. They were greeted with acclaim by the aviation press and in the industry as the first of their kind, a truly pioneering effort which soon was emulated by others. But despite NBAA's good efforts, the problem of aircraft noise became ever more controversial as the years passed. The association early on adopted a position that the Federal government should take responsibility for rational solution to the problem and during the succeeding decades never wavered from that early stance. In 1967 NBAA gave full support to a bill which vested authority in FAA to specify maximum noise levels in newly certificated engines. This legislation led to enactment of Federal Aviation Regulation (FAR) Part 36, which mandated step decreases in engine and aircraft noise. And in 1972 NBAA helped to halt attempts in the U.S. Senate to turn over the FAA's authority to the Environmental Protection Agency (EPA). The landmark Noise Control Act of 1972 retained FAA's lead role but unfortunately did not give any specific direction concerning limits on the power of airports to impose noise limits.

A second major challenge was the eruption of the air traffic-airport congestion crisis in mid-1967. Acrimony and confrontation between elements of aviation, and between them and the government soon appeared. First to be affected were the New York airports and then greater Pittsburgh. Within months the term Golden Triangle was created to describe the region extending from New York to Pittsburgh to Washington and back to New York. All movement by air within the triangle was soon subject to congestion, real or imagined. Intra-industry bitterness began when Stuart Tipton, pipe-puffing, tweeded President of ATA uncharacteristically called for restrictions on general aviation at Washington National Airport, in spite of continuing underutilization at nearby Dulles and Baltimore-Friendship.

In November DOT Secretary Boyd added fuel to the fire during Senate hearings by saying that "airport operators might charge fees for peak hour use or ban general aviation flights at busy times." Despite NBAA efforts to create an aviation user forum to work out the problems, the battle lines became ever more fixed. The issue was on a collision course which led within a year to one of the most contentious FAA rules proposals in the agency's history. But as with so many issues, rules would not provide solution. The traffic crunch eased only when a major economic recession deeply curtailed air travel.

Meanwhile, NBAA's efforts to enhance managerial skills in company aviation departments was on course and moving fast. The 1967 spring symposium was held at Purdue University in April. Among the topics covered were budgets and fiscal planning, personal communications techniques and professional management, the last topic being much in vogue at business administration schools. The annual meeting held later in the year in Boston featured a panel on pilot compensation factors, with Peabody acting as chairman.

The October 10–12 meeting was held at the Boston Sheraton and the adjacent War Memorial auditorium. Attendance rose to 2,800, another record. Three-year Director terms were voted for Dunsworth, Winant and two new Board members, Ronald J. Guerra of Kaiser Industries, and Michael J. Murphy of Marathon (formerly Ohio) Oil Company. Mayfield moved up to the Presidency, Dunsworth became Vice President and Teel, already the longest serving Treasurer, was elected for two additional years. Keif submitted his resignation from the Board and Peabody was named to the one-year remainder of the term. Shortly thereafter, Keif retired from Texaco and settled in Sedona, Arizona. On June 22, 1975, NBAA received word that he had died.

Povey was redesignated as Associate Advisor, the first to be given a second one-year term. Additionally, it was determined that henceforth there would be two Advisors, named in alternate years, with each serving two year terms. In 1968, Jesse

The War Memorial Auditorium, exhibition center for the 1967 annual meeting, was inspected in the spring by members of the Boston host committee and the NBAA Board. From left, Clyde Coppage, Worcester Airport, B. Owen Mayfield (profile), Hercules Powder, Joseph Garside, Wiggins Airways, E. E. Dunsworth, Trunkline Gas, Don M. Teel, U.S. Steel, Horace E. Wood, Gillette Company and NBAA President, John I. Becker, Van Dusen Aviation, J. G. Fritsch (profile), Butler Aviation, and M. Robert Mulligan, McMillan Ipswich Corporation.

N. Childress, President of the Southern Airways service base in Atlanta, was named to serve until 1970. Thus, it was felt that broader representation could be given to the growing associate segment, along with better continuity. And Wood was given the same honorary title of Chairman as had been granted to Keif two years earlier.

By-laws amendments enacted at Boston deleted reference to the executive advisory group which had existed very briefly in the 1950's and raised the number of directors to 13. Named to the two openings for one year each were Norman L. Mitchell of the Minneapolis Star and Tribune Company and Charles E. Morris, Mobil Oil.

Mitchell, a Minnesota native, was an active force in CAOA-NBAA, having been in attendance at the first Washington forum in August, 1948, while flying for S. J. Groves & Sons, Inc., of Minneapolis. A World War II Marine Corps dive bomber pilot, he, like many others in business aviation, chose a piloting career after completion of wartime service. Morris became an institution in business aviation as long-time head of Mobil's worldwide aircraft fleet. An Ohio native, he was an anti-submarine pilot in the war, joining Pan Am World Airways in 1946. Later, with Peruvian International Airways, he flew DC-4's, and then joined All American Airways. Going with Mobil in 1951 as a DC-3 captain, he was given managerial responsibility for the entire operation, based at Westchester County Airport, New York, in 1956.

As Wood left the Presidency he was credited for his diligence and efforts to increase the size of the membership. Bauer probably reflected a widely-held opinion when he said[18] "he was probably not the administrator or overall organizer that some of his predecessors were. He was essentially a pilot and leaned that way in his performance." A New Jersey native, Wood was a student at Rutgers University when

World War II took him into Naval Aviation. Prior to joining Gillette after the war, he was an FAA flight examiner. Retired early from Gillette, he was involved in several aviation service organizations in the 1970's and 1987 was engaged in semi-retirement activities in Charlottesville, Virginia.

Additional tragedy visited NBAA's Board in late 1967 and early 1968. Gex died of a heart attack before Christmas and early the next spring Timken was dead. In both cases the Board expressed its deep regret on the loss of active, resourceful leaders. Louise, Timken's widow, maintained a close and warm relationship with NBAA over succeeding years and was present at virtually every annual meeting. For her exceptional loyalty and support she was given special recognition at the association's 1985 annual meeting.

April of 1968 also brought the resignation of Thera from the Board, occasioned by his leaving Minnesota Mining. Named to take his place was A. E. Townsend, a management employee of Columbia Gas Systems Company. Baldwin and John B. Bean, Corporate Director, International Milling Company, Minneapolis, were named to the Board in July, succeeding Gex and Timken, and the unofficial title of Chairman was put in the discard pile.

As it celebrated its 21st birthday in 1968, NBAA had much for which it could be thankful. Recent growth brought expansion of Suite 401, Pennsylvania Building in the spring of the year, and headquarters could boast it occupied more than 2,000 square feet. Membership stood at 750 companies. Cumulatively, they accounted for one-third of U.S. gross national product and spent a half-billion dollars a year on airline tickets. The members' own fleet of aircraft contained 700 turbine powered ships, 330 of which were jets. Members' aircraft flew more than a million hours a year, consumed 165 million gallons of fuel and had an estimated value of $769 million.

Preparations for the 1968 annual meeting included yet another round of by-laws changes. The frequency with which amendments had been made over the years, beginning only months after the first by-laws were adopted, was strong evidence that structural evolution of NBAA was not complete. While the general course of association affairs had long since been clearly charted, the ability to eliminate unanticipated side trips was as yet unrealized.

The 1968 changes, enacted at Houston, eliminated the seldom used and little understood honorary membership category, defined more clearly Regular and Associate membership qualifications, put the Associate Advisor positions on a permanent footing, renamed the Executive Director position as Executive Vice President and fine-tuned the Executive Committee description to include former NBAA chief executives as long as they remained on the Board.

While the by-laws changes were being refined for submission to the membership, matters heated up on the legislative agenda. Senator A. J. (Mike) Monroney of Oklahoma sponsored a bill (S.3641) which called for a massive airways-airports improvement program to solve the congestion crisis in a decisive, long-range fashion. The measure called for an airline passenger ticket tax and fuel taxes on general aviation of 7 cents a gallon, rising to 10 cents in 1972. Also provided was a dedicated aviation trust fund which would serve as the bank account for the improvement program. Monroney's bill met with cautious, mixed response by NBAA and other general aviation groups. All had serious reservations over the size of the fuel tax proposals and over the equity of benefits which the improvement program would bring to general aviation. It took two years of push and pull for Monroney's bill to work its way through the Congressional mill. Finally, it emerged as the Airway and Airport Improvement Act of 1970, substantially changed from the original 1968 version.

The summer of 1968 also brought forth a different, shorter range approach to solving the congestion crisis. It was a quarrelsome FAA rules proposal, NPRM 68-20, one of the most irritating in aviation history, so contentious that NBAA for the first time went to the court system to try to set matters right.

Aimed at easing traffic problems on a temporary basis, the rule proposed hourly landing and takeoff slot allocations for all classes of users at five airports, Newark, LaGuardia, Kennedy, O'Hare, and Washington National. General aviation, lumped with a jumble of users called "other" in the rule, received the smallest number of slots, ostensibly in accord with historic patterns of use. The incendiary proposal was such a traumatic break with the historic first-come, first-served principle, that a special membership briefing was held at the Marriott Twin Bridges Hotel near Washington to explain its intricacies and thus rally opposition. FAA's plan was judged as unjustly discriminatory and a violation of the open access provisions of the 1958 Aviation Act. And it was also short-sighted. One example, in FAA's own backyard, was the huge, unused capacity to serve Washington, D.C., which existed at Dulles and Baltimore. Why not attempt to shift traffic to those points, rather than impose quotas at National Airport?

The topic made the annual meeting in Houston buzz October 8–10. About 2,700 persons took part in events at the Shamrock Hilton and saw the largest aircraft display, 100 ships on the line at Hobby Field. Mayfield, Morris, Peabody and Townsend were voted three-year terms as Directors; Baldwin and Bean were each elected for one year. Mayfield was voted a second term as President and Dunsworth and Teel were re-elected Vice President and Treasurer. George E. Haddaway, *Flight* publisher, was named an Associate Advisor to serve in tandem with Childress.

In November, FAA's 68-20 high density role proposal was enacted, with June 1, 1969 set as the operative date. Among the slot allocation rules were spinkled requirements that 64-code transponders were to be required in the affected airport areas, along with the ability of aircraft to maintain 150 miles an hour speed.

Responding, NBAA's Board met December 29, 1968, with Bruce G. Sundlun of Amram, Hahn and Sundlun, who had been designated NBAA Counsel when the storm clouds gathered during the summer. Unanimous agreement was reached to use every avenue of protest, including a court test if necessary. The way would have to be prepared by January 31, 1969, to satisfy legally-imposed time requirements. There were two grounds for NBAA's objections: exclusion of aircraft

Exhibit booths at annual meetings grew larger and became more attractive as the years passed. In 1968, the relatively high-ceilinged Hall of Exhibits at the Shamrock Hilton in Houston provided an incentive for designers to add new touches, including aircraft mock-ups.

contravened the Federal Aviation Act, and FAA/DOT consideration of the rules proposal failed to produce evidence to support it. In fact, 98 percent of the 3,041 responses to FAA's public comment docket (officially Docket 9113, Amendment 93-13, NPRM 68-20) were opposed to the rule.

Briefs were filed January 15, 1969 in the U.S. Circuit Court of Appeals, Washington, but that court quickly declined jurisdiction. Meanwhile, Winant and Sprague, Jr., met with DOT Secretary John A. Volpe in early February to urge a stay of implementation. In decisive terms, Volpe refused any reconsideration. The die was irretrievably cast.

NBAA's lawsuit, along with one filed by AOPA, was moved to the Federal District Court in Washington, where motions and cross motions for summary judgment were made by all parties. July 2 brought the shocking news that District Judge Howard F. Corcoran had upheld FAA on grounds it could take emergency action where drastic events so dictated. And while there was limited talk of appeal, it appeared certain the rule would remain in effect. But some good came from the lawsuits. FAA set a December 31, 1969 expiration for the rule and rescinded a three hour block of time during which only air carriers could have use of Kennedy airport. Most important, an airport reservation office (ARO) was set up by FAA to handle general aviation slot requests on an advance planning basis. A small but significant dent was put in the FAA armorplate.

As the high drama of 68-20 unfolded, NBAA's continuing interest in the setting of objectives and in long range planning went into high gear. In mid-1969, Mayfield designated a standing committee of the Board to take charge of these matters and convince Bean to chair it. Highly experienced in corporate planning in his work with International Milling, Bean was the ideal candidate. Soon, he had assembled a committee consisting of Dunsworth, Teel, Townsend, Winant, and Haddaway, with Mayfield and Ward holding ex-officio rank. At the first meeting agreement was reached that the group would aim at establishing five-year planning cycles beginning with the 1971–1975 period. While not realizing it, the committee selected a starting-point which became a major transition year for NBAA.

Bean's long range planning group recognized at its inception that the world outside NBAA was entering a period of moderate to heavy turbulence. As 1969 lengthened, a world-wide and deep recession gripped the economy. Belt-tightening measures were soon in effect resulting in reduced business flying and in some cases, layoffs or aviation department closings. Sales of aircraft dwindled and UAC predictions for future sales turned gloomy. The crisis of air traffic-airport congestion eased, ironically just at the moment the full impact of slot allocation was hammered home.

Senator Monroney's broad gauged bill continued to receive Congressional interest in 1969. At hearings held midyear, NBAA urged that the measure give considerably more emphasis to reliever airport development and use of area navigation (RNAV) equipment to expedite travel. The association said it would agree to a fuel tax provided the monies received were wholly used solely for the intended purposes. NBAA would consider a 5 cent tax as fair, provided the program was bold and the tax levied on all users, general aviation and airlines alike. It opposed the government scheme, which the airlines and general aviation manufacturers had accepted, to impose a passenger ticket tax rather than a direct levy on air carriers themselves.

Washington, which had last hosted the NBAA annual meeting in 1951, was the site of 1969's gathering, held September 23–25 at the Washington Hilton Hotel, with Dulles Airport furnishing static aircraft display facilities. Attendance soared to 3,373, mostly because of the large number of government personnel attending.

Secretary Volpe addressed the opening night banquet and heard near-deafening cheers when he gave the high density rule short shrift: "I don't like it any more than you do and as far as I'm concerned, December 31st can't come too soon." December 31st came and went as did many, many subsequent New Year's Eves. On

At 1969's annual meeting in Washington, the Presidency of NBAA passed from B. Owen Mayfield (left), to E. E. Dunsworth, Trunkline Gas Company. The session was the first to be held in Washington since 1951 and set a new attendance record of 3,373.

December 31, 1986, the high density rule was still in effect at four of the five airports. There was additionally, more than idle talk at FAA that additional airports might need to be brought under the rule. So, 18 years after enactment, there was no end in sight to the temporary regulation, an admission that no perceptible actions had been taken during the many intervening years to increase the capacity of the airports.

Unique among major events of the meeting was presentation of NBAA's Award for Meritorious Service to Aviation, now one of the industry's major honors, to Olive Ann Beech. She became the first woman to receive the award, and through 1986 retained that distinction. Her acceptance was characteristically modest and for the most part consisted of a visual review of the contributions she made to development of business aviation, first with her husband, Walter, and later, during the many years since his death. Haddaway, typically resourceful, put the presentation together with flair and humor. The citation engraved on the award plaque hailed Mrs. Beech for "personal faith, dedication and efforts which have contributed immeasurably to the development and progress of business aviation."

Dunsworth moved into the Presidency at Washington and noted in his inaugural remarks that "at no other time in our history has . . . business aviation faced more crucial issues." Bean was named Vice President and Mitchell Treasurer. Haddaway, whose term as Associate Advisor was to expire, was persuaded to remain another two years. Baldwin, Bean and Teel were re-elected to three-year Director terms. And James F. "Skeets" Coleman, Ziff-Davis Publishing Company official and winner of the Harmon Trophy for his test piloting work, was elected to a three-year term, replacing Wood, who left the Gillette Company on an early retirement basis mid-1969.

As he left the Presidency, Mayfield was cited for "strong and untiring leadership" during his two-year tenure.

Summing up 1969, and in a sense, the decade which was drawing to a close, *Flight* editorialized[19] that NBAA "had delivered the goods both in quality and quantity . . . any objective rating will have to be E for Excellent." Citing the vexatious problems which erupted as the 1960's grew older, *Flight* commended staff and Board for "having established a positive position on all matters affecting the flexibility of . . . business airplanes."

Rough going lay ahead but there was no doubt the association had resources and intelligence to do the job well, come what may.

NOTES TO CHAPTER 6

1. John A. Pope, Arlington, Virginia, memorandum to J. H. Winant, March, 1988.

2. Letter, Robert H. Wood, *Aviation Week,* to Jean H. DeBuque, NBAA, October 7, 1953.

3. *Flight,* October, 1963.

4. Letter, Scott E. Miller, Garrett General Aviation Service Division, to J. H. Winant, March 10, 1988.

5. *Business/Commercial Aviation (B/CA),* December, 1964.

6. John Fricker, *Aeroplane and Commercial Aviation News,* November 19, 1964.

7. Earle W. Bauer, Findlay, Ohio, Audio tape interview with J. H. Winant, October 22, 1987.

8. *B/CA,* December, 1964.

9. Bauer tape, October 22, 1987.

10. *B/CA,* October, 1964.

11. Bauer tape, October 22, 1987.

12. *B/CA,* October, 1965.

13. Cole H. Morrow, McLean, Virginia, audio tape interview with J. H. Winant, May 5, 1987.

14. Bauer tape, October 22, 1987.

15. Telephone call, H. E. Wood to J. H. Winant, May, 1966.

16. *B/CA,* October, 1966.

17. Ibid.

18. Bauer tape, October 22, 1987.

19. *Flight,* December, 1969.

Chapter 7

COMING OF AGE: 1970–1976

"**T**HERE IS A GREAT NEED FOR BUSINESS AVIATION TO improve its image," E.E. Dunsworth said in an interview conducted soon after his installation as President of NBAA. "It has come of age and it must be recognized as the important adjunct to American business that it really is."[1]

Events of the next few years would prove him correct on all counts. Major issues were elevated to crisis proportions, one following hard on the heels of the other. A rising clamor over aircraft noise made NBAA the protagonist in a lengthy New Jersey court battle. A disastrous airplane accident in Colorado threatened imposition of strangling new regulations on business aircraft. And the very life of business aviation hung in the balance during a devastating national fuel shortage. Business aviation's importance to the nation's economic welfare became the determinant in test after test. Through perseverance, a renewed sense of purpose and the use of long range strategic tools, the association by mid-decade reached a position of lasting eminence.

Dunsworth, arguably NBAA's hardest working chief executive, devoted enormous amounts of time and energy to his duties. Born in 1925 in an Oklahoma town prophetically named Jet, he became a U.S. Marine Corps fighter pilot in World War II, serving in the South Pacific region. Dedicated to a career in aviation, he organized the Aviation Department of Trunkline Gas Company in 1950 and headed it until retirement in 1985, with 13,000 hours in his log book. In addition to leadership positions in NBAA spanning the years 1960 to 1978, Dunsworth was a prominent figure in Houston aviation circles, chairing two key panels of the area's Chamber of Commerce, as well as the Business Aviation Committee and the Aviation Advisory Council. His loyalties to NBAA were famed. Many years later he said "retiring from NBAA was more of a psychological blow than retiring from the (Trunkline) company."[2] In 1987, he was a resident of Rockport, Texas and while retired from the aviation world, was deeply involved in Republican Party political and campaign activities.

As the 1970's began, vexing regulatory and political issues tested the mettle of NBAA staff. Frederick B. McIntosh, left, Manager of Technical Services, and Robert B. Ward, Executive Vice President, gave their full attention to discussion of problems posed by imposition of the FAA's high-density airport slot reservation and allocation system.

The vexing issue of aircraft environmental concern, long simmering through the 1960's, came to a boil in 1970. The effects of Federal Aviation Regulation (FAR) Part 36 began to be felt. Militancy among airport neighborhood citizens groups grew rapidly, and the Congress began to examine new aspects of the situation. In February, Donald A. Baldwin of Texaco convinced the NBAA Board to restate strongly its good neighbor precepts which urged operators of turbine powered aircraft to use noise abatement piloting techniques. Further, the Board at Baldwin's urging directed staff to contact engine manufacturers and fuel production companies. These were asked respectively to tell NBAA what specific design or modification steps they were taking to meet Federal noise standards, or what they were doing about rising apprehension over air pollution caused by petroleum-based fuels. One immediate result of NBAA pressure was adoption by Teterboro Airport, New Jersey, a key business aviation center, of NBAA's noise abatement recommendations as the preferred local flight procedures.

NBAA's even handed approach to the problem of aircraft noise was summarized many years later by Harry C. McCreary, who served as a Director and officer in the late 1970's.

In the late sixties and through the seventies, the problem . . . became more of an issue. The days when a pilot could shove the throttles forward and go, any time he wanted to do so, were fast coming to an end, as airport neighbors began to assert their rights . . . Wisely, the NBAA recognized this and adopted a policy which tried to accommodate some restrictions on aircraft operations, while trying to prevent absolute 'curfews' from interfering with the interstate commerce aspect of business aviation.[3]

At the February, 1970 Board meeting Charles E. Gates, Jr., Chief Executive of Gates Rubber Company, was appointed as a Director, replacing A.E. Townsend. Gates Rubber had a two-pronged interest in business aviation: its own internal flight department and its control, since 1967, of the Learjet manufacturing operation.

In that same month, John P. Woods, a highly valued staff manager charged with airspace/air traffic control matters, left the association to become chief staff executive with the National Association of State Aviation Officials (NASAO).

Ways of communicating better with members were a challenge to the new Dunsworth administration. Two innovations were made in early 1970. A series of Eyeball Meetings, face-to-face gatherings of staff and member company personnel began, with Cleveland the first site. The idea was to take NBAA to the membership in regional meetings, hoping this would improve member understanding of issues and at the same time give an increased sense of direction to staff. Considerable change was also made in the association's forms of written communication. The long-standing format of Reports and Bulletins was scrapped. In its place were created For Your Information (FYI) reports on light blue paper and Action Bulletins (AB) on pink. The former were purely informational, meaning to give insight into the nature and status of important topics; the latter were devoted to matters of regulatory or legislative nature on which member company action was desired. The role of the *News Report* periodical was sharpened. The new aim was to focus on reporting staff and Board actions, and on reviewing major projects. The *News Report's* circulation was broadened to reach far beyond the membership. Multiple copies were sent to aviation service organizations and other airport-centered bodies where they could serve as consciousness-raising member recruitment tools.

Another information channel was opened in April of 1970, testifying to the reality that the 1970's were to be the Era of Internationalization of business aviation. Twin forces were at work: evolution of the multinational corporation and the development of intercontinental range business aircraft. April's *NBAA Maintenance Bulletin* contained a new section titled "International Notes". This became a regular vehicle through which aircraft operators reported on international travel conditions. In 1982 the section was converted into a stand-alone publication, IBAC (International Business Aviation Council, Ltd.) *International Update*, published by NBAA on behalf of the newly formed international federation.

The same month also brought formation of a new attempt to unify general aviation interests on an informal basis, a quest which had not been tested since dissolution of the General Aviation Council (GAC) in the mid-1960's. Dunsworth was the prime mover in the new effort, proposing the need in a telephone conversation with Dwane Wallace, Cessna's chief executive.[4] Wallace agreed. Dunsworth and he soon met in Wallace's Wichita office and they then contacted J.B. "Doc" Hartfranft of AOPA, Frank Sain of NATA, James Tilford, Tilford Aviation, and other key general aviation association figures. On April 2, 1970, senior elected (no staff) officers of NBAA, GAMA, ADMA, NATC, NATA, AOPA and NPA met at the Hunt Club near Houston and GENAVAC (General Aviation Associations Council) was born. Simply put, the search "was to talk with, not at, each other,"[5] in the hope that individual association positions would thus become more similar, or at the least, not destructive of each other. Staff executives were excluded from the contemplated semi-annual sessions in the belief that personality conflicts and ego-centered puffery would be avoided. But, since a built-in irregularity to the rule existed from the beginning in the inclusion of Hartfranft, an AOPA employee, this precept was doomed. By the mid-1970's senior staff personnel were present, provided the chief executive was also there. GENAVAC proved durable as well as helpful and it not only grew in membership over the years but remained an active force. Its cardinal operating rule, discussion without binding decision, remained intact.

At April's Board meeting William F. Gilbert, Manager of the Weyerhaueser Company's flight department, Tacoma, Washington, was appointed to the Board to fill a vacancy created by Owen Mayfield's resignation in late 1969. Gilbert, long active in committee work and a Chairman of the Airspace/Air Traffic Control panel, later rose to prominence as NBAA's Chairman. Mayfield retired from Hercules in 1970, and later became owner of a motel-marina complex in Stuart, Florida. On March 17, 1982, he was victim of an accident or sudden disability, falling into the water and drowning while working on one of the boats docked at his premises.

The late spring brought significant news from NBAA's legal front lines. In April the U.S. Circuit Court of Appeals ruled against NBAA on the high density airport slot allocation rule. An appeal to the U.S. Supreme Court was considered but not pursued; the odds and the financial drain were too discouraging.

One month later, however, the Board decided to make a vigorous assault on imposition of a noise-inspired jet curfew at the Morristown, New Jersey airport. Negotiations to lift the ban were begun with others in the industry. Air lines showed a particular interest since Morristown was a designated reliever airport for the New York area. Use of noise abatement procedures was urged on the airport as an alternative to the general 9 p.m. — 7 a.m. curfew, which was tightened on Sundays to permit operations only between 1 p.m. and 3 p.m. If direct negotiations turned out fruitless, NBAA's Board was prepared to take the issue to court since it had grave implications as a possible national precedent.

In 1970, NBAA pilot safe flying awards for the first time totaled more than one billion miles; additionally, there were 623 million-miler pilots, 190 half million milers and 166 million mile companies.

During the summer the Board was approached by Sain, Chairman of NATA (National Aviation Trades Association), who proposed merger talks between NBAA and his organization, which for the most part represented aviation service organizations (also known as FBO's) and air taxis. While lacking spontaneous enthusiasm, the NBAA Board nevertheless agreed to look into the prospects. At NBAA's annual meeting in Denver, September 22–24, Dunsworth announced that "the feasibility of merger between NBAA and NATA will be studied." Sain, present at the meeting, endorsed the concept.

The Denver gathering was a major breakthrough in several ways. Most important, the exhibition area for the first time was in a discrete 100,000 square foot civic center hall built for the purpose of housing major conventions. John A. Pope, staff member who had responsibility for annual meeting plans, ranked this breakthrough first among notable events in his NBAA career.[6] "Number one was the decision to take the annual meeting out of hotel basements, garages, ballrooms and whatever into civic centers . . . The Board opted for Denver and their Currigan Hall in preference to other possible sites," he wrote.

> *What that decision did was to open up a whole new exhibit world for aviation suppliers, enlarge the scope of products displayed, and give the buyers a lot more to see. After the 1970 meeting opened and closed, there was no great immediate reaction. Exhibitors ... were about to face a couple of years of downturn in the economy and NBAA's meetings in 1971 in Minneapolis and 1972 in Cincinnati grew only slightly in size as to numbers of exhibitors and booths and numbers of attendees. My recollection is that 1973 in Dallas was the first year that exhibitors grasped what could be done with exhibit size and flair and NBAA's meetings began to grow in every which way every year thereafter.*

> *What this meant to NBAA was steadily increasing revenue which then allowed for adding to the staff and services. In addition, the annual meeting grew in prestige internationally and, in time, gained recognition as the premier aviation event in the United States.*

At Denver the airport static display was in operation for all three days of the annual meeting. This was an innovation, making a clear statement that a special airport day was an idea whose time had expired. Don Murphy of Combs Gates, Denver, ably chaired the local committee but 1970 was the final year in which exhibitor arrangements were handled by the host city committee. The move into major civic center surroundings was too daunting for volunteer management. Staff took on the responsibility beginning the next year and then paved the way for professionally managing the explosive growth of the NBAA exhibition from 279 booths in 1970 to 1,722 by 1986.

Dunsworth, John B. Bean and Norman L. Mitchell were elected at Denver to second terms as officers. Elected as three-year Directors were Randall H. Carpenter, Time, Inc.; Dunsworth, Ronald J. Guerra, and John H. Winant. Named to one-year terms were Gates and Gilbert. Carpenter, new to the Board, was well known in business aviation circles. Once an American Airlines pilot, he had been a senior official of the Flight Safety Foundation, and in 1956–58, prior to joining Time, was with General Precision Laboratories. D.U. Howard of San Antonio was named to a two-year term as Associate Advisor, replacing Jesse M. Childress.

In late 1970 there were 854 NBAA member companies, 620 of them voting members, and 234 associates. The major recession which had begun a year earlier showed its growing impact at Denver. In spite of NBAA's new showcase approach to the meeting and the attendance level of 2,707, a feeling of unease pervaded the event. During the months which followed, membership eroded, with the voting (business aircraft operating) segment holding steady, but with the associate segment plummeting to 186 by mid-1971. Additionally, the work of Bean's Long Range Planning Committee was beginning to turn up gaps in confidence and satisfaction at the staff leadership level, as well as shortfalls in NBAA's achievement of goals. The planning group, consisting of six Directors, identified four pressing needs. Membership qualifications required redefinition; there was a need to reflect growing demands for professionalism in flight crews; the membership needed to be broadened; and, as Dunsworth said when he became President, there was need for better recognition of business aviation and the association. Since most of these would eventually require member authorization, a By-Laws Committee was created. Winant was named Chairman but also was retained as a member of the planning committee.

A milestone on the legislative pathway was passed in 1970 with enactment, finally, of the airport-airways development bill introduced in 1968. One of its key revenue raising provisions was a $.07 per gallon tax on general aviation fuels. Another was an 8 percent passenger ticket tax. Further, the bill mandated a study which aimed at allocating to users their shares of the costs of operating the national air transportation system. Implicit in this was the theory that the new taxes were provisional. NBAA swallowed hard, acknowledging that even with imperfections the act was better than originally anticipated. The prospect of major airspace-airport capacity improvements was satisfying. But the association's leadership knew in its bones that the cost allocation study would lead to major trouble.

Association staff ranks grew through the late 1960's and into the new decade; in 1967 there were seven senior members; by autumn of 1970 there were ten. Ward was Executive Vice President and staff chief. Pope was Director, Membership Services and Administration; Fletcher Cox, Jr., was Director, Public and Press Relations; Richard D. Chamberlain, Director, Government Relations; Frederick B. McIntosh, Manager, Technical Services; Claire D. Bullington, Manager, Membership

Services; William McMurray, Manager, Airspace/Air Traffic Control Services; Lawrence B. Bedore, Manager, Airport Services; Ann T. Miletich, Manager, Accounting Services; and Myrtle E. Somers, Manager, Office Services. Ward joined staff in 1966. Pope and Miletich had been with NBAA since 1961. McIntosh and Bullington came aboard in 1964 and Somers in 1969. All the rest joined NBAA in 1970. Cox, McMurray and Bedore succeeded others in their positions. Chamberlain filled a new post.

By December the Board determined that a merger with NATA was not in either's interest. Too many questions relating to the inherent vendor-consumer nature of the respective voting memberships were difficult or impossible to answer. The possibility was strong there would be conflicting positions on some major issues. NBAA's announcement stressed the point that there was "no termination of relationship between the two . . . Quite the contrary, we have found (new) areas of cooperation." It fell to Dunsworth "to attend NATA's annual meeting in December and to have to tell them, 'no dice.' It was really a difficult thing to do."[7]

The year ended with explosion of a bombshell which was ignited in the autumn of 1969 by the crash of a chartered aircraft into a Colorado mountainside, killing many members and the coach of the Wichita (Kansas) State University football team. The coach carried the professed lease of the airplane in his pocket. It also perished in the crash. The near impossibility of establishing what party or person had actual operational control of the airplane led the FAA to a radical rules proposal, labeled NPRM (Notice of Proposed Rule Making) 70-41. It proposed to alter the historic "commercial operator" concept and redefine it as "transport of persons or products from which an ultimate profit or sale is realized." As it pondered the various meanings these words might have, NBAA concluded they could cover a huge proportion of its membership. The proposal so altered time-honored "for hire" concepts that it would destroy the bedrock on which private carriage business aviation was founded many years earlier. An alarm bell was sounded throughout business aviation. The proposal might affect as much as 80 percent of the civil fleet. It would result in tight Federal regulation, economic as well as operational, it would restrict flexibility, and worst of all it would give no promise of enhancing safety.

While the association was rallying support for its position on 70-41, time ran out at Morristown on attempts to reach peaceful settlement of the curfew problem. In February, 1971 the Board voted to take the issue into the higher levels of the New Jersey court system to seek overturn of Judge Joseph H. Stamler's Superior Court ruling upholding the curfew. Several air lines and the Air Transport Association joined with NBAA as plaintiffs.

Meanwhile, the dilemma of staff leadership grew during the winter months and on March 5, 1971 Ward resigned. Dunsworth's announcement noted that "in Bob's time we have seen increasing stresses placed on the air traffic control system . . . (and) constraints proposed on civil aviation by men either willfully or accidentally unaware of all aviation's importance to the nation's economy." A personnel search committee was created consisting of Dunsworth, Bean, Guerra,

George E. Haddaway, Mitchell, Don M. Teel and Winant. Dunsworth named Pope to take charge of staff activities pending conclusion of the search.

Late the same month, NPRM 70-41 was declared dead and FAA was sent back to its drawing board to try again. Of 600 docket comments on the defunct proposal only 10 were favorable. Kenneth M. Smith, FAA Deputy Administrator, admitted that corporate aircraft had not been intended to be included anyway. A select committee headed by Willard Smith, Assistant Secretary of Transportation, reported four recommendations to a concerned Congress. Every aircraft lease should be filed with FAA; some form of continuous maintenance program should be used; filing a flight plan should be mandatory; and minimum pilot qualifications should exceed those of FAR Part 91. These mandates should apply, he said, to all turbine powered and "complex" aircraft except those operated by air carriers. Smith's committee moved the subject out of an inferno and on to ground where it could be less heatedly debated.

In May, only a year after taking the post, Chamberlain resigned from the staff government relations job. The position was left open pending selection of a new staff chief.

June 3, 1971 brought news of the death of William K. Lawton, who had served as Executive Director for the decade 1956–1966. Illness cut short his subsequent service with Flight Safety, Inc., and he was an invalid for the last several years of his life. J. Sheldon "Torch" Lewis led a memorial gathering to honor Lawton's life at the National Aviation Club in Washington.

On June 22, 1971 the search committee completed its assignment. Announcement was made that Winant, then Vice President, Industrial Relations and Facilities for Sprague Electric had accepted the Executive Vice President post, to be redesignated President under by-laws proposals approved by the Board for membership action. It was Dunsworth who suggested the staff leadership idea to Winant in May as the two met in the Lambert Field (St. Louis) air terminal on their way to a meeting of the search panel. Dunsworth, arriving at the hotel shuttle bus stop at the airport, found Winant already there, sitting on his luggage. As they waited, Dunsworth proposed the idea. Winant, totally unprepared, asked for time to think the matter through prior to giving a reply, so the proposition was not raised at the committee's St. Louis meeting. But Dunsworth made Bean aware and they settled in to await word. In early June, Winant gave his agreement and the committee was polled at a meeting in Minneapolis. Dunsworth then telephoned all other members of the Board individually. The result was unanimous approval and August 21 was set as the effective date. Thinking back on the event years later, Dunsworth said to Winant, "My claim to fame is that you became President. NBAA has become what it is thanks to you, since that date."[8] Writing in the July *News Report*, Winant described NBAA: "Unlike most trade groups it cuts across all lines of corporate activity and is the stronger for it . . . The common experience is that use of aircraft contributes positively to achievement of corporate goals." The incoming staff chief said his highest priority was "retention of the identity and viability of corporate and business aviation, now threatened (by reduction of) operational freedom and by greatly increased costs."

The organizational thought process which led to Winant's decision has been described by Gilbert as one of NBAA's leading issues during the 1960's and 1970's. "There was a need for organized planning, for a re-evaluation of the association's goals, and most important, a need for strong leadership to keep the association on track toward the goals. NBAA reacted to these needs by hiring John Winant and then proceed to lay out the road ahead."[9]

As 1971 lengthened attention continued to focus on the Smith Committee findings and FAA attempts to grapple with the extraordinarily complicated issues raised by the Wichita State tragedy. McIntosh, always resourceful, sold NBAA leadership on the need to take the initiative in shaping an acceptable regulation which would deal with the issues on operational and safety grounds only. This would eliminate economic stipulations, an area in which FAA had neither experience nor charter.

NBAA's initiative was crafted during the annual Flight Safety Foundation corporate seminar at the Marriott Key Bridge Hotel in Washington. McIntosh recalled the way it went:

> ... I approached people like Don Baldwin (Texaco), Charlie Morris (Mobil), Randy Carpenter (Time, Inc.), Otto Pobanz (Federated Department Stores) and several others. The idea was to get as many members as possible to get together during the one open lunch period of the seminar. I briefed them there on what we thought was going to happen and asked for guidance. Our friends ... suggested that a committee be formed. I was given orders to draft a sample regulation which NBAA could live with, and after soliciting additional committee members was to circulate the draft and call a meeting in Washington.[10]

As was the case on earlier and subsequent occasions in NBAA history, one alternative to 70-41 considered was a separate regulatory identity for professionally-flown business aviation. FAA Flight Standards Director James F. Rudolph soon responded in a classic rejoinder. Separate identity, he warned, would require separate certification. In turn this would mean that each operations manual, each procedure, each operating plan would require FAA approval. Changes in any of these would need approval. Was this what corporate aviation really wanted? Would FAA have manpower to respond promptly to requests for action? The answers were obvious. Other solutions were considered.

McIntosh proceeded to put together the member working group to talk the issues through to satisfactory conclusion. Serving on this unique panel were:

Morton J. Brown, AMP, Inc.
John P. Doswell, American Standard, Inc.
Joseph L. Lacey, Atlantic Richfield Co.
Elmer C. Miller, Brockway Glass Co., Inc.
Harry J. Nystrom, General Mills, Inc.
Charles A. Childs, Gerber Products Co.
James N. Mahle, Hillenbrand Industries.
Stanley C. Smith, The Hoover Co.
S.A. Richards, The Magnavox Co.
Raoul Castro, Marcor Flight Operations
M.L. Nicholson, Mine Safety Appliance Company
Philip B. Henderson, Natural Gas Pipeline Company of America
Cornelius Fulton, Jr., Olin Corporation
Noble L. Utley, Owens-Corning Fiberglas
John W. Kandravi, Pennwalt Corporation
Roger B. Glass, Pennsylvania Glass Sand Corporation
Walter M. Kearney, Sanders Associates, Inc.
Neville B. Watson, C.V. Starr and Co., Inc.
Norris W. Lindsey, Temple Industries
C. Leo Boyd, Tennessee Eastman Company
Arthur Lippa, Jr., United States Steel Corporation
Dunsworth, serving *ex officio* as NBAA President

McIntosh, after completing the draft regulation requested of him at the Marriott meeting, contacted Rudolph and arrangements were made for a meeting of the member working group. Rudolph and Joseph Ferrarese of FAA both attended. McIntosh remembers Rudolph's approach as being soft-gloved. Using the NBAA draft as a reference point, Rudolph expressed FAA's need and desire for help. The working group responded in depth. Slowly, over the next several months, a new FAA rules proposal began to take shape.

Prior to joining NBAA staff in August, Winant saw to circulation to the membership of the proposed by-laws overhaul. The many changes were, with one exception, unchallenged or welcomed enthusiastically. The one exception, however, produced a resounding protest from a minority of members and an annual meeting which was the most turbulent in history.

At issue was a proposal to divide the voting membership into two categories, to be called Corporate and Business members. Corporate membership imposed higher professional qualifications than Business. The former category mandated having an Air Transport Rating (ATR) holder on the flight deck when carrying passengers. Also required were an operations manual and use of a recurring training program. The aim of the changes was two-fold: to encourage greater professionalism, a Long-Range Planning Committee goal, and at the same time give a clear signal that NBAA had its welcome mat out for other than what was called the "big iron," or large turbine aircraft fleet owners.

The annual meeting, held in Minneapolis September 21-23, 1971, turned into a lengthy and heated debate. Robert D. Powell, NBAA's outside counsel (succeeding Bruce G. Sundlun) recommended that the meeting resolve itself into a Committee of the Whole so that the issues could be discussed fully, and votes could even be taken, without making any action official or irretrievable. Dunsworth turned the chair over to Bean, who led the Committee of the Whole discussion for an agreed-upon 60 minute period. The loyal opposition, which felt that second class citizens were being created by the change, was led by Henderson, George H. Wiederhold; Swift and Company, Lloyd J. Parsons, Burlington Northern, and George Gerk, Jr., A.H. Gruetzmacher & Co. They put their case forward eloquently. But when the time came for the meeting to be reconstituted as the association's official body, their arguments failed. By a vote of 331 to 131, in person or by proxy, all by-laws amendments were carried. Pope recalled the meeting as one of the most momentous of his career.

Referring to the second class citizenship argument, he said, "what seemed to underlie that feeling" was the difference in pilot licensing requirements. Those who opposed apparently didn't want the world to know (though NBAA certainly wouldn't tell anyone) that their pilots . . . did not have an ATR. Some backed up their vocal opposition by taking their companies out of membership, either permanently or for a period of time.

"The net result was that NBAA survived that temporary unhappiness and, subsequently, began to acquire an ever increasing stream of new members. When the by-laws were changed, we had around 800 members and 15 years later, NBAA had nearly 3,000."[11]

The actual count of members who dropped out because of expressed dissatisfaction was 11 companies. The change was obviously more an incentive to growth than a deterrent.

The Minneapolis meeting committee was chaired by David M. Woodrow of 3M, later to become Director and chairman of NBAA. There were 2,638 registrants and 256 booths, both slightly down from Denver. But the worst of the recession was over and the clouds on NBAA's horizon were being scattered by fair winds.

Bean was elected to the newly-titled position of Chairman of the Board at Minneapolis. Mitchell moved up to the new Vice Chairman post and Gilbert was named Treasurer. Under the new by-laws, each was elected for a two year term. Winant became President and was also designated Secretary. The changes gave him a full-fledged voting position on the Board, which in effect returned him to a status he had held since 1957.

Wayne Rosenkrans, President of Jeppesen and Co., was named Associate Advisor, taking Haddaway's place. Elected to three years terms as Director were Gilbert, Mitchell and Morris. To bring the Board up to its newly enacted maximum of 15 elected Directors, Earle W. Bauer, Marathon Oil Company, Arthur E. Weiner, Burlington Mills, and Richard I. Hornbeck, General Electric Co., were voted Director positions.

For almost two decades John A. Pope was charged with staff responsibility for annual meetings. In 1971 he and local Committee Chairman David M. Woodrow, 3M, right, made plans for the aircraft display area at Wold-Chamberlin Field, Minneapolis.

New Chairman Bean, a Minneapolis native, was a Corporate Director of International Milling Co., later renamed International Multifoods. An Amherst College graduate, he was a World War II Naval transport pilot and served as a pilot with Pan American Airways as well. Later active in the advertising business in California, he returned to Minneapolis in 1955 to take his position on the Milling Company board. He was particularly active in the company's international operations, with emphasis on South America.

Dunsworth left the Presidency with praise ringing in his ears. Years later Bauer stated his belief that "Dunny was the most enthusiastic of all NBAA chief executives to date. He was a charger . . . He accomplished a great deal of good."[12]

Looking back on Dunsworth's contributions to NBAA, Bean gave him credit for sensing needs for new organizational directions as well as for the setting of new high standards. Many who came on the NBAA stage later, he wrote,[13]

> *. . . little realized how much time Dunny devoted to shoring up the organization . . . It was he who, probably more than anyone else, sensed the problems of the situation and the fact that something quite drastic needed to be done and had to be done rather abruptly. It was he who would*

A turbulent 1971 annual meeting in Minneapolis gave birth to extensive by-law changes. It also witnessed change in NBAA command. John B. Bean, right, International Milling Co. (later International Multifoods) became Chairman, replacing E. E. Dunsworth, center, as chief executive officer. Norman L. Mitchell, at the lectern, made his final report as Treasurer prior to being moved up to the newly-created Vice Chairman position.

have to deal with the then executive director. It was he who had the tough job of informing certain staff members that we would go outside to pick a successor. It was he who insisted that the title of the professional staff leader be changed to President in order to give that person the prestige required in Washington ... It was he who insisted that we must get somebody with the ability and the stature to fill the job of President so that it would not be just another empty Washington title.

And, of course, it was he who had the shrewdness to approach and interest John Winant in accepting the position. These factors and Winant's ability were the crux of making NBAA an important factor in aviation affairs in the United States.

Following his election as Chairman, Bean moved rapidly and forcefully to continue implementing solutions to what he felt were the truly pressing issues of the period. "The first of these," he said,[14]

NBAA's Board of Directors was expanded by 1971 by-laws changes. All members were present for this 1972 photograph. From left, front row, James F. Coleman, Ziff-Davis Publishing Co., Richard I. Hornbeck, General Electric, Thomas P. Roche, Deere and Company, Arthur E. Weiner, Burlington Industries, William F. Gilbert, Weyerhaeuser Company and NBAA Treasurer, E. E. Dunsworth, Trunkline Gas, and Norman L. Mitchell, Minneapolis Star and Tribune and NBAA Vice Chairman; standing, John H. Winant, NBAA President, Wayne A. Rosenkrans, Jeppesen and Company, Associate Advisor, Charles E. Morris, Mobil Corporation, Earle W. Bauer, Marathon Oil, Parker V. Ward, Van Dusen Aviation, Associate Advisor, Milton J. Pugsley, Chrysler Corporation, P. Ray Grimes, American Republic Insurance, Ronald J. Guerra, Kaiser Industries, Morton J. Brown, AMP, Inc., Randall H. Carpenter, Time, Inc., and John B. Bean, International Milling and NBAA Chairman.

was that NBAA had to have good relations with the Congress and take an active part in testifying there on aviation matters. The second was that NBAA needed to computerize its information and then use that information to educate the FAA, the Congress, and other members of the aviation community as to who we were, what we did, the distinction (of) business and corporate aviation from the other segments of general aviation, and the importance of our place in aviation in the United States.

The change in staff leadership, carried out under Dunsworth, was one positive step. But Bean added, "most important of all, it required a change to a more positive attitude on the part of the NBAA Board and staff, particularly with regard to asset allocation and management methods."

The computerization of data requirement was soon initiated under Bean in the form of comprehensive surveys of business aviation's characteristics, conducted for NBAA by Price, Waterhouse & Co. Done for 1972 and again for 1974, the surveys produced statistical information which was of great value in addressing the major issues of the 1970's. The importance to business aviation of major airports (60 percent of all flights, about half of which were to interconnect with air carriers), was exemplary of useful findings. As useful was corroboration that 40 percent of flights did not involve airports served by carriers, a fact which was extremely helpful in obtaining a satisfactory allocation during a major fuel crisis in 1973–1974.

Other data provided convincing evidence of business aviation's extensive activity. There were 37,950 aircraft in the business fleet, 2,250 of them turbine powered, 25,000 with piston engines. Use of helicopters had grown to require a fleet of 550. Business aircraft conducted 6,212,000 flights in 1972, amassing 7,989,000 hours. There were 1,957,000 flights to points outside the United States. And average annual hours of use for turbojets were 483, for turboprops 507, and for piston powered craft 257.

By fall of 1971 NPRM 70-41 was transformed into NPRM 71-32, covering large and turbine powered airplanes. The new proposal was given shape and substance by the NBAA working group's efforts, which included long Saturday or Sunday sessions in Washington, and by a positive attitude in FAA. Among permitted activities in private use would be the carriage of goods or materials so long as no charge was made, interchange of aircraft between companies, time sharing arrangements, and five options for inspection programs. Additional work was needed to make the new NPRM truly workable. But thanks to McIntosh and his volunteer group, NBAA could claim a major victory. The next step taken by McIntosh was to create a rules working group composed of member company attorneys whose task for the next several months would be to comb through the new proposal for adequacy as well as accuracy. McIntosh's handling of this arduous and complex challenge was typical of his skills. Looking back on it in 1988, Gilbert was moved to give him a special accolade. "He contributed much to establish NBAA's credibility in the aviation community," Gilbert said of McIntosh. He "gave himself wholly to serving the membership. If there was a question regarding the technical aspects of utilizing business aircraft all you had to do was call Fred. He would be on top of it."[15]

1972 was NBAA's 25th anniversary year. It brought several causes for celebration.

In January, Pope instituted a new membership service, the issuance of *Management Aids*, a quarterly publication intended to supplement the NBAA Recommended Standards Manual, whose periodic republication Pope had faithfully accomplished over the years. The first issue of the new periodical, titled, "The True Value of Business Aircraft Operations," was a reprint of a speech given by veteran consultant R. Dixon Speas. With characteristically methodical attention, Pope continued the *Management Aids* series, never missing a deadline up to his retirement in 1984.

The Morristown curfew case moved one notch ahead when in February, Judge Stamler refused to review the issue, enabling NBAA and its allies to take the matter to the New Jersey Appellate Court. Meanwhile, a jet curfew which had been imposed at the Burbank, California, airport appeared headed for the United States Supreme Court. NBAA's Board began to consider whether the association should seek participation in the Burbank case as a friend of the court.

In March, Brown of AMP and P. Ray Grimes, of American Republic Insurance Company, Des Moines, Iowa, were appointed to the Board; in April, Thomas P. Roche, Deere and Company, was also named an interim Director.

A month later Bullington resigned from staff to move to Nags Head, North Carolina, and eventually into the real estate business there. In late June, Dorothy W. Cheek joined the organization as Administrative Assistant. Formerly with the National Wildlife Federation, she went on to a distinguished career with NBAA. Her accession came almost at the moment staff headquarters were again moved, this time to a 4,308 square foot suite on the same floor of the Pennsylvania Building. The new space was formerly known as Suite 438. NBAA, however, retained its designation as Suite 401, thus avoiding the cost of reprinting large quantities of paper stock.

So as to give credit where it was much deserved, the Flying Safety Awards program was supplemented to include a maintenance personnel award beginning in 1972. And to further NBAA's technical competence and its already impressive credentials, cognizant staff members began that year to attend the National Transportation Safety Board (NTSB) Aircraft Accident Investigators School. This enabled NBAA to be an official team member in the investigation of major accidents involving business aircraft.

To help with 25th anniversary plans a steering committee was named. Serving on it were Joseph B. Burns, former NBAA President; Walter C. Pague, Director from 1946 to 1964; E. Tilson Peabody, Board member from General Motors; Nelson U. Rokes, pioneer business aviator from Procter and Gamble; Teel and Winant. The celebration would be focused on the annual meeting in Cincinnati in September.

In June, four members volunteered use of their aircraft for noise signature tests conducted by FAA and NBAA at the FAA Research Center near Atlantic City, New Jersey. Participating were Glen Alden Corporation, American Standard, Bethlehem Steel and Cessna Aircraft Corporation. Sixteen fly-bys and eight takeoffs were conducted for each aircraft. FAA's Richard Skully hailed the results: "You couldn't have asked for better cooperation, general interest and knowledge . . . than we received from these flight crews." The program was widely regarded as yet one further piece of evidence that NBAA and its responsible members were making every effort to minimize aircraft noise and at the same time maintain maximum safety standards.

Membership began to grow measurably as the year lengthened. A new category, Affiliate status, created by the 1971 by-laws changes, brought its first application, from Mobil Oil Canada, Ltd. Application from Empaques de Titan S.A., Mexico, soon followed. Affiliate status made NBAA resources available to business operators whose craft were not U.S. registered. The idea was to promote internationalization of business aviation. It worked. By 1986 there were some 30 Affiliates, based in North and South America, Canada, Europe and Africa.

August brought enactment of NPRM 71-32 as new Subpart D of FAR Part 91. A last minute hitch developed when a vocal group of air taxi operators sought to scuttle the entire rule because of their objection to the time sharing provisions. Evidently they felt the provision would establish a new category, competitive to the taxi industry. An appeal by Winant to FAA Administrator John Shaffer, supplemented by a visit with FAA Chief Counsel George Carneal, put things back on track and business aircraft operators, who had expended considerable time and money to comply with the new rules, were able to employ them on schedule. A last minute bonus was worked out by McIntosh. NBAA members would be granted an exemption under the rule if they wished to use it for coverage of aircraft types not specifically addressed by Subpart D. The exemption, still alive in 1986 through annual renewal processes, was credited time and again not only for raising safety standards, but for raising NBAA's membership total as well.

As NBAA prepared for its 25th anniversary meeting, *Flight* magazine paid compliments to the organization. Describing aviation groups as often "heap big smoke but very little fire," the journal said, "NBAA is one of the bright exceptions." Congratulating NBAA for helping develop government policies rather than react to them, *Flight* concluded NBAA's "leadership recognizes that anger and name calling are the best ways not to get your way."[16]

The Cincinnati annual meeting was an upbeat festival. Long time member Arthur Godfrey was opening night banquet speaker, with actor Cliff Robertson toastmaster. Burns, a gifted speaker, presided at the Awards and Honors Night banquet. The NBAA Meritorious Award was shared by the seven companies which maintained continuous membership in NBAA during the entire 25-year period. They were, in the order in which they joined CAOA, Republic Steel, Wolfe Industries, Burlington Industries, ARMCO Steel, Reynolds Metals, Corning Glass Works and General Electric. Among the many contributions which this group made to NBAA not the least was leadership. Six of the seven provided one or more Directors over the years to 1986. Three were the source of chief executive officers of the association.

Elected as three-year Directors at Cincinnati were Milton H. Pugsley, Chrysler Corporation, taking the place of Teel, resigned, Bean, Brown, James F. "Skeets" Coleman, and Hornbeck. Named to one-year terms were Grimes and Roche. Parker V. Ward, Van Dusen Aviation, was designated Associate Advisor, taking Howard's place.

There were symbolic overtones in Teel's departure from the Board, and in his retirement from United States Steel a few months later. The end of a chapter in business aircraft management was being written. The pioneers, characterized by Teel, were beginning to leave the stage, their places to be taken by a younger breed who were not veterans of wartime military service, but who by and large were professional business pilots or managers from the start. *Professional Pilot* magazine, a prominent national journal whose main interest was business aviation, devoted most of an issue to Teel in early 1973. Associates of many kinds, spanning many years, each paid tribute to his devotion to the building of business aviation. Speaking for NBAA, Winant wrote, "It was back in 1934 that he signed on as a captain with Loffland Brothers Drilling Company," a period "before anyone had even

This quintet of NBAA leaders eagerly awaited the opening of the 1972 annual meeting in Cincinnati. From left, Wayne A. Rosenkrans, Earle W. Bauer, Howard V. Gregory, Parker V. Ward and Richard I. Hornbeck. Bauer and Hornbeck served as the association's Chairman in later years. The three others all served as Associate Advisors to the Board.

come up with a name to describe" business aviation. For nine years he served as an NBAA Director, five of them as Treasurer. "He is a rare man in that he has genuinely loved his work, and has had the happy privilege of helping to create and build a great endeavor from the ground up . . . An older order in business aviation is indeed changing. The industry's founding fathers are taking leave of us and a new order is taking its place." Don goes "knowing that he leaves the shaping of the future in good hands."[17]

Attendance at Cincinnati was 2,942, a significant increase over the prior two years, and a sign that business aviation was again on the move.

November brought a decision by NBAA to seek *amicus* status in the Burbank case. The Ninth U.S. Court of Appeals had struck down the curfew and all that now remained was Supreme Court action. The stakes were too high for the association to stand on the sidelines. No matter what, a Supreme Court ruling would necessarily establish national precedent on curfews. Counsel Powell was given instruction to seek status and to prepare NBAA's brief for review by the justices.

Cincinnati's Convention Center housed the 1972 exhibition area. The use of spacious, high-ceilinged, purpose-built facilities led to rapid growth of the exhibition into one of the world's largest aviation events.

Almost concurrent with the Burbank case was Congressional action in creating the Noise Control Act of 1972, a sweeping statute which dealt with aspects of noise as disparate in source as railroad locomotives, highway tractor trailers, and aircraft engines. In most cases responsibility for control was vested in the EPA; aircraft were the sole exception of consequence. FAA, mostly because of the preexisting FAR Part 36 situation, retained control over aircraft and their engines, but EPA was given a strong subsidiary role. Air pollution matters, a separate problem, were wholly an EPA function.

During the December, 1972 Board meeting Otto C. Pobanz, Federated Department Stores and Chairman of the Cincinnati meeting committee, was appointed to the Board. He took a place vacated by Coleman, who had left Ziff-Davis Publishing Company. Pobanz's subsequent long service on the Board was distinguished by his inquisitive mind and by the constant flow of ideas and suggestions which it generated. He was a great, creative source of energy.

The next month brought significant news in the Morristown and Burbank cases. In New Jersey the appellate judges ruled that NBAA and ATA had not acted timely in seeking relief but added that they could seek a new, independent court action. The Supreme Court of the state, agreeing with the appellate ruling, refused to hear the original case. While rebuffed, NBAA and its allies determined to initiate their own new action, starting back at the Superior Court level. The Federal government, meanwhile, executed a totally unexpected about face in its position on Burbank. Whereas it had protested the curfew at the circuit court level, it planned to go to the nation's highest court as a backer of the right to impose the ban. NBAA's decision to enter the case as *amicus* was confirmed as an essential move to protect the rights of business aircraft owners.

William Horn, Jr., joined NBAA staff that same month, taking on the position of Manager, Airspace/Air Traffic Control Services. His accession filled a void created by McMurray's resignation in late 1972 to become a teacher in the Maryland community college system. Horn brought heavyweight credentials as a 30-year U.S. Air Force veteran with 5,000 hours piloting time. As a colonel, his final assignment was as chief of the military coordination staff which worked with FAA on airspace and traffic control matters.

On the user tax front, things began to reach a contentious state in January, 1973, when the Department of Transportation (DOT) unveiled preliminary results of the Congressionally-mandated cost allocation study to which it had devoted almost two years of effort. It was obvious the study would call for massive increases in general aviation charges or taxes. Samuel Ewer Eastman, DOT's policy chief and study director, told Bean, Winant and McIntosh as much over lunch as he probed for the upper limits of resistance, beyond which NBAA would not willingly go. Luncheon ended with Bean declaring that the existing $.07 tax was in many ways an unfair burden and the association would not remain quiet. Dissecting the study's tentative findings, NBAA, working closely with the General Aviation Manufacturers Association (GAMA) and other groups, pointed out glaring flaws. The study wholly disregarded the existence of any public benefit which derived from general aviation. It not only failed to admit that it was the air transportation system which placed demands on the user; it took exactly the opposite position. Further, the study totally missed the point that the air traffic control system was designed to the highest possible, and therefore costly, standards, to insure safety for air carrier and military operations. The system was not designed to meet the specific needs or desires of general aviation. The NBAA Board, sensing a major battle in the offing, created a special team consisting of Bean, Rosenkrans, Winant and McIntosh. A mandate was given to this group to deal with the unfolding problem and to keep the Board alerted to the need for concerted action. Hornbeck, looking back on the issue in the late 1980's, identified it as one of the two most important during his long service on the Board.[18] It was, he said, "an attempt to burden general aviation, and particularly business aviation, with an unduly large portion of the cost of operating the system . . . NBAA took the lead in opposing these taxes (and) . . . in particular protested the lack of recognition given public good accruing from the system." That the 1973 cost allocation failed in the end to increase general aviation taxes was in Hornbeck's opinion "in large measure because of the association's efforts."

By midyear the U.S. Supreme Court listened to the Burbank curfew arguments. It issued an opinion which struck the curfew down. Aviation interests felt both vindicated and jubilant, but there was a catch in the opinion. In a footnote which became ubiquitous, the court said the ruling did not address the situation in which a municipality (or other entity) might impose a curfew at an airport which it owned and operated. Burbank airport was at the time owned by the Lockheed Corporation. And while the court made a mighty declaration, many parts of which were extremely useful in contesting later curfew actions, it tightly circumscribed the scope of its findings. In this regard, the decision contained the same kind of disappointing shortcoming found later in other noise-related cases: the final decision focused only on one small part of a large problem area. Left undecided in each court contest were extraordinarily important and intrinsic portions of a disturbingly broad issue which cried out for resolution.

By mid-1973 there were strong hints that devastating events, sharp and discordant, would soon visit business aviation with an unprecedented new crisis. A major shortfall of petroleum-based fuels was gaining momentum. By July it seemed inevitable that winter would bring a heavy shortage, possibly of disastrous size. NBAA focused much of its resources in preparing for this gathering storm. Winant and McIntosh began an almost daily round of the skeletal Federal agencies responsible for emergency planning. Included among the tools being held in reserve in case of danger was the dreaded device called rationing.

In the midst of this growing turmoil one day stood out as a shining symbol of accomplishment, testifying that despite serious problems, NBAA was moving rapidly forward. On July 25, 1973, announcement was made of the creation of the Associate Membership Advisory Council. The group was the result of several months of study and fine-tuning. The purpose was to further improve communication and support between all elements of the membership and to give associates more direct access to the NBAA Board and staff. It was an extension of the Associate Advisor concept initiated nine years earlier. The Council idea was originated by Winant and proposed by him to Bauer's Support and Service Committee. With Bauer's enthusiastic backing, the idea rapidly moved forward. The July announcement said the membership of the Council would be drawn from diverse parts of the Associate base; the two Associate Advisors to the Board would act as co-Chairmen of the group. One standing assignment would be evaluation of the annual meeting in which associates played such a vital role. Bauer later described the founding of the Council as,

> ... one of the best things NBAA accomplished. It tapped a great mass of good people, companies and facilities, all of which were tied to the aircraft operations of NBAA members. To have these people (generally senior management personnel) giving us their input and their support has been extremely important to the progress of the organization.[19]

Bedore left staff in late July to take a position in FAA's environmental group, and by early September his place was taken by Robert A. Cooke, a U.S. Naval Academy graduate with 5,000 hours piloting experience. Cooke, designated as Manager of Airport Services, soon was drafted as a key player in the rapidly-developing fuel shortage issue. His outstanding efforts in the months which

The aircraft display line at Love Field, Dallas, in 1973 was the largest ever and meeting attendance set a new record. NBAA was on the move, with membership soon to pass the 1,000 company mark.

followed imposition of the October embargo on Middle East oil shipments paved the way for a long and fruitful period of service with NBAA. Also joining staff in September was Donald A. Maunder, another former Naval officer, who filled the newly created position of Manager, Technical Services. Maunder's work with NBAA soon terminated and the following year his place was taken by Willian Fanning, also a former Naval officer. Fanning, like Cooke, became an NBAA institution. His areas of special expertise included aircraft certification, operation, maintenance and safety. In time he became the organization's chief accident investigator, participating in several NTSB teams which dug for the probable cause of major business aircraft tragedies.

As final preparations were being made for the 1973 annual meeting in Dallas, NBAA began issuing Fuel Supply Outlook Bulletins. By October these warned of a bitter winter and a shortfall of petroleum which might be "as large as 10 percent."

In spite of these threatening external problems, the Dallas meeting, held September 25–27, was a triumph. Attendance soared to 4,610, by far the highest ever, and Bean, rounding out his term as chairman, reported that membership stood at 1,009, another major breakthrough. The irrepressible George Haddaway, who chaired NBAA's first great convention in 1954, deftly managed another record in 1973.

Bean's stewardship was remarkable. Gilbert praised him for bringing "a businesslike approach to the activities of the association when it was very much needed. He was largely responsible for developing the long range plans of NBAA and his acumen and sense of humor went a long way toward providing stability when the waters became a little rough."[20] Bauer credited Bean with "driving the Board and organization to better fiscal control and long range planning. He was an expert in those things and was a forceful leader."[21] Dunsworth held an equally high opinion: Bean, in his estimation, was "the one person who was really responsible for NBAA making the changes that moved the organization into the position of leadership it holds."[22]

Mitchell moved into the chair at Dallas, Gilbert advanced to Vice Chairman, and Hornbeck was elected Treasurer. Three-year Director terms were voted for Ross Beach, Kansas Natural Gas Company, Robert E. Breiling, Associated Aviation Underwriters, Carpenter, Grimes and Guerra. Pobanz was named to a one-year term. Rosenkrans accepted a second two-year term as Associate Advisor; his ongoing work on the user charge issue was considered irreplaceable.

Designated as Chairmen of the Association's standing committees were:

Airports: Henry Stuart, Addison Field
Airspace/Air Traffic Control: John P. Doswell, American Standard
Corporate Aviation Management: Edwin L. King, American
    Management Association
International Operations: Donald Jorgenson, Joseph E. Seagram and
    Sons, Inc.
Technical: Eugene J. Zepp, General Motors

The fuel shortage turned from issue to crisis as the fall lengthened. The Energy Policy Office issued a standby plan which was full of errors and omissions. It would have shunted proper Federal responsibilities to the states. And it contained no priority plan for private transportation or even a semblance of a conservation plan.

Meanwhile, good news came from Morristown. The new action resulted in November in a new order from Superior Court which lifted the curfew. The U.S. Supreme Court decision in Burbank was cited as one reason. Three and a half years of tedious, occasionally disappointing, work finally paid off.

On November 20, the new Associate Membership Advisory Council held its first meeting. The impending fuel crisis was the central theme of discussion. Attending the meeting as charter members of the Council were:

Rosenkrans and Ward, Co-Chairmen
Charles Ames, Memphis Aero Corporation
Frederick W. Becker, Airwork Services Division
E. J. Brandreth, Cessna Aircraft Corporation
Thomas W. Gillespie, Piper Aircraft Corporation
Howard V. Gregory, Des Moines Flying Service
Lloyd W. Harris, Beechcraft Hawker Corporation
W. Russell Miller, AirKaman, Inc.
Robert S. Northington, Piedmont Aviation, Inc.
William L. Patrick, Atlantic Aviation Corporation
Gilbert F. Quinby, NARCO Avionics Division
William B. Watt, Executive Air Fleet
Norman Wollberg, Dallas Airmotive

The day after the Council's meeting NBAA put into operation its Fuel Information Center, a multi-line telephone service containing both recorded informational bulletins and direct personal access to staff members. The center was an innovation which helped tremendously to ease the crucial situation, and while not planned to do so, gave NBAA great national exposure and prominence. At truly critical moments it is innovation, rather than coping, which must be the order of the day. NBAA's actions in creating the information center, which received well over 100,000 telephone calls, is exemplary of innovation at its creative best.

November 25, 1973 was Black Sunday for business aviation. NBAA and GAMA staffs joined to wait out a long vigil as the hour for a major television address by President Nixon approached. Contained in the package of allocation plans announced by the President was a 40 percent cut in business aviation fuel supplies. Chaos followed. NBAA undertook to promote conservation rather than allocation, and to urge more fuel-efficient air traffic handling. It also pointed out forcefully that business aviation fuel consumption was literally a drop in the bucket. Business aircraft used only about 1.5 percent of all jet fuel and $^{16}/_{100}$ths of 1 percent of national gasoline stocks. The proposed slashes would devastate business aviation but made no significant contribution to solving the overall shortage. The morning after the Nixon television drama, Winant and GAMA President Edward W. Stimpson were granted an audience with national fuel czar John R. Love, former Governor of Colorado. While Love showed sympathy he indicated clearly that he was powerless and unwilling to help alleviate the Presidential Order or even to request reconsideration.

Figuratively fueled by the Administration's total lack of understanding, a sweeping movement for equality of treatment of business aviation began immediately. NBAA joined with others in general aviation to broaden the movement. All they asked, collectively, were reductions in fuel supplies no greater in percentage size than those being imposed elsewhere. Initial personal automobile fuel cuts were set at 15 percent; why should business aviation be cut by 40 percent or personal aircraft fuel by 50 percent?

At a pace which seemed agonizingly slow at the time, the tide was turned. Two staunch friends were identified in Congress, members rallied around to support NBAA, and strong protestations were made to senior members of the Administration. Barry Goldwater, Jr., Congressman from California, and Fred Rooney, from Pennsylvania, promoted an equitable treatment provision which legislated that no user group would be given more stringent quotas than others. Advocates of equal treatment began to appear in the Administration, and a new energy czar, Rogers C. B. Morton, who also was Secretary of the Interior, took a second look at the aviation situation. Senator Robert Dole, Kansas, pressed for a fair solution. The pace of activity in the Fuel Information Center, costs of which were partially underwritten by GAMA, quickened. As many as 2,500 calls a day were being received at the height of the bleak period which lasted through December, 1973. NBAA relentlessly drove home its principal points: give equitable treatment to all users, provide relief for hardship cases through an established appeals channel, provide for new or changed circumstances, and make fuel available for transient aircraft.

As the year turned, Cox decided to leave NBAA to seek a career as a free-lance writer. His position, vacated at a troublesome time in NBAA affairs, was soon filled by appointment of Frank McGuire, a news writer for *Aviation Daily*, and well versed in the issues of the moment.

January, 1974 was a much brighter period than December, 1973. New energy allocation rules published on the 15th gave a 90 percent share for business aviation and 100 percent to that segment which involved flying directly related to energy production. Aviation service organizations were to get 95 percent, helping resolve the transient aircraft dilemma, and administration of programs would be with the Federal, rather than state, government. The Federal Energy Office was soon to become the Federal Energy Administration (FEA). Winant was moved to say, "We feel quite encouraged about our ability to deal with the situation," and noted that production of aviation fuels was already increasing. By April things were more nearly normal and on the 28th the fuel information hotline service was put on standby. One national publication, *General Aviation News*, listened to the final recorded message and said, "the fuel crisis ended on April 28th. It must have, because John Winant said it did."[23] A half year of disordered doubts was ended.

But even with the worst behind, the fuel crisis left traumatic effect. Its deep marks were covered over, hidden by a powerful resurgence which carried business aviation to new heights in the late 1970's. Underneath, however, was the disturbing legacy of uncertainty bequeathed by the fuel problem. The bedrock of the business aircraft is its versatility, the capability of being used to go wherever and whenever business needs dictate. Unavailability of fuel, even if on a short lived basis, planted a seed of doubt which unquestionably was a contributor to disarray in the business aircraft manufacturing industry a decade later.

Bauer had strong memories of the crisis.

Had it continued much longer I think (we) would have suffered irreparable damage ... Many companies would have gotten out of business aviation. And it did make a permanent change in the cost of aircraft operation because fuel prices were so dreadfully affected. It left a scar and many people are apprehensive that it might happen again ... This has caused many companies to develop 'what if' plans.[24]

Lee L. Robbins, Corning Glass Works, Chairman of the Energy Committee created because of the crisis and later NBAA Chairman, ranked the fuel shortage as one of the major deterrents to business aviation during his career. "Fuel shortages allowed producers to push prices to frightening levels. The fight against increasing fuel prices took more of a tack of getting us fuel rather than trying to contain prices. Through very powerful lobbying, the NBAA was able to get us our fair share of fuel. They also set up the network which could inform the membership where fuel was available."[25]

The dramatic events of late 1973 were not, however, so depressing as to bring to a halt the strong comeback which business aviation launched in 1972. Cessna announced in early 1974 that it had delivered 81 Citations the prior year, an all time record. And GAMA noted that January, 1974 sales of U.S.-built general aviation aircraft were up 14 percent over January, 1973.

NBAA's membership began yet another upward surge, in part because of a mailing list recruitment campaign designed by Pope, but in larger measure because of association performance in the noise, tax and fuel arenas. In March, 1974, the Board determined it could within by-laws criteria accept foreign-based vendor service organizations as Associate members. This action gave impetus to the growing internationalization of the community and helped solidify ties on a global basis. In June, Winant appeared before the board of CBAA and proposed creation of the International Business Aviation Council (IBAC). His argument was that if Canadian and British interests were ready, the project should move ahead. Canada was interested but wanted to see how matters stood across the Atlantic. Later in the year Winant and BAUA's chief met at lunch in London. The British were non-committal. NBAA's Board decided to keep the proposal alive but not to push it. The better course would be for an incentive to organize to come from outside the United States, avoiding any stigma the group was simply an extension of NBAA. Six more years would be required for the incentive to materialize, but finally it did.

June brought a special award, conferred by Ziff-Davis Publishing Company jointly on NBAA and GAMA, for their work in the fuel crisis. The plaque which symbolized the honor praised the two "for raising the call to which everyone in general aviation responded enthusiastically."

1974's annual meeting site was Los Angeles, with the inimitable "Scotty" Miller heading the local arrangements committee for the third time. Attendance topped even that of Dallas, with 4,781 registrants. Exhibiting companies rose to 168, occupying 344 booths at the city's new convention center. Zepp was elected to a one-year Director term, and three-year terms were given to Bauer, Gilbert, Mitchell, Morris, and Pobanz. Northington, Senior Vice President of Piedmont Aviation, was designated as the new Associate Advisor.

The following month brought to the fore yet one more momentous aircraft noise issue. The Town of Greenwich, Connecticut, and a local citizens group began a multi-million dollar suit against Westchester County, New York, and the FAA. At issue were alleged excessive and harmful noise effects caused by operations at the Westchester County Airport in White Plains, one of business aviation's greatest centers and home base of more than 100 business jets. The case was filed at U.S. District Court, New Haven. And while NBAA moved quickly to obtain status as an intervenor for the defendants, its real aim was out-of-court negotiation of the demands for a curfew and other flight restrictions. In 1988, Hornbeck, a central figure in NBAA's efforts recalled the eventual, but not unbroken, accord. "A settlement was reached," he said,

> *which included a court stipulation to form a committee of users and residents to try to resolve amicably major differences of opinion . . . This*

committee has been in being more than a decade, with NBAA representatives playing an active role. Despite a major lawsuit which took place in the 1980's in New York, the committee has managed to prevent further litigation through consultation and the education of both users and residents to the legitimate needs and concerns of each other.[26]

Powell, NBAA's Counsel, also played a leading role in the Westchester County situation over the years, as did McIntosh, and, eventually, Doswell. All were to be put to frequent test, the most trying of which was an unwanted but necessary U.S. District Court case in New York which resulted in 1983 in the lifting of a night curfew.

Early 1975 brought final government approval of NBAA's General Aviation Fuel Reservation System, a scheme by which aircraft operators could telephone ahead to points along an itinerary and be given assurance that designated fuel supplies would be held available. The approval of the Federal Trade Commission was a necessary ingredient. More than 700 service organizations joined the system and a directory was circulated widely by NBAA. While the actual fuel crisis was past, the system was praised widely in the industry and press as a forward looking preventive device. As with other important programs of the period the system carried NBAA's name and its growing reputation to many receptive audiences, including prospective members.

Singled out for individual praise as the year ended was C. Leo Boyd, Chairman of the NBAA Avionics Subcommittee. *Aviation Week* magazine named him one of its "Men of the Year" for his efforts in "development of a comprehensive program for all-weather" corporate aircraft operations."[27]

January of 1975 brought the shocking news that Director Grimes was in a deep coma in a Des Moines hospital, the aftermath of surgery to remove a large brain tumor. For the next several months Grimes hovered on the thin line between life and death, constantly in coma. Faith and strength finally won the battle and by mid-year he was conscious and on a slow road to recovery. But recover he did, perhaps miraculously, for his improvement eventually led to regaining his FAA medical certificate. By 1978 he was a full-time professional pilot again. Grimes' story of return from the brink of death to sound health was an epic in courage, fortitude and the never-failing faith of his family.

On January 1, 1975, FAR Part 36 came into full play with the mandate that all aircraft engines newly manufactured from that date would have to conform to the regulation. Thus were born what came to be called "Stage 2" engine noise criteria, a term much used in the years which followed, and which figured prominently in potential or actual attempts by many airports to limit aircraft operations.

Within five months there was first mention in NBAA circles of an all-out jet ban at the Santa Monica, California airport. A temporary injunction was invoked and NBAA, at least for the time being, decided not to become involved. Events were to change NBAA's position dramatically and led it ultimately into a costly yet productive lawsuit.

New Orleans' Rivergate Center was the setting for the 1975 annual meeting exhibition area. Janice K. Barden became the first woman to chair an annual meeting, a responsibility she would duplicate on two other occasions by the late 1980's. Mock-ups of entire aircraft were much in evidence on the exhibition floor.

The 1975 annual meeting was held in New Orleans, October 29–31, and Janice Barden, principal of Aviation Personnel, Inc., became the first woman to chair a local arrangements committee. Her performance was outstanding in all regards, so much so that she would be called on two more times prior to the end of the 1980's to chair annual meeting committees. There were 4,812 registrants in New Orleans in 1975, exhibiting companies rose to more than 140, and booths to 382. Mrs. Moya Lear cast a spell over the awards night banquet as she accepted the Meritorious Award on behalf of husband Bill. Her platform magic ended with a song, and marked only the second time a proxy was permitted to receive the award. The other was in Lindbergh's behalf in 1953.

At New Orleans, Mitchell stepped down from the chair after an impressive two-year administration. Gilbert became Chairman, Hornbeck Vice Chairman and Beach Treasurer. Three-year Director terms were voted for Bean, Brown, Hornbeck, Pugsley, and Zepp. Howard Gregory, President of Des Moines Flying Service, was named Associate Advisor in place of Rosenkrans, whose four-year record of service earned him deserved and lasting praise.

Executive and staff leaders paused for a moment during the 1975 annual meeting in New Orleans. Norman L. Mitchell, left, was the outgoing Chairman, to be succeeded at New Orleans by William F. Gilbert, center. John H. Winant, left, observed his fourth year as President and his eighteenth as a member of the NBAA Board.

By January of 1976 membership in NBAA passed the 1,300 mark. Of the total, 611 companies were Corporate and 395 Business members. Membership had increased by 35 percent since passage of the contentious by-law requirements a little more than five years earlier.

March brought appointment of Harry C. McCreary, President, McCreary Tire and Rubber, and David M. Woodrow, 3M, to the Board. They took seats vacated by Mitchell and the slowly-recovering Grimes, whose company had sold its aircraft. And the staff Information Director position soon changed hands again, with McGuire leaving to form a helicopter-oriented newsletter. Taking his place was Joseph G. Mason, a highly experienced aviation journalist who came to NBAA from Minneapolis, where he was editor of *Airport Services* magazine.

Horn's staff responsibilities were supplemented by appointment to ATPAC (Air Traffic Procedures Advisory Committee), created by FAA to review all existing regulations and procedures in the aftermath of the horrifying crash in December, 1974, of TWA flight 514 into a Virginia mountainside near Dulles airport. ATPAC became an industry fixture which, often useful and often frustrated by governmental inertia, continued into the 1980's.

In May, Pope was named Secretary of the corporation, and one month later Bauer was elected Treasurer, replacing Beach. The latter found that personal business commitments would likely make it impossible for him to move through the officer chairs.

A review of association dues levels was conducted by the Board prior to the 1976 annual meeting and the decision was taken to make no change from the amounts set in 1969. Growth in membership, combined with ever more successful annual meetings, were generating needed revenues to expand services, make innovations, and build a healthy reserve fund, one large enough to finance major revenue needs. Events which were encountered later in the decade proved the wisdom of creating and building the reserve.

By mid-year, Congress completed a lengthy review of the 1970 airports-airways act. Largely because of strong legislative efforts by all of general aviation there was no change in the fuel tax, meaning the 1972–1973 DOT cost allocation study had failed to convince Congress that the levy should be increased enormously. The new measure, continuing the 1970 act until 1980, was signed into law on July 12 by President Ford.

At annual meeting time in September, Chairmen were named for the various standing committees:

Airports: Gerk of A.H. Greutzmacher
International Operations: Paul R. Stevens, W.R. Grace and Company
Corporate Aviation Management: Parsons of Burlington Northern
Operations: James Crigler, El Paso Natural Gas Company
Airspace/Air Traffic Control: Doswell, American Standard
Technical: Jack H. Piehl, Shell Oil Company

Rosenkrans chaired the 1976 Denver annual meeting, which built the national bicentennial theme into most events. Some 5,382 persons attended the September 14–16 gathering. Growth required that NBAA use the entirety of Currigan Hall for exhibits rather than the half which was needed in 1970. Exhibition participation grew to 165 companies with 486 booths. Elected to Director terms were Beach, Breiling, Carpenter, McCreary and James F. Nields, Chief Executive of Ware Knitters, Inc. of Massachusetts. Woodrow was elected to a one-year term and W. Russell Miller, Air Kaman, Inc., was named as an Associate Advisor. In his address at the annual meeting Chairman Gilbert saluted the strong people involvement which had moved NBAA forward so rapidly in recent years. In particular, he cited the Board, standing committees, *ad hoc* panels, individual actions, and effective staff work. "So," he concluded, "for the great support you good member company representatives have given to NBAA, I give you back the highest of accolades for people involvement. Without your endorsement, your criticisms, your leadership, there would simply be no vibrant NBAA and, perhaps, no business aviation community in the United States."

Perhaps in celebration of his election to the Board, Nields, one of the association's great catalytic forces and a beloved figure, set a new world non-stop record piloting his Beech Baron home from Denver to Boston. Crocker Snow, venerable Director of Aviation for Massachusetts, greeted Nields on arrival at

The exhibition area occupied the entirety of Denver's Currigan Hall in 1976. Symposiums and maintenance-operations meetings were held in the adjacent auditorium complex. New records were set for attendance, exhibitors and exhibit space used.

Boston's Logan airport, uncorking a bottle of champagne as Nields climbed out of the Baron.

Bean brought his long service on the NBAA Board to a close at Denver, resigning as of the end of the annual meeting. J.W. "Bill" Eagleton of Shell Oil Co., Houston, was named to take his place as of December, 1976.

In October, Cooke, still manning the fuel barricades, pleaded with the Congress to deregulate fuel and return it to proper status as a free market commodity. This appearance, fourth by Cooke and seventh by NBAA on the subject, finally had a payoff. In December the fuel allocation for business aviation was raised to 100 percent of need, effectively ending the long period of nominal control.

That same month, Richard Witkin, chief aviation writer for the *New York Times*, made a strong endorsement of the corporate aviation safety record. This segment of aviation was, he said, "... a world of privately owned executive planes that are generally conditioned like thoroughbreds and operated with consummate conservatism (which) has built a safety record rivaling the low accident rate for this country's airlines." The story was triggered by the crashes on September 27 of a

Gulfstream II at Hot Springs, Virginia, and a Learjet at Sao Paulo, Brazil. These, Witkin pointed out in documented terms, were exceptions. In detailing the commendable safety record of such aircraft, he called particular attention to the high number of takeoffs and landings of corporate planes as added credentials.

At year's end the Board, recognizing that staff needs were fairly bursting the Pennsylvania Building suite, agreed to move NBAA headquarters to One Farragut Square South, where it would occupy the entire eleventh floor, some 4,800 square feet. America's bicentennial year ended on an upbeat note for NBAA. As an institution, it was much on the move, growing in size and prestige. Membership, which stood at 859 companies just before the turn of the decade, rose to 1,349 by mid-1976. Total income in 1969 was $267,588; in 1976 it was $714,736. Net return from the annual meeting, also a growing force, rose from $85,862 to $237,891 between those same years. Business aviation, the world NBAA represented, was also on its way to new records. Good years lay immediately ahead.

NOTES TO CHAPTER 7

1. *NBAA News Report,* interview, E.E. Dunsworth, October, 1969.

2. E.E. Dunsworth, Rockport, Texas, audio-tape commentary, February, 1987.

3. Harry C. McCreary, Indiana, Pennsylvania, letter to J.H. Winant, May 11, 1987.

4. Dunsworth tape.

5. Ibid.

6. John A. Pope, Arlington, Virginia, memorandum to J.H. Winant, March, 1988.

7. Dunsworth tape.

8. Ibid.

9. William F. Gilbert, Tacoma, Washington, memorandum to J.H. Winant, March, 1988.

10. Frederick B. McIntosh, Leesburg, Virginia, memorandum to J.H. Winant, April 26, 1988.

11. Pope memorandum, March, 1988.

12. Earle W. Bauer, Findlay, Ohio, audio-tape interview with J.H. Winant, October 22, 1987.

13. John B. Bean, Naples, Florida, memorandum to J.H. Winant, May 17, 1988.

14. Ibid.

15. Gilbert memorandum, March, 1988.

16. *Flight* magazine, editorial, August, 1972.

17. *Professional Pilot* magazine, February, 1973, p. 39.

18. Richard I. Hornbeck, Greenwich, Connecticut, memorandum to J.H. Winant, April 11, 1988.

19. Bauer tape, October 22, 1987.

20. Gilbert memorandum, March, 1988.

21. Bauer tape, October 22, 1987.

22. Dunsworth letter, June 5, 1988.

23. General Aviation News, May, 1974.

24. Bauer tape, October 22, 1987.

25. Lee L. Robbins, Horseheads, New York, memorandum to J.H. Winant, April 8, 1988.

26. Hornbeck memorandum, April 11, 1988.

27. *Aviation Week* magazine, December, 1974.

Chapter 8

THE GREENING OF BUSINESS AVIATION: 1977–1981

MAKING THE 1977 MANUFACTURERS' FORECAST TO THE New York Society of Security Analysts, Russell W. Meyer, Cessna's chairman, painted a vivid word picture. Illustrated were the actual events of that January day and the next. Leaving Wichita at 7:30 a.m. in a Citation, Meyer flew to LaGuardia for the analysts luncheon session. Later in the day he would go to a 3,000 foot grass strip in New Jersey for a visit at the company's avionics plant, then to Dayton for meetings with propeller division people which would continue through lunch the next day. The last leg would take Meyer back to Wichita in time for two or three hours at the office. "This could not have been done without a business airplane," he said. It "was a routine example of business airplane productivity."

The story was exemplary of the thousands of ways in which aircraft were being put to use as the 1970's lengthened. Each year of the decade brought more aircraft into the business of multiplying the productive use of time. Business aviation basked in a period of full bloom, each year more brilliant than any before. Finally, the end was reached in 1979, generating shock waves which ravaged even the top of the line business aircraft marketplace by 1982.

By March of 1977, NBAA's staff was in its new offices at One Farragut Square South (also known as 1634 Eye Street, N.W.). The move took place almost precisely on the thirtieth anniversary of the first post-incorporation CAOA Board meeting. The senior staff members who settled into the impressive new suite were John H. Winant, President; John A. Pope, Director, Membership Services and Secretary; Joseph A. Mason, Director, Information Services; Robert A. Cooke, soon to become Assistant to the President, Government Relations and Energy; Frederick B. McIntosh, Director, Operational Services; William Horn, Jr., Manager, Airspace/Air Traffic Control Services; William Fanning, Manager, Technical Services; Ann T.

Miletich, Manager, Accounting Services; Dorothy W. Cheek, Manager, Administrative Services; and Myrtle W. Somers, Manager, Office Services. Within a few months, Michael J. McCarty, recent honors graduate of Parks College, University of St. Louis, joined the group as Administrative Assistant with responsibility for airport services.

While the association and the business aviation community took advantage of every expansion opportunity in the late 1970's, the vexing issues of aircraft noise and energy shortages continued to chip away at the solid foundation of the growing structure.

EPA in early 1977 suggested that Federal airport development funds (which were really not Federal monies, since the system's users actually provided them) be withheld from airports which did not enforce its proposed, unworkable noise restrictions. Cooke, responding at public hearings, described EPA's ideas as "absolutely anathema." The nation's air transportation system, he said, "is basic to the economy . . . and any national noise policy should support it strongly through pre-emption of local regulations (which are) detrimental to its health and welfare." He urged use of noise suppressants such as NBAA's "fly to the numbers" principle, which endorsed use of safe piloting techniques to bring aircraft noise levels within FAR Part 36 limits. EPA's proposals were not adopted.

Transition of national administration from President Ford to President Carter brought a burble to the energy scene, causing inaction on deregulation of fuels. NBAA took a platform for energy policy personally to James R. Schlesinger, the Carter energy advisor, soon after the President delivered his first televised fireside chat, attired in a wool pullover to ward off the White House chill.

Remove all allocation and price controls immediately, said NBAA, and reject any special treatment based on the specious argument that the pleading party is more energy efficient than someone else. The association restated its bedrock belief that any shortage should demand equitable sharing of existing supplies among all users. It was also pointed out that aviation had a built-in ethic: "you must carry aloft all the fuel to be used on a flight and for every excess pound of fuel, the payload must be lightened."

Spring brought several memorable occurrences. At the suggestion of Director J. W. "Bill" Eagleton, a Helicopter Committee was created, initially to help develop requirements for basic instrument (IFR) routes in the northeastern states, the Baltimore trench in the Atlantic, and Alaska. Anthony Zuma, Tenneco, was named Chairman. McIntosh soon made a tour of the North Sea and Alaskan zones to see first-hand how petroleum industry helicopters were put to use there.

Building on a 1974 innovation, Cooke put together and orchestrated the first of the major International Operations Seminars, attracting 41 attendees from 25 companies to the Washington Hotel.

Membership passed the 1,500 mark in April, registering the largest annual gain in history, with the lowest recorded termination rate, less than 4 percent.

And John P. "Jack" Doswell, American Standard, long-time Airspace/Air Traffic Control Committee head, received Flight Safety Foundation's corporate meritorious service award for his outstanding volunteer work. Later the victim of Guillame Barre syndrome, Doswell spent agonizing months regaining use of his limbs. Eventually he requalified for an airman's license and, in the final years of his life, worked as a consultant, frequently giving substantial time to NBAA causes without charge. In 1987 he died of cancer, depriving the community of a towering symbol of the best in volunteerism.

The 1977 annual meeting in Houston September 27–29 was a standout. *Convention News'* retrospective comment was that when "NBAA connoisseurs get togther to reminisce, 1977's Houston show is the standard against which all other NBAA conventions are judged."

There was unprecedented registration of 7,102 persons, 32 percent more than in record setting Denver. Never before had so many exhibitors (192) occupied so many booths (560).

The annual meeting witnessed election of William F. Gilbert, Weyerhaueser Company, Earle W. Bauer, Marathon Oil, Charles E. Morris, Mobil, Otto C. Pobanz, Federated Department Stores, and David M. Woodrow, 3M, to three-year Director terms. Eagleton was named to a one-year term. Thomas W. Gillespie, Piper Aircraft Corporation, was designated the new Associate Advisor, taking the place of Howard V. Gregory. Effective October 1, Milton H. Pugsley of Chrysler submitted his resignation as a Director.

Houston was also scene of change in command. Richard I. Hornbeck, General Electric, became Chairman, succeeding Gilbert. Bauer was named Vice Chairman and Harry C. McCreary, McCreary Tire and Rubber, was designated Treasurer.

Gilbert was remembered affectionately as a modest Chairman with an engaging, dry sense of humor and a strong loyalty to the organization. A Macalester College graduate, one time air traffic controller and highly experienced pilot, he brought a variety of credentials to his work with Weyerhaeuser and his leadership of NBAA.

Hornbeck served as chief of GE's Air Transport Operation from 1963, taking the post after 10 years as a line pilot. A cum laude, Phi Beta Kappa graduate of Williams College, he was a flight instructor, charter pilot and Colonial Airlines pilot prior to joining GE. Bauer described him as a "very sincere, dedicated person, more than willing to give of himself and his knowledge. His judgment was outstanding."[1] Hornbeck's two years as Chairman were characterized by intelligence and inquisitive leadership. In the particular case of a major and risky lawsuit against the city of Santa Monica, he displayed a strong vein of courage as well.

Named at Houston as standing committee chairman were:

Corporate Aviation Management — Leo L. Brown, General Mills
Airports — George Gerk, Jr., A.H. Gruetzmacher & Co.
Airspace/Air Traffic Control — Doswell
Helicopter — Zuma

International Operations — Paul R. Stevens, W.R. Grace and Company
Operations — Les B. Gerlach, Texaco, Inc.
Technical — Jack Piehl, Shell Oil Co.
Energy — Lee L. Robbins, Corning Glass Works.

Energy conservation was a watchword in energy capital Houston. A panel discussion on energy cost cutting was led by Woodrow. Raleigh E. Drennon, BFGoodrich, spoke about operational means by which pilots could reduce fuel consumption. William M. Flener, FAA's Associate Administrator for Air Traffic and Airways Facilities, described ways traffic control handling could help: towing, gate holds, and elimination of circuitous routing. Direct, rapid descent from cruising altitude to airport approach was a topic of hot interest.

The 1977 meeting is remembered as a sparkling showcase of new aircraft. Seven were shown at Houston and 10 new models were announced for future production. Among the new craft were the 700 model Hawker-Siddeley, with the quiet Garrett TFE731 engines; the Rockwell Sabreliner 65, with similar power plants; the Dassault Falcon 50, a three-engine, long range aircraft which made a seven hour, 52 minute London-Teterboro flight on the way to Houston; the Model 28/29 Learjets with "longhorn" winglets; and the Piper Cheyenne III turboprop. Two new helicopters tailored to business use were displayed: the Bell Model 222 and the Aerospatiale SA365 Dauphin 2.

William P. Lear described his next hoped-for breakthrough aircraft, the Futura, later redesigned as the Lear Fan, built with composite materials. It underwent a tortuous journey toward certification after Lear's death, with his widow, Moya, playing a leading role. With financial backing from the British Government, it went into the developmental-manufacturing stage in Belfast, Northern Ireland, while test models attempted to get a certificate in the United States. Time worked against the project. Months turned to years and it failed when the British withdrew support.

The final major announcement at Houston came from Canadair. Its new widebody business jet, descendant of a Bill Lear concept, was moving on time through development and manufacture. The new airplane, to be named Challenger, would, after initial difficulties, occupy a prominent place among the larger business aircraft.

The year 1978 brought bullish forecasts of aircraft production. GAMA President Edward W. Stimpson predicted that U.S. manufacture of general aviation airplanes would be 18,000 units, a 7.1 percent increase. The Helicopter Association International declared there were 6,000 craft in the current rotor wing fleet. By 1985, 10,000 were forecast, 50 percent of them in business use.

Business Week had a February cover story which said. "Last year . . . the U.S. business aircraft fleet flew several times as many hours as all domestic airlines combined. Corporate aircraft are radically transforming the way many companies do business." The story claimed there were 50,000 business aircraft, up markedly from the 35,000 reported in NBAA's 1972 data bank survey. United Airlines did not consider business aviation a competitor, *Business Week* said. United thought of business planes as a vast feeder fleet bringing customers to it. "Of United's 20 largest corporate customers, 17 fly their own planes," the article concluded.

An NBAA environmental seminar held in March at NASA's Langley Center in Hampton, Virginia, was prophetic. Winant told the more than 200 attendees that "like it or not, this subject is so complex that no single decision, legislative, regulatory, or judicial, can resolve it as a whole." Others pointed out that a 1976 DOT Noise Policy for the most part was ineffective and failed to take the issues head on. Moreover, restrictions were already in effect or pending at Kalamazoo, Michigan; Aspen, Colorado; Flying Cloud, Minnesota; and at Santa Monica, Torrance, Van Nuys and Hayward, California. Hornbeck played on the theme of "Commerce and Tranquility — No One Gets a Free Lunch." In his remarks he characterized the airport as "the one mile bridge between the bustle of commerce and the tranquility of the leisure that commerce accords us."

On May 11, 1978, litigation was filed by a local airport group to strike down the Santa Monica jet ban which, except for a brief injunction, had been in effect since 1975. In August NBAA and GAMA made a decision to intervene jointly in the case, which was scheduled for trial in U.S. District Court, Central District of California, Los Angeles. The process of reaching the decision was anguishing. The die was cast, finally, when U.S. Secretary of Transportation Brock Adams brought the leaders of the two associations together and told them the Federal government had decided to support the action to overturn the jet ban. Knowing that high risks were involved and that costs would be extremely large, Hornbeck bravely recommended to NBAA's directorate that it and GAMA move ahead. The issue of an unfairly discriminatory ban on all jet aircraft could not be ignored. The fact was that many jets were quieter than piston airplanes, which were wholly exempt from the restriction. It also was obvious that hundreds of airport operators all over the United States were awaiting the Santa Monica results and would act in accordance with them. NBAA's and GAMA's Boards gave their unanimous approvals to the plan. Judith Richards Hope, talented Washington attorney who had served as transportation chief in President Ford's Domestic Council, was selected as the association's attorney. McIntosh and McCarty were given principal NBAA staff responsibility for helping prepare materials and arguments for the case. Winant and his GAMA counterpart, Stimpson, were handed the day-to-day responsibility of developing strategy with Mrs. Hope.

The year was noteworthy on other counts. The second major international seminar, held in April, drew 73 participants and earned itself a permanent annual place in NBAA's programs. Knowledgeable speakers addressed the group: Committee Chairman Stevens; Alan White of the United Kingdom's Civil Aviation Authority; Peter Nowlan, Transport Canada; and David Sheftel, FAA. Bill Dennison of Amerada Hess and Ronald J. Guerra, Kaiser Steel corporation and former NBAA Director, made presentations which highlighted the aircraft operators' perspective on international travel and its peculiar challenges.

Citizen groups demonstrated that they disagreed with the Santa Monica, California, City Council's total jet ban at the local airport. NBAA and GAMA, as intervenor plaintiffs, played leading roles in court action that abolished the ban in 1979.

NBAA's invested reserve funds, a planned buffer against unanticipated costs such as those for the forthcoming Santa Monica case, passed through the million dollar mark in the spring, a remarkable increase from the $89,738 reported in 1958.

Another attempt at making pilot loss of license insurance available got underway following July, 1978 Board approval. American Insurance Marketing mounted the sales effort. All concerned crossed their fingers and hoped that the new plan would achieve goals which had proved unattainable in several earlier attempts. Within two years, however, it became necessary to change insurance carriers and by 1981 the plan faltered; work aimed at making it viable continued into 1985, when yet another program was launched.

As a result of misuse of a company airplane for political campaign purposes by Bert Lance, the Carter OMB director, stiff new regulations on carriage of Federal candidates were enacted in August, 1978. Lance resigned in 1977 in a furor involving writeoff of corporate aircraft costs for trips which were judged to be political in nature. Even the President had been a passenger on a campaign tour of the southern states. The Federal Election Commission (FEC) rules permitted payments for political use, and thus ran head on into FAA's not-for-hire regulations. Obligingly and without prompting, FAA issued an exemption for such payments, raising an ineffective din among many in the air taxi industry, which felt business would likely be stolen away.

July marked the successful, yet limited, end of a tortuous two and a half year attempt to have the Federal Communications Commisson (FCC) affirm that a proposed Minnesota broadcasting antenna tower would be a hazard to aerial navigation. NBAA took its protest to FCC when it appeared that two FAA determinations of hazard would be ignored and that permission might be granted to radio station WCCO's owners to build the 1,200 foot tower. Extraordinarily long quasi-judicial hearings before an FCC law judge ended with his declaration the tower would be a hazard. But he stopped short of affirming that FCC should be bound by FAA determinations and thus failed to recognize the latter agency's pre-eminence in navigable airspace questions. Seemingly endless appeals and other actions followed, including parallel cases which dealt only with the broadcast signal aspects of WCCO's proposal. By the early 1980's the idea of constructing the tall tower appeared to have died and NBAA could look back on an incomplete but precedent setting victory.

St. Louis, for the third time, acted as host to NBAA's annual meeting. The 1978 gathering September 12–14 was yet another record setter. Registration was up by 16 percent to 8,226; and there were 215 exhibitor companies using 671 booths at the Cervantes Center. Maintenance and operations meetings alone attracted 1,200 persons.

Three-year Director terms were voted for Hornbeck, Morton J. Brown, AMP, Inc., Eagleton, and Board newcomers Robbins and Thomas M. Miller, Manville Service Company.

The standing committee chairmen who were named at St. Louis were:

Airports — Gerk
Airspace/Air Traffic Control — George Wiederhold, Jr., Esmark
Helicopter — Arthur Lippa, Jr., U.S. Steel
Corporate Aviation Management — Leo L. Brown
Energy — Louis P. Teer, Combustion Engineering
International Operations — Stevens
Operations — Gerlach
Technical — Jack A. Flory, General Motors

Leddy L. Greever, Vice President, Beech Aircraft Corporation, one of the pioneers who attended CAOA's first forum in 1948, was named to a two-year Associate Advisor position, taking the place of W. Russell Miller, who resigned in July.

At the major symposium Clare Rice, president of Rockwell's Collins Avionics Group, looked into his crystal ball and saw major changes on the flight decks of business aircraft. There would be rapid and massive movement to solid state digital systems and microprocessors, eliminating the need for much existing cockpit paperwork. "All of the procedures associated with each piece of paper are becoming more complex and more critical," said Rice. The day of the glass cockpit was fast approaching, providing means by which "the pilot will be fully informed about aircraft perfomance, navigation situations, and systems status." This quantum leap forward would be made over the next few years.

Late summer saw Mason's departure from staff to become the chief staff person of NASAO. The NBAA information services post was taken in November by Richard Lampl, who brought with him sixteen years of public relations experience, much of it with Sikorsky and AVCO Lycoming.

The year's end presented NBAA two headaches of major but transient nature and one major source of fundamental change which was still unfolding into the mid-1980's.

Transitory but vexing FAA proposals called for tight restrictions in the wake of a frightful in-flight collision of an airliner and a single engine piston plane over San Diego. NBAA, GAMA and AOPA presented joint testimony to a U.S. Senate hearing in San Diego, opposing FAA's massive and unneeded reaction. It would have created 80 new Terminal Radar Service Areas (TRSA) and 44 new highly regulated Terminal Control Areas (TCA). Most air traffic above 10,000 feet would be subject to positive control east of the Mississippi River, and at more than 12,500 feet west of it.

Also fleeting but serious at the time was a possible 5 percent shortfall in petroleum supply, the result of an embargo placed on shipments from Iran, where the American Embassy had been stormed and all occupants taken hostage.

Of much more permanent overall impact on aviation was the enactment in October, 1978 of airline deregulation. NBAA, and Winant in particular, felt the long term effects would be beneficial to business aviation. Overcrowding on profitable airline routes and the unreliability of service to less economically desirable points would, it was felt, give impetus to business aircraft use. But the initial years of deregulation did not produce the anticipated windfall. Other forces also came into play and three years after deregulation's onset business aircraft sales began to slide toward a deep pit. Many causes were involved, and while deregulation may have been minor among them, it nevertheless had a role.

McCreary, looking back on the situation 10 years later, saw a continuing challenge of political nature:

> *... As a result of deregulation, more and more ordinary citizens are traveling by air, because it's cheaper. And the bus companies are gradually going out of business, as cheaper airline fares lure their former customers into the crowded skies. The political consequences of this basic shift in market forces are profound, as more and more voters become airline passengers. If the ATC system becomes so crowded that somebody is going to have to be crowded-out, guess who that's going to be! There is the long-term threat (of deregulation) to business aviation.* [3]

January, 1979, was the starting point of a long series of seminars led by staff member John A. Pope on ways to create a business aircraft department operations manual. The basic teaching tool was the NBAA *Recommended Standards Manual.* Board member Robert E. Breiling joined Pope in leading several of these popular seminars, which were conducted on a semi-annual basis over the next five years.

Gerlach's Operations Committee brought 26 member company and staff personnel together in Alexandria, Virginia January 22 and 23 to mull over the FAA's disputed air space proposals. Administrator Langhorne M. Bond and Air Traffic Regulations chief William Broadwater attended the wrap-up session and listened attentively. NBAA urged that positive control remain in airspace over 18,000 feet, with less stringent regulation from that floor down to 12,500 feet. Adamant opposition was expressed to an FAA plan to create a new category of flight, to be called controlled visual flight (CVF). The plan was later dropped.

NBAA's flying safety awards program was broadened in 1979 to include recognition for helicopter pilots and owners. At award time there were 37 helicopter recipients who had each accumulated 2,000 or more safe hours. There were 12 company awards and 9 helicopter maintenance awards. Fixed wing safety awards set new records, with 1,076 million milers, 213 half-million milers, 252 companies, and 147 company maintenance recipients.

Reflecting the rapid growth in membership, NBAA data showed a member company combined fleet of surprising size, totaling 3,959 units:

    306 turbojets, more than 30,000 pounds
    1,120 turbojets, less than 30,000 pounds
    298 turboprops, more than 12,500 pounds
    548 turboprops, less than 12,500 pounds
    1,134 piston powered airplanes
    552 helicopters
    1 balloon (owned by a Cincinnati radio station)

By spring, growing internationalization required additional staff attention. William H. Stine, II, joined NBAA in the new position of Manager, Plans and International Services. Stine came from the Hoffman Pilot Center, Denver, where he was instructor in fixed and rotor wing aircraft. Previously, he had flown for member companies Sprague Electric and Brock Engineering.

The perplexing Santa Monica issues went to trial in early summer 1979, and after six weeks of courtroom argument, Judge Irving R. Hill issued his decision. The jet ban was struck down as unjustly discriminatory, unconstitutional, and a burden on interstate commerce. NBAA and GAMA prevailed on this central point, but Judge Hill let stand most of the other restrictions on training and helicopter flight, and permitted continued use of SENEL (single event) noise measuring techniques.

City Attorney Richard Knickerbocker, reacting quickly, convinced the city council to lower the established noise limit from 100 decibels, measured by SENEL techniques, to 85. NBAA-GAMA attorney Hope quickly protested this, and Judge Hill delivered a tongue lashing to Knickerbocker, terming the council's action as nothing more than a means of circumventing the court decision. The noise limit went back to 100 decibels pending further court action. The Santa Monica Evening Outlook took a dim view of the city's intentions. A November 6 editorial said "the noise issue . . . is now secondary. The primary objective of the city is no longer to limit noise; it is to force airport businesses to move away or close without having to pay them fair compensation."

The Santa Monica litigation dragged on into the early 1980's, both on appeal and in two derivative cases. NBAA's share of legal and associated costs was nearly $500,000. In the end the city agreed to keep the airport open at least until the year 2015, as was stipulated when it received Federal grants.

Bauer's summation of Santa Monica's true meaning was classic.

> *I don't think we did any earth shaking things, and it was costly. But the benefit to general aviation and NBAA is going to well repay the difficulties and the cost in the long term. Someone had to step in at that time. There was a developing trend to close down small airports for various reasons, primarily noise. If logic hadn't prevailed . . . it would have snowballed. The NBAA-GAMA stand slowed it all down and prevented a host of other problems which would have created bitter battles."[4]*

Not mentioned by Bauer was another facet of Santa Monica. It gave NBAA household meaning in aviation in terms of recognition and respect. On the purely practical side, the case was a tremendous boost to growth in membership.

NBAA's continuing efforts in the energy field resulted in publication of *CONSERVE: Energy Efficient Profile for Business Aircraft.* The book, developed under Teer's and Cooke's guidance, was an outstanding success, widely distributed not only in the United States, but offshore as well. It focused on reliable, fuel-saving, safe operating techniques in all phases of flight.

Atlanta was the site, September 25–27, of the 1979 annual meeting, another record breaker with 9,893 attendees and 245 exhibiting companies that used 810 booths. Press registrations reached 225, with 18 countries represented, strong testimony to the global scope of the event.

The Chairman position passed from Hornbeck to Bauer. McCreary was named Vice Chairman and David M. Woodrow, 3M, Treasurer. Three-year Director terms were voted for Beach, Breiling, Leo L. Brown, General Mills, McCreary and Nields. Norman A. Wollberg, Cooper Airmotive, was appointed to an Associate Advisor post.

Membership passed 2,000 for the first time three weeks prior to the meeting and Hornbeck, in his report to members, said that one word could accurately sum up the tumultuous and eventful year: "BIG."

Bauer designated standing committee chairmen at Atlanta:

Airports — Gerk
Airspace/Air Traffic Control — Wiederhold
Corporate Aviation Management — Raleigh E. Drennon, The
    BFGoodrich Company
Energy — Teer
Helicopter — Lippa
International Operations — Guerra
Operations — Gerlach
Technical — Flory

Never before had so many business turbojets and turboprops been produced, and the end of the long growth curve was still not in sight. But 1979 was the peak year for sales of piston powered airplanes. A steep drop began and continued unabated into the late years of the 1980's. The top of the line, the sophisticated new business aircraft market, continued to grow through 1980 and 1981. The 1979 worldwide production data for such aircraft tracked sales of 395 turbojets and 690 medium turboprops. Medium twin piston production for the year was 993; for light twin pistons it was 2,000.[5]

As 1980 began Breiling resigned from the Board, as he was taking a new position with an Associate member firm, SimuFlite. The next month Leslie H. Walker, Standard Oil of California, was named to an interim term.

Yet another major FAA rules proposal resulted in a special Operations Committee session called by Gerlach in Alexandria. This time the agency planned to create a new FAR Part 125 which would cover aircraft with more than 5,000 pounds payload and the capability of carrying 19 or more passengers. The expressed aim was to eliminate "illegal and unsafe unauthorized commercial charter and lease operators." Yet the proposal threw out a much bigger net. NBAA felt the aim fitted none of its constituency, and sought to exclude business aircraft, either as a class or by individual cases. The association's efforts paid off. By autumn of 1980 FAA granted deviation authority to individual operators, removing about 100 member companies from potential coverage under the rule.

Efforts were renewed in the Congress to enact a new airports-airways development program but they ground to a standstill. NBAA and the many other aviation elements with which it had worked cooperatively for enactment (12 national associations) voiced their deep disappointment. Growth in air traffic, along with shifting patterns created by deregulation, was quickly saturating existing facilities and the computer-based system of tracking aircraft. A bold development and renewal program was urgently needed. NBAA on several occasions acted as the spokesman for the unified aviation group before committees of the Congress. Winant chaired the coalition, which met on more than 30 occasions for more than a year to develop consensus and plan tactics. The sticking point for new legislation came when Senator Howard Cannon, Senate Aviation Subcommittee Chairman, announced plans to defederalize the airports aid program by taking major airports

The NBAA Board of Directors was photographed during the summer of 1980 at Indian Lakes, Illinois. From left, seated, John H. Winant, President, William F. Gilbert, Weyerhaeuser Company, David M. Woodrow, 3M and NBAA Treasurer, Harry C. McCreary, McCreary Tire and Rubber and NBAA Vice Chairman, Earle W. Bauer, Marathon Oil and NBAA Chairman, Richard I. Hornbeck, General Electric, and James F. Nields, Ware Knitters, Inc.; standing, Morton J. Brown, AMP Inc., Leslie H. Walker, Standard Oil of California, Ross Beach, Kansas Natural Gas Company, Thomas M. Miller, Manville Service Company, Leo L. Brown, General Mills, Otto C. Pobanz, Federated Department Stores, Charles E. Morris, Mobil Corporation, Norman A. Wollberg, Cooper Airmotive and Associate Advisor to the Board, and Lee L. Robbins, Corning Glass Works. (Absent: J. W. Eagleton, Shell Oil and Leddy L. Greever, Beech Aircraft Corporation and Associate Advisor)

out of it. The House of Representatives walked away from further work on the bill, feeling the Senate concept would derail the prospect for passage. NBAA's actions as spokesman for the aviation alliance was characteristic of its role as mediator. Years later Greever singled out the association for praise. "NBAA was very influential," he said, "in gathering together other associations so that the general aviation segments could work in unison with each other, instead of having some go in one direction, others in another. That was one of the great contributions of NBAA. It was always consistent. It was not above changing its mind when the facts so indicated and it was never above going along with the group in the interest of unity. It did not seek to gather all the glory for just itself."[6]

September 23–25, 1980 was the occasion of the annual meeting in Kansas City. For the first time, attendance exceeded 10,000, with the final count 11,058. The city's convention center was the setting for the 928 booths occupied by 246 companies. One journal was moved to say that "fears that the recession and location of Kansas city would hurt attendance proved groundless. The continued expansion of business aviation and intense interest in NBAA activities proved to be a strong magnet . . ."

Elected to three-year Board terms were Bauer; John S. Broome, Broome Ranches; Max B. Moore, Jr., Southern Natural Gas Company; Pobanz and

Woodrow. Walker was voted a two-year term. McCreary found it necessary to resign as Director and Vice Chairman as of September 30. "Our company had completely changed its marketing approach and our need for a company plane had disappeared ... I'll always regret missing the honor of serving as Chairman," he wrote in 1988.[7] As of October 1, Woodrow became Vice Chairman and Robbins was elected Treasurer.

William B. Watt, Executive Air Fleet Corporation, was designated for a two-year Associate Advisor post, taking Greever's place. Reminiscing about his service, both on the Board and the Associate Membership Advisory Council, Greever said, "I was very deeply impressed with how conscientious and hard working the Board was. They were intense about their committee assignments and were a serious bunch. They're a hell of a group of people." Greever, speaking principally for the companies that were exhibitors at NBAA annual meetings, had high praise for the concept which underlay the Associate council. "It gave people an excellent opportunity to express themselves. (As exhibitors) they are in a sense customers of NBAA. They want to be competitive and impressive in their displays. They deserve a voice in the setting of convention policy. The Council gives them the opportunity to be heard, and they are not bashful about making their opinions known."[8]

The Kansas City maintenance and operations meetings attracted a record 1,910 attendees. The TFE731 engine session alone attracted 560. The Learjet series drew 210.

The Board announced a goal of 3,000 members by the end of Fiscal 1985, believing it "to be realistically achievable." In 1980 there were 2,217 member companies. The reach for 3,000 slightly exceeded NBAA's grasp. In 1985 the total was 2,941, just 59 short of the ambitious goal. Financial strength of the association was first rate in 1980. Woodrow said at the annual meeting that income for the year was $1,504,605, a 21.5 percent increase over 1979. Expenses were $1,388,355, an 11 percent increase.

One portion of the Kansas City meeting was a profoundly moving moment of aviation history. The Award for Meritorious Service to Aviation went jointly to Sir Frank Whittle and Hans von Ohain, English and German born engineers who had, separately and independently of each other, developed the first jet engines which actually powered aircraft. With precious little government backing, Whittle built an engine in 1937 but it was not given a chance to prove itself until 1941. von Ohain's engine powered its first flight in 1939. Together these two men made the first great breakthroughs which in time revolutionized the industry and eventually changed the face of the globe. The most remarkable thing about their stories, and NBAA's role, was that the two had never met before they shared the spotlight in Kansas City.

During the run-up to the 1980 meeting McCarty left staff to work at the Air Transport Association's regional office in Atlanta. The vacant position was filled in March of the next year when E. H. "Moe" Haupt became Manager, Airport Services, with added duties as helicopter specialist. Coming at a critical moment, Haupt brought with him good credentials: a 21-year Navy career with final rank as Lieutenant Commander and 6,000 hours of fixed and rotor wing piloting time. The standing committee chairmen named by Bauer in 1980 were:

Airports — Fred Gammon, Pan Am Services
Airspace/Air Traffic Control — Wiederhold
Corporate Aviation Management — Drennon
Energy — Teer
Helicopter — David O'Keefe, Mobil Corporation
International Operators (new committee name) — Guerra
Operations — John M. Gallagher, Gannett Company
Technical — Flory

The year 1981 brought the nation a new President, a Republican majority in the U.S. Senate, and in August the first air traffic controller strike in history.

Congress again labored over a new airports-airways development act. Winant once more went to Capitol Hill to speak on behalf of a multi-association coalition consisting of NBAA, GAMA, CAAA, NATA, AOCI, NASAO and AAAE. Later in the year, to emphasize the importance of improving the nation's reliever airports, NBAA, GAMA and ATA joined in a unique effort. It was the Reliever Airport Program (RAP), funded by grants from the three associations and staffed by enterprising Richard G. Dinning, Vice President and Special Counsel for U.S. Air, who devoted half of each week to carrying out the program. Specific needs were developed for 15 major metropolitan areas. Dinning visited each one, trying to convince local government leaders of the need for action to turn around the growing loss of vitally needed airports.

In February, Preston S. Parish, The Upjohn Company, was named an interim NBAA Director, taking McCreary's place. Parish soon rose to leadership positions in the association, including the Chairman post.

The year's greatest preoccupation was with the growing threat of a controllers' strike. PATCO, the union for the group, became more militant as the months passed. The contract with the government expired March 15, but talks continued. Robert Poli, PATCO president, headed the union delegation; FAA officials spoke for the government.

A June 22 strike deadline passed when Transportation Secretary Drew Lewis offered a $40 million package which Poli promised to take to the membership. Six weeks later, the offer was rejected, with PATCO demanding new terms 17 times more costly than in the June package.

The strike was on. Beginning at 12:01 a.m., Monday, August 8, 1981, all but a handful of controllers failed to report for duty. President Reagan gave controllers 48 hours to return to work or be considered as having resigned. Only a small number went back to their jobs. This left the system no recourse but to operate at 20 to 30 percent of normal staffing.

Having made extensive preparations, NBAA put its emergency plans into action the moment the strike began, and the association's conference room looked more like a war operation room for the next several months. Building on experience gained in the 1973-74 fuel crisis, NBAA put into motion a massive telephone information service, containing direct lines and incoming 800-line services, manned initially on a 24-hour a day basis. After talking with FAA Administrator Helms on the strike's first day, Winant conferred with NBAA Chairman Bauer. Together, they concluded that NBAA's members would give every support to the government in what unquestionably was an illegal strike. A mailgram went out to all members, asking that flights be restricted to vital missions during a 72-hour period, enabling the government to stabilize the air traffic system and plan how maximum service could be given.

Fortunately the government did not invoke a strike emergency plan it developed in 1980. That plan would have given short shrift to all but scheduled airline flights. For a time progress was slow. At times only aircraft weighing more than 12,500 pounds were given clearances. Slowly, flow control procedures were put into effect. In September, a General Aviation Reservation System (GAR) was devised. It went into effect October 19, and was essentially a gigantic expansion of the concept developed in 1969 for making reservations at the so-called high density airports. Meanwhile, a goal was set to hold IFR (instrument) flying to 75 percent of pre-strike volume. The actual volume handled in the strike's first week was only 25 percent. Later and at snail's pace, restrictions were eased. High altitude flights were exempted from the GAR, and international flights were placed outside its scope. Conditions improved, in large measure because of NBAA staff efforts taken in concert with those of other major aviation groups.

Administrator Helms made his first public appearance of the strike at NBAA's annual meeting in Anaheim, California, September 15-17. In the front row of the huge auditorium was a handful of PATCO members; the others in the standing room only audience of 1,000 were NBAA meeting attendees. Bauer's introduction brought prolonged applause which turned to cheers, lasting several minutes. There was no question of where NBAA stood.

Scott E. "Scotty" Miller put a new record in the books by chairing his fourth annual meeting committee in 1981; as in the past, his work was outstanding, evidence of his devotion to NBAA and its people. Meeting attendance was 11,658. There were 312 exhibitors with 1,146 booths, both new records by a wide margin. Among the many upbeat events of Anaheim were the founding ceremonies of the International Business Aviation Council, Ltd. (IBAC), culmination of 30 long years of window shopping for a global federation.

Bauer left the chair at Anaheim, turning the gavel over to Woodrow, who almost simultaneously became IBAC's first Chairman. Robbins was elected NBAA Vice Chairman and Nields Treasurer. Three year Director terms were voted for Drennon, Frederick Haap, III, The Mead Corporation, Hornbeck, Miller and Robbins. Parish was elected to a one-year term. Frederick W. Becker, Airwork Corporation, was named as the new Associate Advisor.

Scott E. "Scotty" Miller established at least three firsts in NBAA's history. He hosted the first hospitality suite (1950), was the first Associate Advisor to the Board (1964), and was the only person to chair five annual meeting committees (1960, 1965, 1974, 1981, 1986). With his wife, Lila, left, he greeted Moya Lear, widow of the fabled Bill Lear, in 1981.

Woodrow, a Newton, Iowa native, received a Bachelor's degree from Iowa State University in 1947 and a Masters degree in aeronautic engineering from the State University of Iowa. A 3M employee from 1948, he had been a project engineer and worked in three company divisions before being named Director of Aviation in 1968. Extremely active in Minneapolis-St. Paul aviation affairs, he was also an association leader beginning with chairmanship of the 1971 annual meeting.

Bauer's term as Chairman was remarkable. It came during a period when business aviation flourished but at the same time faced intimidating pressures and threats. As Hornbeck had done in the Santa Monica case, Bauer showed great courage when he took a firm position on the controller's strike. It was a bombshell issue demanding strong resolve. It received it. Commenting later, Bauer said NBAA's position "made a precedent for future FAA Administrators. There was NBAA, a sensible, reliable, logical organization that was willing to stand and face the public and press in support of what it thought was good procedure and good policy. NBAA took its position when it was difficult to find people willing to stand up and be counted."[9]

Incoming Chairman Woodrow announced his appointments to the standing committee chairs at Anaheim:

Airports — Gammon
Air Space/Air Traffic Control — Charles F. Harmon, Jr.,
    Carborundum Co.

William Horn, Jr., Manager, Airspace/Air Traffic Control Services, and Frederick B. McIntosh, Director, Operational Services, played central roles in NBAA's vast hot-line telephone information program during the air traffic controller strike in late 1981.

Corporate Aviation Management — Virgil L. Williams,
    The Upjohn Company
Helicopter — F. Lynn Clough, Tenneco
International Operators — Raymond P. Ward, Dresser Industries, Inc.
Operations — Gallagher
Technical — Martin Lipstein, Johnson & Johnson

In the weeks after the annual meeting, NBAA's hot-line strike information service performed amazing feats. The period August through October, the toughest weeks of the strike, brought well over 100,000 calls, either for one-to-one questioning, or for taped messages on the 800 lines. In September, the high point, weekday calls totalled 16,662. Overnight 800-line calls totalled 12,259. Weekend volume dropped, but only to 8,789. The information covered rules, congested areas, flow control status, and individual sectors and airports. It was all obviously of tremendous value, not only to business aviation, but to a much wider audience. There was no question that the service greatly eased the strain and stress of the strike. By November staff member William Horn, Jr., could say "the system is basically safe, but because of its limited manpower is inherently fragile. An overload anywhere in the system can have a serious impact on capacity. Keep NBAA informed."

The end of the year brought a reluctant but determined decision in the Westchester County Airport situation. Negotiations to reach a peaceful settlement of the noise issue became deadlocked, and there appeared to be only one means for getting matters off dead center. NBAA's Board determined it had to take the issues to court. With evident reluctance the FAA agreed to join in the action. The threat of a suit, however, resulted in an agreement to enter a stipulation December 14, 1981. This would trigger a 60-day noise monitoring program which, it was hoped, would help design suitable and acceptable noise abatement procedures rather than result in drastic action such as a curfew.

Year-end figures showed that NBAA was continuing to grow at a healthy pace, even though there were signs of a slowdown in the manufacturing industry. Total membership was 2,466, almost exactly three times the total of 824 at the time of the major 1971 by-laws changes which set a new course for NBAA.

Year end also brought the final crest of the great waves of production of business aircraft. It was the last of the great years which began with 1977.

NBAA data for 1981 showed world production of business turbojets at 592 units. For medium turboprops the total was 911.[10] These were the largest numbers in history, but they heralded the beginning of a steep slide downward. By 1984, turbojet production was down to 268, the turboprop to 227. Together these showed a decline to only one-third of 1981's peak. Almost overnight, the market had gone from boom to bust. Winds of change began to blow over the business aviation landscape. Days of trial, years of challenge began for NBAA and for all elements of business aviation.

NOTES TO CHAPTER 8

1. Earle W. Bauer, Findlay, Ohio, audiotape interview with J. H. Winant, October 22, 1987.

2. *Business Week,* February 8, 1976, pp. 62ff.

3. Letter, Harry C. McCreary, Indiana, Pennsylvania, to J. H. Winant, May 11, 1987.

4. Bauer tape, October 22, 1987.

5. "Business Aviation's Age of Discontinuity," speech by J. H. Winant, Coronado, California, November 21, 1985.

6. Leddy L. Greever, Wichita, Kansas, audiotape interview with J. H. Winant, July 13, 1988.

7. McCreary letter, May 11, 1987.

8. Greever tape, July 13, 1988.

9. Bauer tape, October 11, 1987.

10. Winant speech, November 21, 1985.

Chapter 9

FORGING THE GLOBAL LINK: IBAC, 1980–1981

THE HOPE THAT BUSINESS AVIATION INSTITUTIONS COULD transcend national boundaries was first expressed in 1950 when Canadians sought to examine an affiliation with NBAA. No decisive actions took place, however, until three decades later when, in rapid succession, a series of events created the International Business Aviation Council, Ltd. (IBAC).

Leading up to the conclusive period there were probings, transient interest and periodic contact between elements based on both sides of the Atlantic. And, during most of the 1970's, there was churning activity among United Kingdom and continental European principals, with deep division of opinion as to national versus regional structures, as well as the status of air taxi operations.

The possibility of some type of international bond was a natural byproduct of the creation of the Business Aircraft Users Association (BAUA) of the United Kingdom and an independent Canadian Business Aircraft Association (CBAA) in 1961. These groups added two more national players to the field which NBAA had occupied since 1946.

BAUA's rootstock was planted in 1960, when Tim A. Vigors, Managing Director of Vigors Aviation, United Kingdom Piper distributors, and Ross R. Stephenson, Aviation Secretary for the Royal Aero Club, began to talk. The subject was the need for institutionalizing the interests and needs of business aircraft operators. Their first plan was to form a special committee of the aero club, but a meeting of December 15, 1960, altered the course. The 50 or so attendees, mostly senior management persons, decided an independent organization was required. A steering committee was put into motion and on May 18, 1961, the BAUA was officially registered. Stephenson became the Chief Executive staff head, a position he occupied for more than 20 years.[1]

At almost the same time the Canadians took their organization out of the aircraft owners and pilots group. Eleanor Beck soon was hired as staff secretary and remained in charge of the CBAA office at Toronto's Malton Airport until 1980, when Harvey F. Protheroe became Executive Director.

An April, 1965, meeting at the Queen Elizabeth Hotel in Montreal brought representatives of NBAA, BAUA and CBAA together. There was warmth concerning prospects for an international body, but the fire did not light. William K. Lawton, Kenneth McAlpine and Fred Hotson went back to their organizations with carefully worded, positive recommendations. The goal was an organization which would, "Exchange information . . . (and) become recognized by I.C.A.O. (and) participate, after recognition, in I.C.A.O. matters through volunteer — and later professional staff — representatives."[2] Despite the intentions, no tangible actions followed.

Early contacts, including those of 1965, involved national organizations. A new element emerged in 1969. Separate visits to NBAA's offices by two colleagues from The Netherlands made it clear the idea of a pan-European association was being considered. Captain Splinter Ad. Spierenburg, Manager of N.V. Philips' impressive flight department, was first to call. Later in the year, D. "Dick" Berlijn, who would become staff chief of the Holland Business Aircraft Association (HBAA) in a few months' time, made his inspection visit to NBAA. Writing the following July, Berlijn told of explorations aimed at "sensing the opportunities for a European Business Aircraft Association."[3] He went on to say it had become "evident that the idea has definite possibilities." Contemplated was "an administrative and consultative umbrella (which) should concentrate on the communication between (national groups) in order to keep them as up-to-date as necessary on all relevant information." Berlijn hoped the European organization would be founded soon.

But what emerged, in 1971, was a Conference of European Corporate Aviation Interests (CECAI), a tenuous attempt to reconcile divergent opinions on how to organize the business aviation community. Differences deepened as the years passed, with many on the continent favoring a pan-European federation and those in the United Kingdom leaning toward creation of discrete national bodies. This division was aggravated by a parallel disagreement on whether commercial air taxi operators should have full membership privileges.

In late 1976 an attempt, promoted by Spierenburg, to use the Flight Safety Foundation (FSF) as a means for rallying a European group failed. CECAI, consisting of the existing national groups, HBAA, BAUA and BDI (the federation of West German industries) decided that "the time is not yet ripe, politically, for the setting up of a European Business Aircraft Association (EBAA) with individual company membership;" efforts should be directed at "formation of national associations of business aircraft user companies."[4]

Yet, in June, 1977, evidently without the full implications being explained to or understood by BAUA[5] and BDI, it was announced that the International Business Aircraft Association (Europe) (IBAA(E)) was being formed in Eindhoven. To make way for it, the HBAA was dissolved and its Chief Executive, L. "Len"

Donkersloot took a similar position with IBAA(E). Announcement of the new group said that "contrary to NBAA and BAUA, IBAA (Europe) membership is open to commercial operators of business aircraft, as it is felt they are faced with the same problems as the private business aircraft operators."[6]

Stephenson protested that "It was never made clear, before this, that the H.B.A.A. was actually going to disappear . . . I think many of the recipients of your news will be somewhat surprised . . . when they find out the make-up of the I.B.A.A.'s present membership, which is so very predominantly commercial . . ."[7]

A response from Donkersloot said tartly that "the only difference between our philosophies is that the B.A.U.A. prefers a closed and 'select' shop and we like a wide open approach."[8]

The fragile fabric of CECAI and the *detente* it created were torn apart. For the next several years business aircraft leadership in the United Kingdom and West Germany walked a pathway separate from that of the European entity whose interests centered on Eindhoven.

During the period beginning with 1974 another force was at work on the other side of the Atlantic, trying to drum up serious interest in a business aviation federation which would unite all continents. John H. Winant, NBAA's President, began the pilgrimage at a meeting of CBAA's board in Toronto, June 7, 1974. There, he spoke at length and coined a new name while he urged consideration of "a mini-ICAO, an International Business Aviation Council, which could be a very useful forum for the discussion and solution of problems which affect business aviation across the board," irrespective of national boundaries.[9] The Canadians agreed in principle. Contact between the two organizations continued while they monitored developments across the Atlantic.

Later that year Winant met Stephenson in London. A preliminary discussion of IBAC was cordial but unproductive. Another meeting in 1976 kept the concept alive. NBAA, meanwhile, also continued its dialogue with Canadian and European business aviation leadership, and waited for a serious initiative to come from abroad.

June, 1980 brought a telephone call from Stephenson to Winant. Stephenson had learned that Winant planned a vacation in England in the autumn. Would Winant be interested, asked Stephenson, in "making his pitch" for creation of IBAC to a group in London?

On Guy Fawkes Night, November 5, 1980, interested persons gathered at BAUA's invitation. The discussion, continuing into dinner, took place at Shell Centre, just across Westminster Bridge from the Houses of Parliament. Present were William H. Alexander, BAUA Chairman, and BAUA Council members Simon Dyer, John Feltham, Clifford R. Moss, and Rex A. Smith; Jorg Seizer, BDI of West Germany; John Velenturf, IBAA(E); Stephenson and his wife, Paula; and Winant. CBAA, invited, could not be present, but sent a wholly supportive message.

A 25-minute presentation by Winant identified areas of shared international concern. Included were airspace access and charges, fueling costs and credit problems, airport facilitation, technical and safety matters, certification, and, above all else, the value of unified representation to international authorities, ICAO foremost. Stress was laid on the point that IBAC would be a voluntary federation of independent organizations. No member would cede its autonomy. By evening's end a fundamental decision was made. The governing authority of each organization present, plus CBAA, would be asked to support a working group whose purpose was to build the framework for IBAC.

Among items touched upon November 5 were the challenge of defining commercial operators, use of English as the IBAC language, the thorny issue of national versus regional organizations, and cost sharing to support the contemplated organization. Agreement was reached that the secretariat (later renamed Administration) would revolve among national members and that NBAA would take the first turn. Finally, BAUA agreed to chair the working group, at least through the initial phases.

Ratification of the November 5 accords came quickly and working group sessions were set for March 30 — April 3, 1981 at BAUA's offices, 50 Rochester Row, London. The sessions were sometimes stormy and it was difficult to achieve the goals set the previous November. But in the end, the group agreed on a document titled, "IBAC 5th Final Draft,"[10] in which vital concepts were spelled out. A statement of object led off:

> *To form an International Council of National Business Aviation organizations, in order to ensure that present and future needs and interests of International Business Aviation are clearly presented to, and understood by, those national and international authorities and organizations whose responsibilities include any administration which may influence the safety, efficiency or economic use of Business Aircraft operating internationally.*

Two types of membership were to be established: National and Regional; Council officers would be provided by National members, and the secretariat would rotate among National members.

Alexander joined the working group at its final session, a luncheon meeting April 3 at Browns Hotel, Dover Street. Also present were all those who had spent the previous three days laboring over the basic agreement: J. Rae Audette, CBAA; Seizer, BDI; Velenturf, IBAA(E); Winant, NBAA; and Stephenson, BAUA. Mrs. Stephenson, secretary to the group, also attended.

Many of the broad precepts were refined at Browns. NBAA would take responsibility for drafting articles and by-laws. Agreement was reached that incorporation would preferably take place in the United States, and that the founding of IBAC would be celebrated at NBAA's annual meeting in Anaheim, California, September 14, 1981.[11]

Left open for clarification in the months leading up to Anaheim were some of the troublesome issues, principally those relating to IBAC's granting of jurisdiction to regional groups. Better geographical definition was needed, and most agreed that representation could include only specified nations in which a regional body actually had members.

Finally, those present at the working group sessions agreed that their organizations would be the founder members of IBAC. Further discussion of interest on the part of a South African association would be pursued separately by Winant.

Soon after the London sessions, BAUA turned the working group chair over to NBAA. Ratification of the agreements was given promptly by all bodies and IBAC was incorporated in the District of Columbia, June 23, 1981.

NBAA's circulation of draft by-laws in June resulted in one final contentious aspect of the national versus regional dispute. Final resolution, tightening the London accord, was that Regional members would be given IBAC recognition in those specified nations where they had members and where no national organization existed. This and several other last minute changes to by-laws were worked out in a Sunday afternoon session at Anaheim, September 13, 1981, with Earle W. Bauer, NBAA Chairman, presiding.

The next morning the founders, except for BDI, assembled in the grand ballroom of the Disneyland Hotel to take part in a ceremonial by-laws signing. Each organization's principal officer spoke briefly of hopes for the future. High level officials of the United States Department of State and Federal Aviation Administration, as well as Transport Canada, congratulated the founders[12] and welcomed creation of a potentially powerful international aviation voice.

Among the stated purposes of the new organization was provision of a pool of knowledge, experience and general information on which members could draw. Further, IBAC tasked itself with promoting ever widening recognition of the importance of international business aircraft flights. The new organization also would support and, wherever possible, work with ICAO. Finally, a principal purpose was to encourage the formation of independent national business aviation organizations.

IBAC's first group of officers were elected to terms expiring at the end of 1984. David M. Woodrow, NBAA, was named IBAC Chairman; Alexander, BAUA, Vice Chairman; James F. Nields, NBAA, Treasurer; Winant, NBAA, Corporate Secretary; and William H. Stine, II, NBAA, Executive Officer. Two months after Anaheim, BDI's signature was placed on the founding document at a London dinner which celebrated BAUA's twentieth anniversary.

Years later Bauer looked back on IBAC's formation as one of the most important events of his NBAA years. "The world is shrinking all the time. The avenues (which IBAC has opened) for international cooperation are tremendous. IBAC fills the bill. I'm delighted I had a small part in its beginning."[13]

The events of September, 1981, brought to a successful conclusion 30 years of unfulfilled promise. A new global organization was, finally, brought into being. But its founding did not dam the currents of disagreement which swirled around the

IBAC's Governing Board held its second regular meeting in Hannover, Federal Republic of Germany, in May 1982. From left, seated, Bernd Gans, BDI of West Germany (later German Business Aviation Association), James F. Nields, NBAA and IBAC Treasurer, David M. Woodrow, NBAA and IBAC Chairman, William H. Alexander, Business Aircraft Users Association (UK) and IBAC Vice Chairman, J. Rae Audette, Canadian Business Aircraft Association; standing, John Velenturf, IBAA (Europe), later European Business Aviation Association, J. Frank McFarlane, IBAA (E) staff, William H. Stine, II, NBAA staff and IBAC Executive Officer, John H. Winant, NBAA staff and IBAC Corporate Secretary, Ross R. Stephenson, BAUA staff, and Cor Z. A. Beek, CAA of Southern Africa staff.

national and regional organization advocates. IBAC's creation was, in one view, "the hammer"[14] needed to help forge new national organizations on the European continent, thus circumscribing the role of a regional group. Yet some in the new federation took a different position in the years ahead, feeling that a regional umbrella group could shelter a growing number of national organizations.

Despite internal differences, however, IBAC was an idea whose time had come. Woodrow, describing it in the late 1980's, said, "the formation, founding, nurturing and blossoming of IBAC was certainly a milestone for business aviation. . . . IBAC is NBAA all over again—this time on a global scale. In my opinion, this giant step toward international recognition could not have succeeded without the support and encouragement of NBAA from its very inception."[15]

NBAA's support, given freely in both tangible and intangible ways, continued strongly in the years after IBAC's founding. The global link which IBAC provided was essential to the operations of all its members, and through them, to the growing international business aircraft world. IBAC's formation was a crowning achievement of the era of internationalization of business aviation.

NOTES TO CHAPTER 9

1. Ross R. Stephenson, London, England, audio-tape interview with J.H. Winant, February 8, 1988.

2. BAUA file document, April, 1965, two pages, untitled.

3. Letter, D. Berlijn, HBAA, to R.B. Ward, July 28, 1970.

4. Len Donkersloot, CECAI Circular No. 7, September, 1976, Eindhoven, The Netherlands.

5. Letter, Stephenson to L. Donkersloot, 29 June 1977.

6. Press Release, International Business Aircraft Association (Europe), June 7, 1977, Eindhoven.

7. Stephenson letter, 29 June 1977.

8. Letter, Donkersloot to Stephenson, 5 August 1977.

9. CBAA document, "Notes on Talk by Mr. John Winant, President of NBAA — June 7, 1974," three pages, unsigned.

10. Document, "IBAC 5th Final Draft," BAUA Letterhead, one page, unsigned.

11. Document, "Minutes of a Meeting of the Steering Committee, Held Friday, 3rd April, 1981, at Brown's Hotel. . .," BAUA Letterhead, eight pages.

12. Remarks, Charles H. Dudley, U.S. Department of State; Donald R. Segner, U.S. Federal Aviation Administration; Richard P. St. John, Transport Canada, copies attached to minutes, IBAC Meeting, September 14, 1981.

13. Earle W. Bauer, Findlay, Ohio, audio-tape interview with John H. Winant, October 22, 1987.

14. Stephenson tape.

15. David M. Woodrow, Edina, Minnesota, memorandum to J.H. Winant, April 29, 1988.

Chapter 10

DAYS OF FAITH — YEARS OF CHALLENGE: 1982–1986

THE CLOSING YEARS OF NBAA'S FOURTH DECADE LAID enormous demands on the organization's human and fiscal resources. The sudden, painful crash of the market for new business aircraft shocked both the user community and the supportive industry. Early on, there was no way of judging whether it was a brief aberration caused by the recession which began in 1981, or whether the slump was a sign of deeper fundamental change. Time would confirm it was not a brief pause; the reasons became visible slowly and were extremely varied and complex. Traditional signposts of industry health seemed no longer applicable. Five years later, root causes were still not fully identified.

But NBAA's leadership, stimulated by faith in the Association's mission and spurred by the practical requirements of grappling with challenge, moved the organization onward.

The old spirit of conquest was still alive in the business aviation community. The year 1982 was less than two weeks old when a Gulfstream III, newest model in one of the most successful aircraft families, set a new world record. With Harold Curtis, former NBAA International Operations Committee chairman, heading the flight crew, N100P, owned by National Distillers, flew 23,314.55 statute miles around the world in the record time of 47 hours, 39 minutes. The achievement added one more laurel to those gained in earlier models (first marketed under Grumman's name): the first nonstop transatlantic business flight in 1968, the first United States to Australia/New Zealand flight in 1969, with Ronald J. Guerra, Kaiser Aluminum, and also an NBAA International panel chairman, at the controls; and the first trans-polar flight in 1972 with Louis P. Teer, Combustion Engineering and later on an NBAA Energy Committee chairman, in command.

On January 20–21, IBAC's Governing Board held the new international group's first working meeting. Montreal, capital city of ICAO, was the appropriately chosen site. G. Gamacchio, chief of external relations for ICAO, and Duane W. Freer, Director of the Bureau of Air Navigation, met with IBAC's leaders. Their appearances, along with a reception attended by ICAO delegates from the countries represented in IBAC, helped to begin a process of recognition of the new federation. Major issues discussed by the board included global aspects of the growing aircraft noise dilemma, the need for a precise, ICAO-oriented definition of business aviation, and the conversion of NBAA's international travel and affairs publication into *IBAC Feedback*. In order to build and maintain momentum, the Governing Board decided on a fast paced semi-annual meeting schedule for the first two to three years, with sessions generally alternating on each side of the Atlantic.

As the Westchester County Airport noise-related stipulation went into effect, NBAA called a meeting of member companies to urge cooperation. The purpose was to promote use of safe noise abatement techniques and to request adherence to the modified curfew which extended from midnight to 6:30 a.m. Present at the session, held in Armonk, New York, were many who took prominent roles in the attempts to bring about a peaceful accord: N. S. "Mike" Waterman, International Aviation Services; Joan Caldwell, Northwest Greenwich Association; Samuel Yasgur, Westchester Attorney; FAA Tower Chief Richard Smith; and NBAA Counsel Robert D. Powell. The meeting also served as a showcase for the new Westchester County Airport Advisory Committee (WCAAC), which was for many years co-chaired by Caldwell and former NBAA Chairman Richard I. Hornbeck, General Electric. By March a second stipulation was crafted. It contained a freeze on the curfew and granted an additional 120-day noise monitoring period, making possible collection of spring and early summer data.

NBAA's General Aviation Reservation System (GAR) telephone hot line service reflected slow but steady improvement in air traffic control staffing. By March, calls for information dropped to a monthly total of 8,108. By mid-year the service was provisionally deactivated.

In the Congress the process of renewing the expired airports-airways development bill continued into 1982. General aviation attention began to focus on the fuel tax provisions, with NBAA urging a single tax both for aviation gasoline and jet fuel. GAMA went along with proposals for a double-track system, with a higher levy on jet fuel. Proponents of the higher tax argued that jet powered aircraft made greater use of the traffic control system and thus should pay more. NBAA argued that there was a built-in differential with a single tax: jet engines consumed considerably more fuel than smaller, piston powered plants, and jet owners were thus paying substantially more in taxes. Congress bought the dual tax proposal, originally put forward by DOT. The new levy was $.12 a gallon for aviation gasoline, $.14 for jet fuel.

Leslie H. Walker, Standard Oil of California, resigned from NBAA's Board in March. The vacancy was filled by appointment of Ronald J. DeSerrano, a 21-year Dresser Industries veteran who had been a leader in recent, successful efforts to prevent imposition of stringent noise constraints at Love Field, Dallas.

May brought creation of the National Airspace Review (NAR), a multi-year program charged with examining every existing air traffic regulation and procedure, and proposing changes wherever indicated. John H. Winant, NBAA President, was named to the NAR Steering Committee, which was charged with acting on all recommendations which stemmed from a host of task groups. The total job requirement was monumental, far exceeding staff manpower capabilities. NBAA issued a call for volunteers to serve on those task forces judged to be of greatest importance to business aviation. A need for 500 man days of effort was anticipated. First of several volunteers was Byron M. "Skip" Reed, H. B. Zachry Company. Over the next two years, staff and member volunteers were able to enunciate business aviation requirements of thousands of provisions examined in the arduous review process.

By summer of 1982, continuing growth of membership and the coincident need to provide more and broader services demanded increased office space. A satellite location was found at 1625 Eye Street, N.W., about 200 feet east of the main offices. The additional space, Suite 824, consisted of 1,333 square feet and was configured to house the membership services and records group, computer operations, mailing services, and central stock storage area. J. Johanna Sigmond (marriage later changed her surname to O'Toole), Supervisor of Membership Support, was put in charge of the satellite, reporting to Dorothy W. Cheek.

Despite the recession and the growing gloom in aircraft manufacturing, NBAA's ranks grew to 2,656 members by mid-summer, and the collective aircraft fleet reached 5,373 units. Both figures were all time highs.

A survey by staff to identify airports judged to be most important to members resulted in 650 responses. The 10 ranked as most frequently used were Washington National, Teterboro, Houston Hobby, Dallas Love, Westchester County, Newark, Denver Stapleton, Chicago Midway, Los Angeles International and Chicago–O'Hare International.

Association interest focussed on St. Louis and its airport September 21–23, when 10,892 persons gathered for the annual meeting. A large audience listened attentively in hopes the question "The ATC System . . . Will It Ever Be the Same?" would be answered by a knowledgeable panel of speakers. Michael J. Fenello, FAA Deputy Administrator, and Raymond Van Vuren, FAA Air Traffic Control Chief, gave interesting presentations but the answer was elusive. Lee L. Robbins, Corning Glass Works, moderated the session. Staff members Frederick B. McIntosh and William Horn, Jr., spoke for members, evidencing their prolonged concern over post-controller strike inhibitions on unconstrained use of the airspace. The rigidity of the GAR system was being replaced by a more subtly pervasive means of metering air traffic. It was the technique known as flow control, which permitted flights to begin only when there was assurance they could land at destination without circling or holding delays en route. Flow control had positive aspects in that it diminished waste of fuel during a flight. But it frequently was the signal that the system could not absorb more than a fraction of planned air traffic. The obvious solution was to increase capacity of the system but political and legislative indecision bottled up the needed funds, year after year.

There were 321 exhibiting companies at the St. Louis meeting, and 128 aircraft were in the static display lines at Bi-State Parks airport. This was the largest number in history and it was obvious that many were not true display models, but were pieces of evidence that the used aircraft market was reaching the glut stage.

Elected to three-year terms as Directors were Leo L. Brown, General Mills, Preston S. Parish, The Upjohn Company, DeSerrano, Dresser Industries, John J. Gallagher, the Gannett Company, and James F. Nields, Ware Knitters. Hal Spragins, III, Memphis Aero Corporation, was named to a two-year term as Associate Advisor, but a change in occupation made it necessary for him to resign mid-1983.

Appointed as standing committee chairmen at St. Louis were:

Airports — Fred Gammon, State of Wisconsin
Airspace/Air Traffic Control — Charles F. Harmon, Jr., Carborundum Co.
Corporate Aviation Management — Virgil L. Williams, The Upjohn Company
Energy — Thomas F. Gordon, General Dynamics
Helicopter — F. Lynn Clough, Tenneco
International Operators — Raymond P. Ward, Dresser Industries
Operations — William Meadowcroft, Consumers Power Company
Technical — Martin Lipstein, Johnson and Johnson

One of the notable operational events of the meeting was presentation to NBAA Chairman David M. Woodrow of a plaque marking completion of a million flight hours by Lockheed JetStar aircraft. Presented by Lockheed Georgia Company Executive Vice President A. H. Lorch, the plaque lauded the record of 204 JetStars which had compiled the impressive record since 1961.

A third Westchester County Airport stipulation was signed in the autumn, calling for seven additional months of noise monitoring. A principal aim was to keep aircraft noise levels below 87 dba on approach and 76 dba on takeoff from 11:00 p.m. to 6:30 a.m. daily. Accumulation of the additional data would, it was hoped, give a comprehensive year-round database on which acceptable operating practices could be built. Hopes, unfortunately, would soon be dashed by implacable county government inaction to carry out the intent of the stipulation. Time was running out on compromise.

IBAC, meanwhile, continued its efforts under Chairman David M. Woodrow to establish its credentials. A pioneering event which took place at IBAC's November, 1982 meeting, helped measurably. The senior airworthiness officials of the United States, the United Kingdom, Canada, France, the Federal Republic of Germany, and The Netherlands all attended the IBAC Governing Board meeting at the Waldorf Hotel, London, to discuss the development of Joint Airworthiness

Regulations (JAR) under which aircraft receive certification on a multi-nation basis. The IBAC precedent led to continuing periodic meetings of the group, bringing the United States more closely in touch with evolving unity among European Economic Community (EEC) countries.

Major staff changes were made January 1, 1983. John A. Pope was given the title of Staff Vice President, Membership Services; McIntosh was designated Staff Vice President, Operations, to serve as such until his retirement on June 30. Robert A. Cooke was named to take McIntosh's place on July 1, and William M. Flener, former FAA Associate Administrator, joined staff as Director, Government Relations. Flener was no newcomer to NBAA, having served as its consultant and roving ambassador during the darkest days of the controller strike.

As the new year began, the outlook for new aircraft production remained bleak. Edward W. Stimpson, GAMA President, predicted there would be only 2,800 deliveries of U.S. built general aviation aircraft during 1983, a pittance measured against the towering 1978 total of 17,811.

Meanwhile, the effects of air line deregulation and resurgence from the recession in the U.S. economy began to place renewed pressures on the capacity of many airports. Congress mandated creation of an Airport Access Task Force, with CAB acting as administrator, to look into the problem and propose solutions. Winant was selected as a member and toward the end of the probe acted as lead man in opposing takeoff/landing slot auctions as a means of relieving pressures. Some of the major air lines favored the auction idea; smaller carriers, the regional and commuter groups, and all of general aviation were opposed to it. The fear of the opposition, whose arguments prevailed, was that cash-heavy major carriers would likely buy up every favored slot time and force all others off the airport. Most of the task force findings dealt with equitable means of changing ground and air traffic procedures, of changing air line scheduling practices to avoid bunching flights, and of better utilizing airport runway and taxiway potentials.

In March of 1983 the Westchester County situation came unglued. NBAA put the county government on notice it would take the issues to court. The association's attorney, Robert D. Powell, stated in a letter that NBAA was "driven to this action by the manipulation of the County." During the preceding months the stipulation had been shunted aside while politicians jockeyed for position. The departure of County Executive Alfred Del Bello to become New York State's Deputy Governor created a chaotic late 1982 campaign. The airport issue became a political football and as a result the county failed to abide by its promises to conduct a meaningful monitoring program aimed at an acceptable compromise solution. FAA subsequently entered the case, filing a complaint against the county and the curfew issues were taken to U.S. District Court, Southern District of New York, in early July. A three-week trial, vigorously prosecuted by Powell, FAA attorney Leonard Ceruzzi, and AOPA attorney John Yodice, brought a clearcut and decisive ruling from Judge Robert Ward. He struck down the curfew as "an unreasonable, arbitrary, discriminatory and overbroad exercise of power by the county." He also took note that "the FAA has been delegtaed exclusive regulatory responsibility for regulating aircraft noise." The judge imposed a permanent injunction on the curfew.

A kneejerk reaction soon followed. The county initiated, but then quickly abandoned, action to invoke stringent noise standards. Instead, it asked for voluntary compliance with a program to control midnight to 6:30 a.m. operations.

The victory was complete, and while the court decision did not set national conditions, it served as a mighty deterrent to hasty, poorly conceived actions at airports all over America.

Flener left staff in June, 1983, his place taken by J. E. "Jeb" Burnside, Manager, Government Relations, a young and hard driving man with Congressional office and committee staff experience.

While overall congestion problems grew in scope, summer brought easing of some of the strike related air traffic rules. Return to more nearly normal FAA staffing levels resulted in removing nine key airport pairs from the reservations system. The remaining 11 key airports were scheduled for similar action in early 1984. In September of 1983, constraints on movements between ARTCC's were lifted, and traffic was back to 90 percent of pre-strike volume. A two-year period of difficult, often agonizing constraint under tight rules was ending. But the ongoing problem of a shortfall in system capacity was still building.

The hope that major system improvement program would begin was dashed in mid-1983. A three-way handshake agreement between Congress, the Administration, and the aviation industry was breached only a year after it had been made. Symbol of the agreement was the 1982 airports-airways act, under which the new user taxes would be used for massive system upgrading. But the Administration threatened to veto the Fiscal 1984 appropriations bill unless $800 million were cut from it. The veto threat was successful. Woodrow, speaking at 1983's annual NBAA meeting, deplored the situation: "A bold FAA program, funded wholly with dedicated user tax dollars (has fallen) victim to Administration attempts to produce a slightly less imbalanced budget."

The 1983 meeting, held in Dallas, October 4–6, was a huge success and despite the sluggish aircraft manufacturing picture, it set all time records. Attendance rose to 14,753, and there were 370 exhibiting companies with 1,428 booths.

Woodrow, bowing out as Chairman, announced that for the first time in 13 years there was a decline in membership. The fiscal year end total was 2,638, a decline of 18, less than ½ of 1 percent. But the numbers were an indicator of slowdown in portions of business aviation. Association financial status had never been better. Income for the year was $2,238,801 and expenses were $1,991,786. NBAA's reserve funds exceeded $3 million. The association was well positioned to weather whatever storm might come.

Three-year Director terms were voted for Howard O. "Tad" Evans, General Motors, A. M. "Skip" Penizotto, RCA, Woodrow, John S. Broome, Broome Ranches, and Max B. Moore, Jr., Southern Natural Gas Company. Dwayne K. Jose, Bell

Lee L. Robbins' first official duty as NBAA's Chairman was to present the Award for Meritorious Service to Aviation to United States Senator Barry M. Goldwater, left, at the 1983 annual meeting in Dallas.

Helicopter Textron, was named to a two-year Associate Advisor term; M. A. "Dutch" Barbettini, Teledyne Neosho, was designated for one year, filling the unexpired Spragins' term.

Robbins of Corning Glass succeeded Woodrow in the Chairman position. Nields was elected Vice Chairman and Parish became Treasurer.

A director since 1978, Robbins brought a no-nonsense, shirtsleeves attitude to his new duties. His leadership was characterized by true hands-on interest. His judgment was close to uncanny, his ability to get at the heart of the matter superb. Robbins joined Corning after working at the Elmira Aeronautical

Corporation as "an all around handyman, taking pay in flying time." Starting as a Corning co-pilot in 1954 he was in 1970 Manager of the company operation, and later was given the title of Director, Aircraft Operations.

Woodrow, looking back on his years with NBAA, later named three groups which he felt had most beneficially affected the organization:

> *The first group is the staff, because the scoreboard of their accomplishments is on the record, and it is, indeed a remarkable record. The other measure, if one is needed, is the expressed respect they have from the people with whom they work in the agencies and with the members.*
>
> *The second group are the Associate Members, without whom NBAA would not be able to sustain the current level of accomplishment. In capsule form, NBAA brings the user to the table and the Associates bring the products which enable the operators to accomplish their missions — a strong combination. The Associate Members have particularly brought great credit to this union by the quality of their exhibits at the annual convention. They deserve a grand measure of recognition for the total success of the NBAA venture.*
>
> *The third group are the NBAA member volunteers — all of those persons who have given so much, as an elite group, to make NBAA work by virtue of their time and their talents, on committees and otherwise. They have a special place in my heart because they make the system work so much more efficiently. All we have ever needed was more of them.[1]*

A sense of genuine modesty would have prevented Woodrow from deservedly placing his own name in the roster of outstanding contributors. Parish years later named him as one of the Directors whose influence in NBAA was greatest in the 1980's, and cited in particular his dedication both to the association and to the task of launching IBAC on a successful journey.[2] An even-handed, judicious manager, Woodrow led NBAA through troubled times and to new heights of accomplishment. Concurrently he gave the IBAC Chairmanship enormous amounts of time and energy. While he vacated the NBAA Chair in 1983, he would continue as chief executive officer of IBAC until the end of 1987.

Named by Robbins as NBAA standing committee chairmen were:

Airports — Gammon
Airspace/Air Traffic Control — Harmon
Helicopter — Duane S. Moore, Illinois Department of Transportation
Operations — Meadowcroft
Corporate Aviation Management — Williams
International Operators — Ward
Technical — Lipstein

As NBAA's annual meeting evolved over the years into one of aviation's premier events, news about it grew to first rank significance. Many of the monthly aviation magazines devoted large portions of autumn issues to previewing and later summarizing the highlights of the convention. Unique, however, was the on-site publication early each morning of two news organs, copies of which seemed to be everywhere in the convention city. *Aviation Show Daily* began its coverage at Los Angeles in 1960. Cincinnati's 1972 meeting was the birthplace of *NBAA Convention News*. The *Daily* started as an American Aviation Publications effort and subsequently was a property of Ziff-Davis, Murdoch and McGraw-Hill. Editorship of the *Daily* revolved among a number of key employees. *NBAA Convention News* was founded by James Holahan, its editor, and Wilson Leach, publisher. Both continued to serve in those positions during the years which followed. Their publication broadened its scope and eventually took the name *Aviation International News,* but the NBAA convention issues retained the original title.

Late 1983 witnessed completion of a major effort to restructure the NBAA Flying Safety Award program. Given particular impetus by Robbins, the changes converted the base lines for awards from miles to hours. There were two principal goals. Hours were a much more common yardstick for measuring experience throughout aviation. Further, hours would be a fairer measure to apply to the piston engine element of the business fleet, which in general flew at lower altitudes and slower speeds than turbine craft. Membership was polled on the proposed changes and based on its strong support the Board gave the revisions a green light in December, 1983.

The end of the year brought Horn's retirement from staff. His departure and that of the veteran McIntosh in June, brought great regret. McIntosh took into his retirement accolades of NBAA and government as well. FAA conferred on him its highest distinction, the Distinguished Service Award. Horn was also a highly respected figure. Among staff he acquired the nickname of Mr. Acronym for the vast number of technical committees he served which were generally known by initials.

Cooke moved quickly to fill the gap and took a firm grip on the senior operations duties relinquished by McIntosh. And early in the new year C. Dennis Wright, a highly qualified expert, occupied the airspace/air traffic control position vacated by Horn. An Auburn University graduate, Wright served in the U.S. Navy, worked in airport planning and was a prominent air traffic control spokesman for AOPA before joining NBAA's staff.

Early in 1984 storm clouds began to gather ominously around the issues of fringe benefits and personal use of company aircraft. At the heart of the matter were questions which had been long left unanswered and which had proved vexing for many years both to members and to staff. At the center of the storm were personal use of aircraft and the occasional occupancy of seats which otherwise would have been empty on company flights.

The Deficit Reduction Act of 1984 propelled the issues toward resolution. Debate over whether to include tax provisions in the act was inconclusive. But the legislative report which accompanied the act to the floor of each house of Congress issued a mandate to the Internal Revenue Service (IRS). It called for an early review of all areas of fringe benefits not specifically dealt with in existing laws. Further, it gave IRS the power to issue regulations. Within a year, the Congressional mandate created a major battleground on which contentious company aircraft proposals would be fought.

At mid-year Pope announced his plan to retire December 31, ending a 23-year career with the association. Flight Safety Foundation commended him with its Business Aviation Meritorious Award for "advancement of business aviation safety," citing the Recommended Standards Manual, Management Aid series, and company operations manual seminars.

NBAA's member company aircraft fleet grew to 5,309 units in 1984, with 2,143 turbojet aircraft, 1,311 turboprops, and 727 helicopters forming substantial blocks.

In June the Board gave a go-ahead to a major innovation which had been initiated in April, 1983, by Director Raleigh E. Drennon, BFGoodrich. The Drennon initiative aimed at establishing means by which NBAA could sponsor graduate school level studies in business aviation management. Investigation conducted during 1983 and early 1984 included examination of the interest and credentials of several prestigious schools of business management. The June Board action singled out the Colgate Darden Graduate Business School of the University of Virginia. Drennon and the study group, Parish, Wigton, Williams and Winant, were given authority to enter negotiations to form an alliance with the school and develop a graduate level educational and research program.

Drennon's concept was a momentous breakthrough. It recognized the growing importance of strong professional credentials in business aviation management. Further, it was evidence of the long transition which began after World War II and led by the 1980's to a requirement that flight departments be headed by persons whose credentials went far beyond an airman's certificate. Looking back on Drennon's leadership in promoting education, Parish cited it as one of the great contemporary contributions by Directors.[3]

In August, Alan N. Darrow joined staff as Assistant to the President, with the understanding he would succeed Pope with the title of Vice President, Administration, at the end of the year. A professional association executive, Darrow brought strong experience in convention management and in association administration. An American University graduate, he was keenly aware of business league practices and requirements. His selection proved to be an extremely wise choice. Testimony to this was given by Parish in 1988, when he expressed particular praise for Darrow for his skills and for his execution of an administration reorganization plan.[4].

U.S. Secretary of Transportation Elizabeth Hanford Dole paid NBAA a compliment later in 1984 when she named Winant as a member of a select Commission on Reorganization of the Metropolitan Washington Airports. The purpose was to devise a plan by which the Federal government could divest itself of ownership of Washington National and Dulles International Airports. Chaired by former Virginia Governor Linwood A. Holton, the commission labored under heavy conflicting pressures but devised a plan which was enacted by Congress in 1985. Operations of the airports was subsequently turned over to a regional authority on a long-term lease agreement which was structured to lead eventually to outright ownership.

Atlanta was host to the 1984 annual meeting, with 12,777 attendees and a record press registration of 265. The number of exhibiting companies jumped to 412, an increase of 42, and 1,400 booth spaces were occupied. Three-year Board positions were voted for Robbins, Drennon, Frederick Haap, III, Mead Corporation, and Hornbeck. Harry J. Christopher, Reynolds Industries, was a nominee but personal circumstances led him to withdraw his name shortly before the meeting. John P. Kennedy, Airport Corporation of America, was named an Associate Advisor.

Robbins' selections for standing committee chairmen were:

Airports — Gammon
Airspace/Air Traffic Control — Byron M. Reed, H. B. Zachry Company
Operations — Curt Treichel, United Technologies Corporation
Corporate Aviation Management — Williams
Helicopter — Moore
International Operators — Bob J. Weinwurzel, Philip Morris
Technical — Jon Haag, Caterpillar Tractor

Special emphasis was laid on announcement that an agreement had been concluded with the Darden School. First efforts were to be a special on-campus, week-long seminar in business aircraft management, and the development of management case studies using real life situations. The case study material would be made available to all members.

Pope was honored at the Atlanta awards night banquet and at the end of the year left staff with a Board expression of "good wishes that his retirement be a period of fruitful activity."

By late 1984 the spreading airports-airways congestion problem became acute. Using the same technique which it had successfully employed in the past, NBAA set up a new 800-line telephone information service. Wright coined an acronym, FASST, to describe it (Fly Around Saturated Sectors and Terminals). Information supplied by the message system, updated daily or more frequently if needed, dealt with flow control patterns, significant weather trends, en route flow and gate holds. The service helped measurably to alleviate flight planning problems. Feedback on its utility was extremely positive. Criticizing lack of action on plans to upgrade the traffic system, Winant spoke at RTCA's annual luncheon. "The mid-1980s are no better than 1968," he said. "We cannot afford to have this situation continue in a seemingly open ended series of cycles in which strong resolve is followed by inept or weak action."

The end of 1984 witnessed two important decisions. NBAA agreed to remain IBAC's Administration for a second three-year period expiring at the end of 1987. And the Board approved consolidating NBAA's offices in a 12,376 square foot area comprising most of the second floor of the Ring Building, 1200 Eighteenth Street, N.W. The move was completed in March, 1985.

Aircraft production for 1984 proved beyond any doubt that the collapse which began in 1982 was a long term, worrisome problem. World wide manufacture totalled only 268 turbojects, 227 medium turboprops, 94 medium twin pistons and 329 light twins.[5] GAMA's data for U.S. production of all general aviation aircraft, excluding helicopters, showed a total of only 1,600 units, less than 10 percent of 1978's record crop.

What went wrong? Why the dramatic 1982 crash in production and why had there been no recovery? By early 1985 complex answers emerged, identifying many causes laid out in a discouraging, interlocking pattern. Each depressant seemed to follow right on the heels of another, stringing the ordeal out into what seemed an endless procession. Prominent among contributors to the problem were:

- A deep recession from 1981 through 1983, not only in the U.S. but in most of the industrialized world. Recovery was slow and spotty.

- A rapidly growing trend of mergers and acquisitions among U.S businesses, often resulting in curtailment or elimination of aircraft.

- Rapidly rising aircraft prices, driven sharply up by the heavy costs of product liability insurance.

- A perception of deep uncertainty generated by the controller strike, the constraints of the GAR and the imposition of noise-related restrictions on airports. This perception planted seeds of doubt as to whether an owner could utilize his aircraft as he wished.

- Air line deregulation, which concentrated service on profitable routes, imposing heavy demand on air traffic and airport functions and added to the growing congestion problem.

- The after effects of double digit inflation in the late 1970's, which caused many to purchase aircraft, or production slots, as an investment rather than as a transportation tool. Many of these aircraft, with very low operating time, ended up in the used aircraft market.

- A lingering state of depression in the energy industry, causing selloff of many aircraft in what was historically the major business aircraft user category.

- Growth of aircraft management companies through which use could be pooled among owners, lowering total needs for aircraft.

- Major growth in chartered aircraft use in place of direct ownership.

- A host of tax law changes which eliminated the Investment Tax Credit incentive to ownership, tightened depreciation rates, and aimed at placing high taxes on personal use of aircraft and "empty seat" occupancy.

These many causes, along with subtle societal changes difficult to define precisely, led by 1985 to restructuring of the manufacturing industry. General aviation manufacturers, known for proud independence, joined forces with larger organizations in rapid order. Beech became part of Raytheon; Piper was absorbed into Lear Siegler; Gulfstream Aerospace was acquired by Chrysler; Cessna merged into General Dynamics; Hughes Helicopters became McDonnell Douglas.

But while the aircraft manufacturers were sorely wounded during the long period of trial, other elements of business aviation flourished, some as never before. The used aircraft market was swollen. For the most part, aircraft offered in this marketplace were of extraordinarily high quality, with relatively little airframe time. The service segment operated at a fast clip as owners kept older but extremely sound aircraft for longer and longer periods. The avionics business and replacement parts industry flourished. A host of specialized new services emerged. Included were flight planning organizations, computerized record keeping and maintenance-related programs, real time weather information services, and aircraft-sharing schemes.

There also was no dearth of innovation in aircraft manufacture. Beech announced development of its all-composite Starship. Gulfstream unveiled its Model IV. Dassault planned to introduce its new three-engine 900 Falcon. Piaggio promoted an advanced, partly composite turboprop. And helicopter manufacturers vied to outdo one another with turbine equipment. The first half of the 1980's was truly the best of times and the worst of times in business aviation.

To help carry out the new, greatly expanded educational program, Hilary Harris joined NBAA staff in early 1985 as Manager of Educational Programs. Hers was a new position, tailored to the results of Drennon's Educational Steering Committee efforts.

IRS left an unwanted new year's present on NBAA's doorstep: massively complicated and grossly unfair proposals to tax personal use of company aircraft and the occupancy of seats which would otherwise have gone empty. Personal use would result in income imputed at comparable aircraft charter cost. Empty seat taxation would be taxed at full, unrestricted coach fare levels for the distance involved.

The proposals triggered a furious reaction among general aviation groups. Several disparate attempts to find a viable set of alternatives resulted in formation of a coalition consisting of NBAA, GAMA, AOPA and NATA. The group placed great stress on IRS's shocking errors. The personal use proposal took no account of the fact that a healthy portion of charter cost consisted of profit for the vendor, a factor entirely missing in not-for-hire aircraft use. The empty seat formula called for valuation at an air line fare level which was paid only by a small fraction of passengers in the coach section.

Representative Dan Glickman of Kansas introduced legislation to repeal the IRS empty seat rule and to exempt such use from taxation. After considerable debate the coalition associations brought forth a plan by which increments of first class or coach fare would be charged for personal use based on the weight of the aircraft used.

Senator Dole of Kansas reached a late night compromise in June with Assistant Treasury Secretary Ronald Pearlman. The agreement was stated in a brief Pearlman letter. The scale of imputed taxable income on personal use would extend from a low of 50 percent of unrestricted coach fare for aircraft less than 6,000 pounds, to a high of two times first class for an aircraft of more than 25,000 pounds. Definitions of key or "control" employees who could decide on aircraft use would be amended to cover a much smaller group of truly senior policy making officials using aircraft. And there would be no empty seat tax imputation where "50 percent or more of the regular seating capacity of that plane as used by the company is occupied by individuals whose flights are primarily for the employer's business."

The letter's real worth was open to question. Pearlman soon left government service. The issues seemingly resolved by his letter were still not settled by the end of 1986, and the IRS rules were as vague, complicated and unfair as when originally proposed.

While the IRS controversy raged, good news came to IBAC. Its request for full Observer status, highest category given to a non-government body, was approved in respect to membership on the ICAO FANS committee (Future Aerial Navigation Systems). The approval was granted after an intense effort made by the IBAC Governing Board in Montreal. Included in the effort were visits to senior delegates of nations represented in IBAC, and to senior ICAO officials, including Dr. Assad Kotaite, President of the Council. Heinz Lichius, active both in GBAA and EBAA, was named to serve for IBAC and did so with distinction for the next two years.

Additional welcome news came with conferral of the 1985 NBAA Flying Safety Awards. The new rules, using hours instead of miles, resulted in a 36.5 percent increase in awards from 1983. Awards for accident free hours ranging from 1,500 to more than 12,000 went to 2,276 persons. Maintenance personnel awards were given to 944 persons. Some 434 companies received aggregate flying safety awards, and 193 received maintenance awards.

New Orleans, scene of 1975's great convention, hosted the 1985 version with characteristic verve. Janice Barden carried out the chairman's duties with competence and flair for the second time. Attendance was 12,667, with another

United States Representatives Norman Y. Mineta, at the lectern, and Dan Glickman, seated to the left of Mineta, gave the opening addresses at the 1985 annual meeting in New Orleans. Mineta urged strong support of plans to modernize the airways system; Glickman endorsed efforts to repeal income tax imputation on casual occupancy of aircraft seats which otherwise would have been unused. Members of the Board listened attentively. From left, front row, John S. Broome, Broome Ranches, Leo L. Brown, General Mills, Ronald J. De Serrano, Dresser Industries, Raleigh E. Drennon, BFGoodrich and newly-elected NBAA Treasurer, Howard O. Evans, General Motors, John M. Gallagher, Gannett Company, Frederick Haap, III, Mead Corporation, Richard I. Hornbeck, General Electric, Max B. Moore, Jr., Southern Natural Gas Company, and Anthony M. Penizotto, RCA; second row, David M. Woodrow, 3M, James F. Nields, Ware Knitters and NBAA Vice Chairman, Lee L. Robbins, Corning Glass Works and retiring NBAA Chairman, and far right, John H. Winant, NBAA President.

record being set for exhibitors. There were 452 companies and booth occupancy reached 1,700 for the first time. Sixty companies were first time exhibitors, underlining the growing diversity of the supportive industry.

The trade side of the convention was lively despite the ongoing aircraft manufacturing slump. The Gulfstream IV paid an unexpected visit, with both Allen Paulson and Lee Iacocca putting in cameo appearances. The Falcon 900 was there in the flesh, having made a nonstop Paris-Little Rock flight the previous week. The Astra, latest development on the Westwind theme, was on display and went on a two-

Two Lees met at New Orleans in 1985. Outgoing NBAA Chairman Lee L. Robbins, left, enjoyed a chat with Chrysler Corporation Chairman Lee Iacocca aboard a Gulfstream IV mock-up in the exhibition area.

month national tour after the meeting. Learjet president James B. Taylor annouced a 17.6 percent cut in Lear model 25 and 55 prices and General Dynamics President David S. Lewis was on hand to discuss the new Citation IV model and hint of a Model V. The PHH Group solidified its position as America's largest aircraft management firm by acquiring Beckett Aviation, the pioneer in the field. And while helicopter sales were flat, there was no lack of displays at New Orleans. Present were the Sikorsky S-76, Hughes McDonnell Douglas 500 series, Bell's new flight test 400 Twin Ranger, Aerospatiale's A365N twin Dauphin, MBB's twin BK117, and Agusta's 109A.

Three-year Director terms were voted for Reed, DeSerrano, Gallagher, Parish, and Nields. A two-year term was given to Richard S. Wigton, The Clorox Company. Robert G. Lambert, Aviall, Inc., was designated the new Associate Advisor.

Robbins retired from the Chairman position and later commented that during his years with NBAA the two issues "which had more to do with the decline in corporate aviation were fuel shortages and the loss of free access to airports."[6] Parish was elected as new Chairman, Nields was re-elected Vice Chairman, and Drennon moved into the Treasurer position.

Parish brought extraordinary experience to the Chair. Vice Chairman of the Board and Chairman of the Executive Committee of The Upjohn Company, he

By 1985 a high degree of complexity and sophistication was a routine ingredient in NBAA annual meeting exhibits and the annual event attracted world-wide attendance and media coverage.

was active in a large number of civic, charitable, and educational causes. A U.S. Marine officer in World War II, he served in combat on Guadalcanal, New Britain, and Peliliu. Senior trustee of Williams College in 1985, he had previously served on the boards of the Eaglebrook School and Holderness School. A high time pilot, he was a member of the General Aviation Safety Panel under FAA Administrator Helms and was founder and chairman of the Kalamazoo Aviation History Museum. Highly intelligent and resourceful, Parish gave distinction to his new NBAA position.

Drennon, a BFGoodrich employee since 1972, was for 12 years a design engineer and test pilot for Lockheed. The JetStar was one of the several aircraft in whose design and development he played a part. His Goodrich career began in international operations and resulted in his being named Director of Aviation in 1978. A Georgia Institute of Technology graduate, he had the inquiring mind of a seasoned engineer and an extremely strong sense of imagination. His work with NBAA began in the mid-1970's, when he authored *Management Aid* publications and was speaker or panelist at several annual meetings.

Parish's appointment to the chairs of standing committees were:

Airports — Ed Lovings, Southern Company Services, Inc.
Airspace/Air Traffic Control — Edwin G. Fox, Jr., Manufacturers
   Hanover Corporation
Corporate Aviation Management — Williams
Helicopter — Moore
International Operators — Weinwurzel
Operations — Treichel
Technical — Herb Willford, Dana Corporation

In the preparation and execution of the 1985 and subsequent annual meetings, Dorothy W. Cheek played a continuously growing role of importance, with greatest emphasis on exhibitor arrangements and relations. Additionally, she was elected Corporate Secretary of NBAA as of January 1, 1985, succeeding Pope in that position.

Just prior to the New Orleans meeting Mrs. Ann W. Devers joined NBAA staff, taking the Educational Programs place of Hilary Harris, who resigned to enter law school. Mrs. Devers was well known in the industry, having worked with *Commuter Air* and *Airline Executive* magazines, and with *World Aviation Directory.* She also served as Secretary of the Aviation/Space Writers Association.

Having discussed his intentions at length with Parish and others on the Executive Committee in October, Winant announced at the December 12, 1985 Board meeting that he would retire at the end of November, 1986. His hope in giving long notice was that no pressure would be placed on the organization to seek a successor in haste. By the time of his retirement he would be 63, would have been President for 15 years, and a Director for almost 29 years. Reluctant as he was to end his service with NBAA, his carefully studied opinion was that both he and the organization could profit from a change in staff leadership. Parish, prepared for Winant's announcement, immediately named Woodrow to chair a search committee and designated Hornbeck and Robbins to serve with him.

The hope was to choose a successor President no later than early summer of 1986, and to have the incoming staff work in tandem with Winant beginning in September.

Early 1986 produced the first fruits of the NBAA-University of Virginia alliance. From May 4 to 9 the initial seminar, "Managing the Corporate Aviation Function," was held on the Darden School campus in Charlottesville. The course, restricted to 35 participants, was a sellout and met with general acclaim. Meanwhile, a series of case studies in business aviation management problems was being put together. They called into play the true experiences of NBAA member companies in such diverse areas as aircraft selection, fleet upgrading, allocation of costs within the company, and the challenge of choosing between aircraft ownership, leasing or chartering. The complete studies were issued to all member companies in workbook form, along with a floppy computer disc which acted as a tutorial aid.

Two other seminars, developed by staff, were held back to back in Philadelphia and Dallas. One dealt with corporate helicopter management, the other with maintenance management.

Ann T. Miletich ended her 24½ year career as NBAA's chief accountant on April 30. At a reception honoring her, she was presented a certificate noting that she had earned "the respect of the association's financial, insurance, pension and banking institutions, as well as its independent accountants, and is widely known as a person of integrity and faith." To take her place, Mrs. Patricia M. McMillan, a highly qualified accountant, joined the staff as Manager, Financial Services.

The search committee, busy through the winter, considered applications from more than 40 candidates for the President position. The several finalist candidates were personally interviewed at length by committee members, and a qualified management search consultant. By late April the committee narrowed the field to one candidate whom it would recommend to the Board. At Woodrow's request, Parish convened a special meeting May 15, 1986.

Woodrow reported in detail on the committee's efforts and then proposed that Jonathan Howe be named as President Designate, to take Winant's place December 1.

The Board concurred unanimously. Howe appeared to be the best choice on several counts. In FAA's Service since 1963, he was in 1986 Director of the Southern Region headquartered in Atlanta. In a statement issued on Howe's selection Parish said, "we are delighted and are particularly fortunate that Jonathan Howe will be NBAA's next President. He will bring us exactly the right set of credentials, knowledge, and experience needed to manage the many and great challenges which business aviation will face in the coming years." Howe was 48. He served in many FAA legal affairs posts, becoming Deputy Chief Counsel in 1978. There, he was lead attorney in all litigation arising from the DC-10 crash at O'Hare airport in June, 1979. For that work he received the Presidential Meritorious Service Award. Prior to becoming Southern Region Director, he was Deputy Director of the Northwest Mountain Region. Howe received his bachelors and law degrees from Yale.

At Parish's urging the Board adopted a detailed set of broad association objectives at its June 25 meeting, refining precepts first identified in the 1971 reexamination of NBAA. The newly stated objectives were intended to be a road map for association planning for the balance of the decade. Parish used them as the central theme of his report to the membership at the 1986 annual meeting. (See Appendix section for full text of objective statement.)

The convention, held in Anaheim September 30–October 2, was another West Coast success story. "Scotty" Miller of Garrett Aviation Services chaired the convention committee for a record fifth time. Attendance reached 13,906 and there was yet one more record on the exhibition side, with 456 companies using 1,727 booth spaces. Membership dipped to 3,902 companies, down 39 from the previous year. But association reserve funds were at $4,035,913, a quantum increase from the $342,000 level which existed 15 years earlier.

Director terms of three years were given to Broome, Woodrow, Moore, Myron W. Collier, Cyclops Corporation, and Richard J. Van Gemert, Xerox

Preston S. Parish, elected as NBAA's Chairman in 1985, presided at the Awards Night banquet during the 1986 annual meeting in Anaheim, California.

Corporation. Just prior to the meeting, Nields resigned from the Board and the Vice Chairman post. He did so with deep regret but strong conviction that the time to do so was exactly right. He would be sorely missed, both for his warmth and his keen insight. Drennon was named to take his place as Vice Chairman and Haap was designated Treasurer. J. Robert Duncan, Duncan Aviation, was named to a two-year term as Associate Advisor.

Among vendor announcements at Anaheim, prominence was given to Canadair's new model 601 with General Electric CF 34 engines, and to Beech's acquisition of the Mitsubishi Diamond turbojet program. The name of the aircraft would henceforth be Beechjet.

Sales of new aircraft continued to be flat, but the used aircraft market gave signs that the long period of glut was nearing an end. Of more lasting importance than the dearth of sales since 1981, however, are data on business aircraft production measured over a much longer run. The figures on just a sampling of some of the medium sized turbojets and the best selling turboprop illustrate the huge popularity of business aircraft. Through 1986, 641 craft of the 125 family (HS, DH, BH and British Aerospace) were sold. Cessna, through 1987, delivered 1,490

Citations of the original, Model I, II, S-2, and III versions. Learjet sold 1,577 of its Models 23 through 55. And Beech King Air deliveries of all models, counting only civil aviation customers, totalled 3,422 through 1986. Because business aircraft are built so sturdily, most of these thousands of aircraft, and of the many other makes and models in the post-1965 fleet, were still in service in 1986.

Standing committee chairmen appointed by Parish at Anaheim were:

Airports — Fred Ware, Illinois Department of Transportation
Airspace/Air Traffic Control — Fox
Corporation Aviation Management — Williams
Helicopter — Moore
International Operators — Franklin Davis, American International
    Group
Operations — Treichel
Technical — Willford

In saddening contrast to the many convivial happenings at Anaheim was the death of E. Tilson Peabody, former NBAA Director and retired General Motors employee. Stricken by a heart attack while in the exhibition area October 1, he died despite prolonged efforts of paramedical personnel to revive him.

Anaheim was Winant's final meeting as President. The awards night banquet was the setting for an expression of praise for his service. Among honors listed by Parish was announcement that the Board Room at Washington headquarters would be named for Winant. Concurrently, Gates Learjet made it known that it was establishing a permanent bachelor level scholarship in his name for study in aeronautical engineering or aviation management.

During the months leading up to retirement, other honors were given to Winant. Among them was RTCA's highest distinction, its annual Achievement Award, a special Medallion Award from the Air Traffic Control Association, and FAA's highest honor, the Distinguished Service Award, given for "outstanding leadership in aviation." Embry-Riddle Aeronautical University earlier had recognized him by awarding him an honorary degree of Doctor of Aviation Management.

Woodrow named Winant as "the individual who has most beneficially affected NBAA," and described him as the "personification of the image and integrity by which NBAA has become known."[7] In Robbins' opinion "he was, is and always will be Mr. NBAA."[8] John B. Bean, association Chairman from 1971 to 1973, said he "brought the experience and demeanor of a seasoned executive to the presidency of NBAA."[9] In particular, Bean cited Winant's achievement in making "the necessary contacts in government both personally and using the considerable talents of staff. He (also) made a special point of talking with the members and giving that personal touch ... which is so essential in a trade organization's affairs."

FAA Administrator Donald D. Engen gave the most succinct compliment. "Even on the few occasions when he lost on an issue, he has won friends," Engen said.[10]

Jonathan Howe, left, appointed as NBAA President in December, 1986, was soon interviewed outside a U.S. Senate hearing room. With him, center, is Duane W. Ekedahl, President of the Regional Airline Association.

Incoming NBAA President Howe quickly made it clear he would establish his own imprint and would utilize his own style of leadership.

In his maiden speech, delivered at RTCA's annual awards luncheon in late November, 1986, Howe reemphasized three great challenges which had been of great concern to NBAA and which he said plagued all of aviation: lack of aviation system capacity, underfunding of urgently needed improvements, and a poor public image which shed a negative light on the industry. Howe challenged his audience to present a unified front and "to take our story to the grass roots of America."

Parish, looking back on "the record of the first half of the 1980s," spoke of how NBAA's actions had gained the organization great respect.

> *What appears to me to be of greater significance, however, is the impact these activities have had in more firmly establishing NBAA as a responsible spokesman for the most active segment of general aviation — business aviation. The choice of the term 'responsible' is deliberate because NBAA's advocacy for any position has always been balanced. It has represented a recognition of the needs of all members of the aviation community not just its own constituency. That is not to suggest NBAA has not pressed the case of business aviation before whatever forum, but rather to note that its advocacy has been more than just self serving.*
>
> *Furthermore, NBAA's interests have not been limited to domestic issues. It is not only a founding member of IBAC but it also shouldered the administrative burden of the Council's initial years providing the*

NBAA Vice Chairman Raleigh E. Drennon, left, and Chairman Preston S. Parish welcomed FAA Administrator T. Allan McArtor, center, to the 1987 annual meeting in New Orleans.

> *chairman, secretary and staff services. Without the leadership, direction and support of the NBAA staff and the Board of Directors, it is unlikely that a network of international organizations could have been created.*

> *Here again, the moderate yet forceful approach to coordinating the efforts of its members for the benefit of the whole aviation community has been the hallmark of IBAC's positions and evidence of NBAA's influence.[11]*

Parish's insight also zeroed in on the cold fact that NBAA in the late 1980's faced daunting challenges. Reporting to the membership on the changing circumstances of the period, he said,

> *Given the increasing complexity of life in the aviation business, and the many challenges facing us, it will take all of Jonathan Howe's skill, the efforts of the staff, and that of the many NBAA members who give so much of their time as volunteers, to make NBAA an even more visible and effective advocate for business aviation.[12]*

Forty years after its incorporation the association faced serious problems which in many ways seemed to have come full circle. Congested airports, lack of system capacity, and government misunderstanding of business aviation's vitally important role in transportation all had hauntingly familiar resonance.

But 40 years of uphill efforts had brought great vitality, respect, determination, authority, and financial strength to what began as a tiny, visionary endeavor of a handful of concerned men.

NBAA's leaders of the late 1980's were well prepared to manage the far-reaching affairs of the organization and to continue the good fight to "attain wider recognition of the fact that the aviation interests of its members are of primary importance to the domestic economy of the nation,"[13] and to a much larger world as well. It could be said fairly that NBAA's leadership, past and current, was marked by the types of "Dauntless Resolution, and Unconquerable Faith"[14] which were made incarnate below that windswept dune in December, 1903.

NOTES TO CHAPTER 10

1. Letter, David M. Woodrow, Edina, Minnesota, to J. H. Winant, April 19, 1988.

2. Letter, Preston S. Parish, Kalamazoo, Michigan, to J. H. Winant, March 29, 1988.

3. Ibid.

4. Ibid.

5. "Business Aviation's Age of Discontinuity," speech by J. H. Winant, Coronado, California, November 21, 1985.

6. Letter, Lee L. Robbins, Horseheads, New York, to J. H. Winant, April 8, 1988.

7. Letter, David M. Woodrow, April 19, 1988.

8. Letter, Lee L. Robbins, April 8, 1988.

9. Letter, John B. Bean, Naples, Florida, to J. H. Winant, May 17, 1988.

10. *Business and Commercial Aviation,* "Washington" column, pg. 202, September, 1986.

11. Letter, Preston S. Parish, March 29, 1988.

12. Preston S. Parish, NBAA Annual Report, Fiscal 1987.

13. Excerpt from CAOA Articles of Incorporation, February 13, 1947.

14. Excerpt from inscription on the Wright Brothers National Memorial, Kill Devil Hill, North Carolina.

Appendix A

EARLIEST BY-LAWS OF THE CORPORATION AIRCRAFT OWNERS ASSOCIATION

THE BY-LAWS WHICH FOLLOW BEAR ALL THE MARKS OF those which were adopted as temporary on November 21, 1946 and then perfected in some few regards by the CAOA Board of Directors, January 9, 1947. A copy is bound into the corporate minutes book with the Association's incorporation papers.

CORPORATION AIRCRAFT OWNERS ASSOCIATION, INC.

* * *

BY-LAWS

* * *

ARTICLE I

The name of the Association is Corporation Aircraft Owners Association, Inc.

ARTICLE II

The location of the office of the Association shall be designated by the Board of Directors.

ARTICLE III

The purposes of the Association shall be those enumerated in the Articles of Agreement and as determined from time to time by the majority of the members voting at a meeting.

ARTICLE IV

Membership

The membership of the Association shall consist of Regular Members, Associate Members and Honorary Members.

1. *Regular Members.* Any corporation, company, partnership, institution or individual owning or operating aircraft as an aid to the conduct of its business is eligible for membership, provided the business of the application is *not* primarily in the field of aviation. Each Regular Member shall have the right to one (1) vote at all meetings of the Association. A Regular Member shall designate in writing one of its officers or other individual to represent it and vote on its behalf at meetings of the Association, and may from time to time, in the absence of such designee, designate in writing an alternate to represent it and vote on its behalf. The term "Regular Member," as hereinafter used, shall mean either a Regular Member or a duly constituted designee.

2. *Associate Members.* Any corporation, company, partnership, institution or individual owning or operating aircraft as an aid to the conduct of its business, which business is primarily in the aviation or air transportation field is eligible for membership as an Associate Member, subject also to the approval of the Board of Directors. An Associate Member may be heard at any meeting of the Association on any matter pertaining to aviation and within the scope of the Association's activities, but shall not vote or be deemed part of a quorum at any meeting of the Association. An Associate Member may designate in writing one of its officers or other individual to represent it at meetings of the Association and may from time to time, in the absence of such designee, designate in writing an alternate to represent it at meetings of the Association.

3. *Honorary Members.* The Board of Directors may by vote of two-thirds of its members elect as an Honorary Member of the Association any corporation, company, partnership, institution, or individual who in its opinion has made a noteworthy contribution to the field of aviation, particularly as it applies to industrial aid air transport or to the work of the Association. An Honorary Member shall be exempt from the payment of dues. The Board of Directors may by a vote of two-thirds of its members elect an individual Honorary Member or representative of an Honorary Member, an honorary officer of the Association. An Honorary Member or an honorary officer shall not vote or be deemed part of a quorum at any meeting of the Association and shall not be a member of the Board of Directors except in an ex officio capacity.

4. *Application for Membership.* Application for membership shall be submitted in writing on a form approved by the Board of Directors and shall set forth the qualifications of the applicant for membership as a Regular Member or as an Associate Member. The application, when accepted, shall be an agreement on the part of the applicant to be bound by the Articles of Agreement and the By-Laws now or hereafter in effect.

The application shall be submitted to the Executive Committee for approval or rejection. To be elected to membership, each applicant must receive the affirmative vote of a majority of the members of the Executive Committee. Notice of acceptance or rejection shall be given the applicant promptly.

A Member's liability for dues shall commence on the first of the month following the date of approval by the Executive Committee of his application for membership. No member shall have the right to vote until he shall have paid his dues.

5. *Expulsion.* A member may be expelled from the Association by the Executive Committee for conduct prejudicial to the welfare of the Association or its members, or for failure to pay dues in accordance with these By-Laws, after notice of and opportunity for hearing.

6. *Resignation.* Any member may resign at any time upon first discharging any indebtedness due the Association and submitting his resignation in writing to the Secretary. The resignation shall be effective fifteen (15) days after receipt by the Secretary or upon the discharge of all indebtedness, whichever occurs last.

7. *Voting Rights.* Only regular members (sic) of the Association in good standing shall be entitled to vote. The Executive Committee may determine from time to time the condition upon which members in arrears may vote at any meeting.

8. *Dues.* The Board of Directors shall determine the amount of dues and the manner of payment, but any charges in the amount of the dues shall not be effective until thirty (30) days after the members are notified in writing of such change. The initial dues which shall cover the year 1947 shall be One Hundred Dollars ($100.00) for each Regular Member (or each Associate Member).

ARTICLE V

Membership Meetings

1. *Annual Meeting.* The Annual Meeting of the Association for the election of Directors and for the transaction of such other business as may properly come before the meeting shall be held at a time and place determined by the Executive Committee.

2. *Quorum.* A majority of the Regular Members of the Association represented in person or by proxy shall constitute a quorum for doing business, but any number may adjourn a meeting to a subsequent date without further notice.

3. *Special Meetings.* Special Meetings shall be held at such times and places as the Board of Directors shall determine. Special Meetings shall also be called by the Chairman of the Board of Directors upon the request in writing of not less than twenty (20) percent of the Regular Members who shall specify in their request the business which they desire to be considered at the proposed meeting.

4. *Notices.* All meetings of the members shall be called by forwarding notice thereof to each member at its address of record not less than fifteen (15) days prior to such meeting.

5. *Voting and Amendments.* A majority vote of the Regular Members present at a meeting, in person, shall decide any question except an amendment to the By-Laws which shall require a vote of the majority of the membership, voting in person or by proxy, and except an amendment to the articles of Agreement which shall require a majority vote of two-thirds of the membership, voting in person or by proxy.

6. *Proxies.* At least twenty (20) days before each Annual Meeting of the Association the Secretary shall mail a blank form of proxy to each Regular Member. Proxies shall be recognized only if held by Regular Members.

7. *Place of Meetings.* Membership meetings shall be held at the principal office of the Association or at any other place in the United States which the Executive Committee shall select.

ARTICLE VI

Board of Directors

1. *Election of Directors.* The Board of Directors shall consist of no more than nine (9) members. Only Regular Members shall be eligible for election and Directors.

2. *Staggered Terms.* The first Board of Directors shall be elected to serve until the next meeting of the members at which meeting one-third (⅓) of the members of the Board shall be elected for three (3) years, one-third (⅓) for two (2) years and one-third (⅓) for one (1) year. Thereafter, one-third (⅓) of the members of the Board shall be elected each year for three (3) years each.

3. *Vacancies.* In the event of any vacancy in the Board of Directors, the remaining members of the Board shall have the power to appoint a successor to serve until the next Annual Meeting of the Association or until his successor shall have been elected and shall have assumed the duties of his office.

4. *Nominations.* The Directors shall be elected at the annual meeting of members. Nominations for Directors to be elected at such meeting shall be made in the manner determined by a majority vote of the members present. Additional nominations may be made by any member.

5. *Duties.* Except as herein otherwise provided, the Board of Directors shall have supervision and management of the affairs and property of the Association. They may authorize any expenditure not exceeding the balance in the treasury at the time, and shall fill any vacancy in any office of the Association for the unexpired term or until the next annual meeting. The Board shall, without limiting the power above granted, have authority to engage employees, fix their compensation, prescribe their duties, dismiss, suspend or remove any employee.

6. *Meetings.* The annual meeting of the Board of Directors shall be held immediately after their election at the place of the annual meeting of the members. Regular meetings shall be held as determined by the Board. Special meetings of the Board may be called by the Chairman of the Board, or by the Secretary, at the request of any four (4) members of the Board of Directors.

Notice of meetings shall be mailed, telegraphed or telephoned at least three (3) days prior to the date of such meeting.

Meetings may be held without notice upon a waiver of notice by all the Directors by letter or telegraph.

7. *Quorum.* Five (5) Directors shall constitute of quorum and any action of a majority present shall be the act of the Board.

8. *Failure to Attend Regular Meetings.* In any case where a director fails to attend three consecutive regular meetings of the Board of Directors, the Board may, at the third consecutive meeting, declare the office of such director vacant and elect a new director for the unexpired term.

ARTICLE VII

Executive Committee

1. *Members.* The Board of Directors shall appoint an Executive Committee consisting of five (5) of its members.

2. *Duties.* The Executive Committee shall have all the powers of the Board of Directors during intervals between meetings of the Board, and shall arrange the program and details of the annual meetings, prepare a budget for the approval of the Board of Directors, and make recommendations from time to time. Its actions shall be subject to the approval of the Board of Directors.

3. *Meetings.* The meetings of the Executive Committee may be called by the Chairman, or by the Secretary at the request of any three (3) members of the Committee, or three (3) days' notice by mail, telegraph or telephone.

4. *Quorum.* Three (3) members shall constitute a quorum, and the act of a majority present shall be the act of the Executive Committee.

ARTICLE VIII

Officers

1. *Election.* The officers shall consist of the Chairman of the Board of Directors, one or more Vice-Chairmen who shall be elected with due regard to representation of various sections of the country, a Secretary, and a Treasurer, all of whom, except the Secretary, shall be elected by the Board of Directors from among their number at the annual meeting for a term of one (1) year, or until the next annual meeting, but no person shall be elected Chairman of the Board for more than two successive terms. All directors shall serve without compensation.

2. *Removal.* Any of said officers may be removed without cause by a vote or a majority of the entire Board of Directors, who shall also fill any vacancies for the expired term.

ARTICLE IX

Chairman of the Board

The Chairman of the Board shall preside at all meetings of the members. Except as otherwise provided, he shall appoint all special and standing committees. He shall have all the usual powers and duties of a presiding officer.

ARTICLE X

Vice-Chairman

In the absence or disability of the Chairman of the Board, a Vice-Chairman selected by the Board shall perform all the duties of the Chairman of the Board.

ARTICLE XI

Secretary

The Secretary shall attend all meetings of the Association, the Board of Directors and the Executive Committee, and keep a record of their proceedings. He shall have the custody of all the records of the Association and have charge of the reporting of the activities of the Association. All records shall be open to the Executive Committee or the Board of Directors when acting as a board. The Secretary shall collect the dues and charges and turn same over to the Treasurer for deposit as and when received. Any of the duties of the Secretary may be delegated by the Board to a Vice-Chairman.

ARTICLE XII

1. *Treasurer.* The Treasurer shall receive and disburse all moneys of the Association and keep an accurate account thereof. All sums shall be deposited in a bank or banks designated by the Board of Directors in the name of the Association as and when received, and may be withdrawn only on the signature of the Treasurer and/or such other officer as the Board of Directors may designate.

The Treasurer shall keep proper receipts and vouchers for all disbursements and report to the Board of Directors or the Executive Committee as required. His records shall be open for inspection by the Executive Committee of the Board of Directors when acting as a board. He shall make a report at the annual meeting and exhibit vouchers and receipts for all expenditures. His books shall be audited annually and copies of the auditor's report supplied to the members of the Board of Directors.

2. *Bond.* The Treasurer may be required by the Board of Directors to file a surety bond for the faithful performance of his duties, any expense in connection therewith to be paid by the Association.

ARTICLE XIII

Notices, and Manner of Voting

1. *Waiver of Notice.* Any notice required to be given under these By-Laws may be waived in writing, signed by the person or persons entitled to such notice, whether before or after the time stated therein.

2. *Manner of Voting.* A vote of the members of the Association, of the Board of Directors or the Executive Committee, or of any Committee may be taken on any proposition, except a proposition to amend the Articles of Agreement or these By-Laws, or to elect officers, by mail or telegraph, without a meeting. A majority of the votes received within a reasonable time fixed in the call for a vote shall be decisive, provided that if twenty percent (20%) of the Regular Members, or any five (5) members of the Board of Directors, or any three (3) members of a committee so request in their reply, a meeting shall be called to determine the proposition.

3. *Notices and Addresses.* Every member shall furnish to the Secretary an address to which all notices and documents may be sent, and such notices and documents shall be held to have been duly sent to and served upon a member when mailed or telegraphed to him at the address so furnished. In default of his having furnished such an address, any notice or document shall be held to have been duly sent to or served upon a member if mailed or telegraphed to him at his last known address.

ARTICLE XIV

Indemnity. Each director shall be indemnified by the Association against expenses actually and necessarily incurred by him in connection with the defense of any action, suit or proceeding in which he is made a party by reason of his being or having been a director of the Association, except in relation to matters as to which he shall be adjudged in such action, suit or proceeding to be liable for negligence or misconduct in the performance of his duties as such director and such right of indemnification shall not be deemed exclusive of any other rights to which he may be entitled.

Appendix B

MEMBERS OF THE BOARD OF DIRECTORS, CAOA/NBAA 1946 THROUGH 1986

Donald A. Baldwin	Texaco, Inc.	1968	1971
Earle W. Bauer	Marathon Oil Company	1971	1983
Ross Beach	Kansas Natural Gas Company	1973	1982
John B. Bean	International Multifoods Corp.	1968	1976
Eugene M. Beattie	General Electric Company	1957	1963
William B. Belden	Republic Steel Corporation	1946	1956
B. J. Bergesen	Ford Motor Company	1957	1966
Donald J. Bixler	Sinclair Refining Company	1946	1952
Henry W. Boggess	Sinclair Refining Company	1952	1962
Robert E. Breiling	Associated Aviation Underwriters	1973	1980
John S. Broome	Broome Ranches	1980	*
Leo L. Brown	General Mills	1979	1985
Morton J. Brown	AMP, Inc.	1972	1981
Joseph B. Burns	Fuller Brush Company	1950	1965
Randall H. Carpenter	Time, Inc.	1970	1979
James F. Coleman	Ziff-Davis Publishing Company	1969	1972
Myron W. Collier	Cyclops Corporation	1986	*
Paul C. Craig	Champion Paper & Fiber	1946	1949
Ronald J. DeSerrano	Dresser Industries, Inc.	1982	*
Raleigh E. Drennon	The BFGoodrich Company	1981	*
J. R. Dunham	United Cigar-Whelan Stores	1947	1954
E. E. Dunsworth	Trunkline Gas Company	1964	1973
J. W. Eagleton	Shell Oil Company	1976	1981
Howard O. Evans	General Motors Corporation	1983	1986
Gerard J. Eger	International Harvester Co.	1954	1963
Cornelius Fulton, Jr.	Mathieson Chemical Corporation	1950	1952
John M. Gallagher	Gannett Company	1982	*
Charles C. Gates, Jr.	Gates Rubber Company	1970	1971
Donald L. Gex	W. R. Grace & Company	1965	1967
William F. Gilbert	The Weyerhaeuser Company	1970	1980
P. Ray Grimes	American Republic Insurance Co.	1972	1976

Ronald J. Guerra	Kaiser Industries	1967	1976
J. G. Guess	Burlington Mills	1947	1949
Frederick Haap, III	The Mead Corporation	1981	*
Richard I. Hornbeck	General Electric Company	1971	*
T. William Hotze	Reynolds Metals Company	1947	1948
Jonathan Howe	President, NBAA	1986	*
J. C. Jones	R. M. Hollingshead Corporation	1949	1949
Aubrey Keif	Texaco, Inc.	1962	1967
Arthur Kelly	BFGoodrich, Inc.	1946	1947
Jim Ketner, Jr.	Texas Eastern Transmission Co.	1956	1963
John C. Kruse	Minnesota Mining & Manufacturing	1961	1964
Palmer J. Lathrop	Bristol-Myers Company	1946	1949
Harry C. McCreary	McCreary Tire and Rubber Co.	1976	1980
William R. Martin	Bristol-Myers Company	1949	1949
Howard L. Maurhoff	National Dairies Company	1949	1953
B. Owen Mayfield	Hercules Powder Co.	1965	1969
John P. Meyers	The Hubinger Company	1958	1964
Thomas M. Miller	Manville Service Company	1978	1984
J. B. Mitchell	Howes Brothers Co.	1946	1949
Norman L. Mitchell	Minneapolis Star & Tribune	1967	1976
Max B. Moore, Jr.	Southern Natural Gas Co.	1980	*
Charles E. Morris	Mobil Corporation	1967	1979
Cole H. Morrow	J. I. Case Co.	1949	1957
Michael C. Murphy	Marathon Oil Company	1967	1970
James F. Nields	Ware Knitters, Inc.	1976	1986
J. J. O'Brien	The Garrett Corporation	1964	1967
Preston S. Parish	The Upjohn Company	1981	*
Walter C. Pague	ARMCO Steel Corporation	1946	1964
E. Tilson Peabody	General Motors Corporation	1967	1971
Anthony M. Penizotto	RCA Corporation	1983	1986
Ralph E. Piper	Monsanto Company	1952	1955 (Oct)
		1955 (Nov)	1958
Otto C. Pobanz	Federated Department Stores	1972	1983
Milton J. Pugsley	Chrysler Corporation	1972	1977
Byron M. Reed	H. B. Zachry Company	1985	*
Delos M. Rentzel	Auto Transport Inc.	1953	1955
Lee L. Robbins	Corning Glass Works	1978	*
William M. Robinson	Sears, Roebuck & Co.	1963	1965
Thomas P. Roche	Deere & Co.	1972	1973
Eugene T. Spetnagel	Wolfe Industries, Inc.	1952	1958
Robert C. Sprague, Jr.	Sprague Electric Co.	1955 (Oct-Nov)	
		1956	1957

Charles W. Summers	Security Elevator Co.	1964	1967
Curt G. Talbot	General Electric Co.	1955	1957
D. M. Teel	United States Steel Corp.	1963	1972
Henry H. Timken	Timken Roller Bearing Co.	1966	1968
A. E. Townsend	Columbia Gas Systems Corp.	1968	1969
Frank J. Thera	Minnesota Mining & Manufacturing	1964	1967
Richard J. Van Gemert	Xerox Corporation	1986	*
Richard S. Wigton	The Clorox Company	1985	*
Leslie H. Walker	Standard Oil of California	1980	1982
Arthur E. Weiner	Burlington Industries	1971	1973
John H. Winant	Sprague Electric Co.	1957	1971 (Aug)
	President, NBAA	1971 (Sep)	1986
Horace E. Wood	The Gillette Co.	1961	1969
David M. Woodrow	3M	1976	*
John R. Yost	Armstrong Cork Co.	1950	1952
Stetler B. Young	Rynel Corporation	1953	1954
Eugene J. Zepp	General Motors Corporation	1974	1978
C. F. Zimmerman	Continental Oil Company	1958	1964
Anthony Zuma	Tennessee Gas Transmission Co.	1952	1953

* — Serving on the Board as of the end of 1986

Note: Harley W. Lake, Socony-Vacuum Oil Co., and Howard L. Jennings, General Motors Corporation, were elected to the CAOA temporary Board, November, 1946, but neither subsequently served.

Appendix C

CHIEF EXECUTIVE OFFICERS, CAOA/NBAA, 1946 THROUGH 1986

CAOA

William B. Belden	Chairman (Temporary)	1946–1947
	Chairman	1947–1951
Cole H. Morrow	Chairman	1951–1953

NBAA

Cole H. Morrow	Chairman	1953–1954
Henry W. Boggess	Chairman	1954–1955
	President	1957–1957
Joseph B. Burns	President	1957–1959
B. J. Bergesen	President	1959–1961
John H. Winant	President	1961–1964
Aubrey Keif	President	1964–1965
Horace E. Wood	President	1965–1967
B. Owen Mayfield	President	1967–1969
E. E. Dunsworth	President	1969–1971
John B. Bean	Chairman	1971–1973
Norman L. Mitchell	Chairman	1973–1975
William F. Gilbert	Chairman	1975–1977
Richard I. Hornbeck	Chairman	1977–1979
Earle W. Bauer	Chairman	1979–1981
David W. Woodrow	Chairman	1981–1983
Lee L. Robbins	Chairman	1983–1985
Preston S. Parish	Chairman	1985–*

*Serving at the end of 1986

Appendix D

ASSOCIATE MEMBER ADVISORS TO THE NBAA BOARD, 1964–1986

	Appointed	Term
Scott E. Miller, Airesearch Aviation Services Co.	1964	1 year
Robert B. Ward, Atlantic Aviation Corporation	1964	2 years
Len J. Povey, Mackey Aviation Services	1966	2 years
George E. Haddaway, *Flight* Magazine	1968	3 years
Jesse M. Childress, Southern Airways, Inc.	1968	2 years
D. U. Howard, The D. U. Howard Company	1970	2 years
Wayne A. Rosenkrans, Jeppesen and Company	1971	4 years
Parker V. Ward, Van Dusen Aviation	1972	2 years
Robert S. Northington, Piedmont Aviation, Inc.	1974	2 years
Howard V. Gregory, Des Moines Flying Service	1975	2 years
W. Russell Miller, AirKaman, Inc.	1976	2 years
Thomas W. Gillespie, Piper Aircraft Corporation	1977	2 years
Leddy L. Greever, Beech Aircraft Corporation	1978	2 years
Norman A. Wollberg, Cooper Airmotive	1979	2 years
William B. Watt, Executive Air Fleet Corporation	1980	2 years
Frederick W. Becker, Airwork Corporation	1981	2 years
Hal S. Spragins, III, Memphis Aero Corporation	1982	1 year
M. A. Barbettini, Teledyne Neosho	1983	1 year
Dwayne K. Jose, Bell Helicopter Textron	1983	2 years
John P. Kennedy, Airport Corporation of America	1984	2 years
Robert G. Lambert, Aviall, Inc.	1985	*
J. Robert Duncan, Duncan Aviation, Inc.	1986	*

*Serving as of the end of 1986

Appendix E

CHIEF STAFF OFFICERS, CAOA/NBAA, 1946–1986

Name	Position Title	Dates	Status
K. H. Kalberer	Acting Secretary	November, 1946–May, 1947	Volunteer
Palmer J. Lathrop	Secretary	June, 1947–November, 1948	Volunteer
C. H. Colby	Executive Secretary	November, 1948–August, 1949	Part-time Employee
Nathaniel F. Silsbee	Executive Secretary	September, 1949–February, 1952	Part-time, 1949–1951; Full-time Employee 1951–1952
Herbert O. Fisher	Executive Director	March, 1952–August, 1952	Full-time Employee
Jean DuBuque	Executive Director	August, 1952–July, 1956	Full-time Employee
William K. Lawton	Executive Director	August, 1956–July, 1966	Full-time Employee
Robert B. Ward	Executive Director	August, 1966–September, 1968	Full-time Employee
	Executive Vice President	September, 1968–March, 1971	
John H. Winant	Executive Vice President	August, 1971–September, 1971	Full-time Employee
	President	September, 1971–November, 1986	
Jonathan Howe	President	December, 1986	Full-time Employee

Appendix F

NBAA ANNUAL MEETING CHAIRMEN

1953 — Ralph E. Piper
1954 — George E. Haddaway & Al Harting
1955 — Robert Kusse
1956 — William K. Lawton
1957 — Corbin Douglass
1958 — Robert Morrison
1959 — S. Keating
1960 — Scott E. Miller
1961 — Henry W. Boggess
1962 — Don M. Teel
1963 — C. C. Holt
1964 — Frank Hart
1965 — Scott E. Miller
1966 — Ralph E. Piper
1967 — Parker V. Ward
1968 — Stewart Ayton
1969 — Charles Abel

1970 — Don Murphy
1971 — David M. Woodrow
1972 — Otto C. Pobanz
1973 — George E. Haddaway
1974 — Scott E. Miller
1975 — Janice K. Barden
1976 — Wayne A. Rosenkrans
1977 — C. F. Zimmerman
1978 — John T. Tucker
1979 — F. W. Hulse, IV
1980 — Dan Meisinger, Jr.
1981 — Scott E. Miller
1982 — John T. Tucker
1983 — J. Patrick Murphy
1984 — F. W. Hulse, IV
1985 — Janice K. Barden
1986 — Scott E. Miller

ANNUAL MEETING SITES AND ATTENDANCE

Year	Place	Attendance	Headquarters Hotel	Exhibition Center
1947	New York	18	Biltmore	None
1948	No Meeting			
1949	New York	20*	Bristol-Myers	None
1950	Washington	75*	Statler	None
1951	Washington	100*	Statler	None
1952	Chicago	150*	Blackstone	None
1953	St. Louis	233	Chase-Park Plaza	Hotel
1954	Dallas	432	Adolphus	Hotel
1955	Detroit	517	Sheraton Cadillac	Hotel
1956	Miami	—	McAllister	Hotel
1957	Denver	800	Cosmopolitan	Hotel
1958	Philadelphia	—	Bellevue Stratford	Hotel
1959	Minneapolis	750	Leamington	Hotel
1960	Los Angeles	1,000	Ambassador	Hotel
1961	Tulsa	898	Mayo	Theater
1962	Pittsburgh	873	Penn Sheraton	Hotel
1963	Houston	1,000	Shamrock Hilton	Hotel
1964	Miami	1,700	Americana	Hotel
1965	Los Angeles	1,800	Ambassador	Hotel
1966	St. Louis	2,263	Chase-Park Plaza	Hotel
1967	Boston	2,800	Sheraton Boston	War Memorial Auditorium
1968	Houston	2,700	Shamrock Hilton	Hotel
1969	Washington	3,373	Washington Hilton	Hotel
1970	Denver	2,707	Denver Hilton	Currigan Hall
1971	Minneapolis	2,638	Leamington	Minneapolis Convention Center
1972	Cincinnati	2,942	Netherlands Hilton	Cincinnati Convention Center
1973	Dallas	4,610	Dallas Hilton	Dallas Convention Center
1974	Los Angeles	4,781	Biltmore	Los Angeles Convention Center

Year	Place	Attendance	Headquarters Hotel	Exhibition Center
1975	New Orleans	4,812	Marriott	Rivergate Center
1976	Denver	5,382	Denver Hilton	Currigan Hall
1977	Houston	7,102	Hyatt Regency	Thomas Convention Center
1978	St. Louis	8,226	Stouffers	Cervantes Convention Center
1979	Atlanta	9,893	Peachtree Plaza	World Congress Center
1980	Kansas City	11,058	Muelebach	Bartle Hall Convention Center
1981	Anaheim	11,658	Disneyland	Anaheim Convention Center
1982	St. Louis	10,892	Stouffers	Cervantes Convention Center
1983	Dallas	14,753	Hyatt Regency	Dallas Convention Center
1984	Atlanta	12,777	Atlanta Hilton	World Congress Center
1985	New Orleans	12,667	New Orleans Hilton	New Orleans Convention Center
1986	Anaheim	13,906	Anaheim Hilton	Anaheim Convention Center

Note: * = estimated figure

Appendix G

ASSOCIATION MEMBERSHIP TOTALS, 1947–1986

Year	Total Members, Fiscal Year Ending	Voting Members and Affiliates	Associate Members
1947	19	18	1
1948	*	*	*
1949	51	50	1
1950	75	75	*
1951	128	128	*
1952	191	178	13
1953	214	192	22
1954	267	215	52
1955	322	241	81
1956	366	270	96
1957	390	279	111
1958	415	289	126
1959	455	314	141
1960	505	337	168
1961	503	342	161
1962	494	349	145
1963	493	346	147
1964	525	362	163
1965	574	389	185
1966	647	445	202
1967	737	516	221
1968	783	544	239
1969	868	612	256
1970	862	620	242
1971	824	638	186
1972	860	676	184
1973	966	768	198
1974	1,099	869	230
1975	1,212	946	266
1976	1,349	1,046	303
1977	1,510	1,159	351
1978	1,712	1,298	414

Year	Total Members, Fiscal Year Ending	Voting Members and Affiliates	Associate Members
1979	1,972	1,458	514
1980	2,217	1,601	616
1981	2,466	1,756	710
1982	2,656	1,876	780
1983	2,638	1,844	794
1984	2,835	1,964	871
1985	2,941	1,972	969
1986	2,902	1,946	985

Note: * = Data not reported for year

Appendix H

ASSOCIATION FINANCIAL RESULTS, 1947–1986

Fiscal Year Ending	Income	Expense
1947	$ 1,900	$ 660
1948	2,598	1,155
1949	8,745	5,710
1950	10,620	9,788
1951	7,951	7,824
1952	24,609	18,826
1953	30,240	29,269
1954	64,281	68,372
1955	54,972	39,527
1956	59,882	45,374
1957	71,031	46,959
1958	84,451	67,524
1959	98,894	67,724
1960	108,353	90,811
1961	107,018	86,633
1962	104,880	89,982
1963	106,323	112,741
1964	123,620	115,612
1965	130,241	133,034
1966	149,861	149,950
1967	185,482	176,752
1968	199,187	171,446
1969	267,588	272,581
1970	411,022	315,355
1971	414,618	339,123
1972	430,311	405,313
1973	504,929	511,339
1974	589,285	540,406
1975	644,228	653,715
1976	714,736	675,939

Fiscal Year Ending	Income	Expense
1977	853,729	741,655
1978	1,022,739	933,183
1979	1,237,506	1,246,405
1980	1,504,605	1,388,355
1981	1,758,409	1,456,067
1982	2,169,313	1,693,540
1983	2,358,801	1,991,786
1984	2,744,802	2,049,952
1985	3,128,717	2,844,952
1986	3,313,245	3,172,091

Appendix I

NBAA AWARD FOR MERITORIOUS SERVICE TO AVIATION

The meritorious service award evolved over a period of years, beginning with a "Citation" given to Arthur Godfrey at the 1950 CAOA Washington Foum. First use of the permanent title is associated with 1956. The award, one of aviation's most prestigious, is given to those individuals who, by long lasting, personal dedication, have made significant identifiable contributions that have materially advanced aviation interests — not necessarily confined to business aviation.

Following is a list of recipients, and in most instances, pertinent wording from the inscription on the plaques given to them.

Citation

1950   *Arthur M. Godfrey,* "for his outstanding contribution to the use of aircraft as an aid to business during 1949 by operating aircraft in his own business and by promoting the idea on his radio and television programs."

Merit Award

1951   *Colonel J. Francis Taylor, Jr.,* Chief, All Weather Flying Division, Air Materiel Command, U.S. Air Force, "in recognition of his outstanding individual initiative and leadership . . . in the development, test, and evaluation of aerial navigation aids and instruments which have contributed substantially toward increasing safety and utilization of aircraft in all forms of air transportation."

1952   No award made.

NBAA Annual Award

1953   *Colonel Charles A. Lindbergh,* for "his many outstanding contributions of immeasurable and enduring value to aviation and the defense of the nation."

NBAA Special Award for 1954

1954   *Donald M. Stuart,* Director of the Technical Development and Evaluation Center, Civil Aeronautics Administration, "in recognition of his substantial contributions to the progress of aviation in the development of air navigation systems and devices."

Special Citation for Distinguished Service

1955   *Frederick B. Lee,* CAA Administrator, for "outstanding individual initiative and leadership . . . and his loyalty and devotion to the advancement of safety, navigation and utilization of aircraft."

NBAA Award for Meritorious Service to Aviation

1956   *Captain Eddie Rickenbacker,* cited for leadership and his contributions to both military and commercial aviation.

1957   *Igor I. Sikorsky,* Engineering Manager, Sikorsky Aircraft Division, United Aircraft Corporation, "whose half century of vision, resourcefulness and determination in pioneering and developing fixed and rotary wing aircraft has given new dimensions to the world community of commerce."

1958   *No record of the award.*

1959   *Lt. General James H. Doolittle,* first pilot to fly across the country in less than 24 hours; a pioneer in instrument flight; winner of the Mackay, Bendix, Harmon and Thompson trophies; one of the first to earn a doctorate degree in aeronautics, and leader of the first American bombing raid on Tokyo in World War II.

1960   *Donald Wills Douglas,* founder, board chairman and chief executive officer, Douglas Aircraft Company, "in recognition of his enterprising spirit and contributions to the advancement of the aeronautical sciences from which his country and fellow men have immeasurably benefitted . . ."

1961   *William T. Piper, Sr.,* "in recognition of his vision and determination which have brought the realm of flight to untold thousands of pilots and passengers the world over, and in tribute to his dynamic leadership of Piper Aircraft Corporation — producers of more civil aircraft than any other airframe manufacturer in the world."

1962   *A. S. "Mike" Monroney,* United States Senator, "in grateful recognition of his legislative leadership, statesmanship, and aeronautical knowledge which measurably have contributed to safety in the air for his fellow man."

1963   *Edwin Albert Link,* for his "outstanding contribution to worldwide civil and military flying safety through invention and development of the Link Trainer."

1964   *William J. Schulte,* Assistant Administrator for General Aviation, FAA, for his "untiring efforts to present business aviation's requirements and capabilities to the highest government levels."

1965   *Captain E. B. Jeppesen,* "pioneer airline pilot whose enterprise and devotion to air safety led to his establishment, development and management of aerial cartographic and information services which provide immeasurable security and progress of aviation throughout the world."

1966   *James S. McDonnell,* chairman, chief executive officer, founder, and director, McDonnell Aircraft Corporation, whose "aeronautical, scientific and management talents have contributed immeasurably to the progress of civil and military aviation throughout the nation."

1967   *Henry D. Dupont,* founder of Atlantic Aviation, whose "vision, courage, determination, and personal efforts helped create and encourage the business aviation industry."

1968   *Henry J. Schiebel, Jr.,* vice president, Grumman Aircraft Engineering Corporation whose "personal efforts have contributed immeasurably to the development and progress of business aviation."

1969   *Mrs. Olive Ann Beech,* chairman of the board and chief executive officer of Beech Aircraft Corporation, "whose personal faith, dedication and efforts have contributed immeasurably to the development and progress of business aviation."

1970   *Juan T. Trippe,* retired chairman and chief executive officer of Pan American World Airways, "whose vision, resourcefulness and pioneering spirit in developing international air travel created new dimensions for all phases of aviation."

1971   *Michael C. Murphy,* manager of aviation division of Marathon Oil Company, Findlay, Ohio, whose "prudence, skill and dedication expanded aviation's horizons and created a corporate/executive flight operation that is recognized internationally for safety and excellence."

1972   *NBAA's Silver Anniversary member companies* — those which maintained continuous membership since 1947. The citations acknowledged "leadership in advancing business aviation since 1947 through active and continuous membership during NBAA's first quarter century."

The recipient companies were as follows:

The American Rolling Mill Company, (ARMCO), Middletown Ohio.
Burlington Mills Corporation, Greensboro, North Carolina
Corning Glass Works, Corning, New York
General Electric Company, Schenectady, New York
Republic Steel Corporation, Cleveland, Ohio
Reynolds Metals Company, Richmond, Virginia
Wolfe Industries, Columbus, Ohio

1973   *Dwane L. Wallace,* chairman and chief executive officer of Cessna Aircraft Company, Wichita, Kansas, "whose engineering, management and marketing accomplishments led general aviation to its integral, yet unique, position in the world's transportation network, from Arctic and jungle strips to the most sophisticated hub airports."

1974   *Edward J. Swearingen,* chairman of the board, Swearingen Aviation Corporation, San Antonio, Texas, "for perception and innovative leadership in expanding the Utility, Performance, and Economics of the nation's business aircraft fleet through development and modification programs involving Learstar, Super Ventura, Queen Air 800, Excalibur, Merlin, Comanche, JetStar and supersonic business aircraft."

1975   *William P. Lear, Sr.,* president, Lear Avia Corporation, Reno, Nevada, "for innumerable contributions of incalculable value in the field of aviation safety, navigation, operation and efficiency, spanning more than half a century."

1976   *George E. Haddaway,* founder and editor/publisher of *Flight* magazine since 1934. "For his dedication and unflagging spirit in supporting and promoting business aviation as a vital economic and social resource to our nation."

1977   *William F. Remmert* and *D. Robert Werner,* (joint award), "for their pioneering contributions to making business aviation a safe, efficient, and practical transportation tool."

1978   *Dr. Richard T. Whitcomb,* "one of the nation's most distinguished engineers. He discovered a method for designing aircraft to reduce drag and increase speed without the need to add power. He is also the inventor of the supercritical wing."

1979   *Dr. Charles Stark Draper,* "The father of inertial navigation." Dr. Draper is widely recognized as the scientist who developed inertial navigation instruments and guidance systems.

1980   *Sir Frank Whittle* and *Hans von Ohain* — "for their separate and independent development of the jet engine."

1981   *Robert B. Hotz* — ". . . for his unique ability to motivate with the written and spoken word and to impress upon its leaders the wisdom of vigorous technical advancement in air transportation, space and defense."

1982   *Charles L. (Kelly) Johnson,* "aircraft engineer who set and attained goals never before imagined; whose designs have spanned every conceivable flight vehicle known today and some that will reach into the next century."

1983   *Senator Barry M. Goldwater* — "Outspoken aviation advocate and bold supporter of maintaining America's leadership in military and civil aeronautics."

1984   *A. Scott Crossfield* — "In the right place at the right time with the right stuff in the development of aviation technology."

1985   *NASA Space Shuttle Crews* — "who personify all that is best of current combined advancements in aviation and aerospace technology."

1986   *The Personnel of the Air Traffic Control System* — "the men and women whose skill and dedication through fifty years of service have consistently met the challenges of an ever-expanding national airspace system." Award accepted by FAA Administrator, Donald D. Engen.

Appendix J

COMPLETE LIST OF AIRFRAME MANUFACTURERS

Airplane Manufacturers

    Aeritala
    Aerospatiale
    Airmaster, Incorporated
    Avions Marcel Dassault-Breguet Aviation
    Beech Aircraft Corporation
    British Aerospace PLC
    Canadair, Ltd.
    Cessna Aircraft Company
    Construcciones Aeronauticas, S.A. (CASA)
    de Havilland Aircraft of Canada, Ltd.
    Dornier GmbH
    Empresa Brasileria De Aeronautica, S.A. (Embraer)
    Fairchild Aircraft Corporation
    Fokker-B.V.
    Gates Learjet Corporation
    Gulfstream Aerospace Corporation
    Hawk Industries
    International Aviation Corporation
    Israel Aircraft Industries, Ltd. (IAI)
    Lockheed-Georgia Company*
    Mitsubishi Heavy Industries
    Mooney Aircraft Corporation
    Nurtanio Aircraft Industry, Ltd.
    Partenavia Construzioni Aeronautiche, S.p.A.
    Pilatus Britten-Norman, Ltd.
    Piper Aircraft Corporation
    Rinaldo Piaggio, S.p.A.
    Saab-Scania AB
    Sabreliner Corporation*
    Short Brothers, Ltd.
    Skytrader Aircraft Corporation
    Swearingen Aircraft Corporation
    United States Aircraft Corporation

*Indicated company which in 1985 was not manufacturing aircraft but was servicing those previously manufactured.

Helicopter Manufacturers

Aerospatiale Helicopter Division
Bell Helicopter Textron
Boeing Vertol Company
Enstrom Helicopter Corporation
Construzioni Aeronautiche Giovanni Agusta S.p.A.
Hiller Helicopter
Hughes Helicopters (McDonnell-Douglas)
Hynes Helicopters, Incorporated
Kawasaki Heavy Industries
Messerschmitt-Boelkow-Blohm GmbH (MBB)
Rinaldo Piaggio S.p.A.
Robinson Helicopter Company, Incorporated
Schweizer Aircraft Corporation
Sikorsky Aircraft
Westland Helicopters, Ltd.

General Note: Many of the companies named above manufactured aircraft primarily for the "commuter" airline industry. Some such aircraft are adaptable to business transportation uses.

Source: *Business and Commercial Aviation,* April, 1984, adapted for *A Study of Business Aviation in 1985,* Colgate Darden Graduate Business School Sponsors, and NBAA.

Appendix K

STATEMENT OF NBAA OBJECTIVES, JUNE, 1986

I. Business Aviation Management

Objective: Provide sound, multi-level educational programs to improve and sharpen skills needed for effective professional management of business aircraft operations.

Means: 1. Darden Graduate School of Business Case Studies

2. Management Seminars

3. Recommended Standards Manual

4. Management Aids

II. Federal Regulations and Legislation

Objective: Represent the interests of the business aviation community to Federal agencies and Congressional committees concerned with aviation, maintaining and further improving NBAA's effectiveness and standing. Promote inter-association coordination and cooperation in these endeavors.

Means: 1. Improve the utility and capacity of the national aviation system.

2. Maintain reasonable aviation user charges, taxes, and airport fees.

3. Strive for solution of environmental concerns through adoption of national noise criteria governing airport regulations.

4. Provide unconstrained access to the airport-airways system for business aircraft.

5. Work to affect federal, state, and municipal regulations beneficially.

III. Safety

Objective: Promote programs which improve the safety record of business and corporate aviation.

Means: 1. Enhance training programs through seminars.

2. Encourage development of refresher programs for the business-man pilot.

3. Provide technical forums, such as the annual maintenance and operations meetings.

4. Continue the NBAA Flying and Maintenance Safety Award Program.

IV. Membership

Objective: Promote the maintenance and growth of NBAA membership.

Means: 1. Enhance relationships among members (Corporate, Business and Associate)

2. Provide useful NBAA programs which enhance the utility and effectiveness of business aircraft.

3. More closely identify NBAA with the interests of the business-man pilot.

4. Maintain the NBAA annual meeting and convention's position as the premier forum for exchange of information and for display of products and services used by business aviation.

V. International

Objective: Seek and maintain the strongest possible voice in international aviation affairs.

Means: 1. Assist business aviation in expeditious conduct of international flight.

2. Work with IBAC and through it, ICAO and other major international aviation forums and governing bodies.

VI. General:

Objective: Improve the image of business aviation and the public's awareness of it.

Means: 1. Publicize the utility and effectiveness of business aviation in promoting commerce and industry.

2. Publicize NBAA's accomplishments to enhance public perception of business use of aircraft.